BATMAN
MASTERPIECES

BATMAN MASTERPIECES

PORTRAITS OF THE DARK KNIGHT AND HIS WORLD

RUTH MORRISON

ORIGINAL STORY BY DOUG MOENCH

WATSON-GUPTILL PUBLICATIONS
New York

Batman created by Bob Kane.

This edition first published in the United States in 2002 by
Watson-Guptill Publications
770 Broadway, New York, N.Y. 10036

ISBN 0-8230-0466-x

Library of Congress Cataloging-in-Publication Data

Morrison, Ruth.

Batman masterpieces : portraits of the Dark Knight and his world / Ruth Morrison : original story by Doug Moench : [featuring art by Carl Critchlow . . . et al.].

p. cm.

Based on a trading card series from DC Comics.

Copyrighted by DC Comics.

ISBN 0-8230-0466-x

I. Moench, Doug. 1948– . II. Critchlow, Carl, 1963– . III. DC Comics, Inc. IV. Title.

PN6728.B36M683 1998

741.5'973--dc21 98-8484

CIP

Senior Editor: Candace Raney
Editor: Sylvia Warren
DC Comics Editors: Eric Fein and Elisabeth Vincentelli
Book and Cover Design: Jay Anning, Thumb Print
Production Manager: Hector Campbell
Printed in Italy
First paperback printing, 2002
1 2 3 4 5 6 7 8 9 / 10 09 08 07 06 05 04 03 02

INTRODUCTION

Batman Masterpieces is based on the DC Comics/Fleer Batman Master Series card set, which was made available in 1996 and which rapidly gained cult status among card collectors because of its unique approach. "There are certain things that every trading card in a set has," says editor Larry Daley, "a 'pretty' picture full of action on the front, and relevant copy explaining the image's context on the back. But we felt we'd done that kind of card to death. We wanted something different." Designer Richard Bruning concurs: "We were looking for a new way to introduce and present the characters in a card set." Traditionally, card backs are filled with information about the character featured on the front; instead, Daley wanted to "create a story in the cards." Other sets, most notably Topps' famous *Mars Attacks!,* had hinted at an overall narrative, but none had ever attempted to link all the cards in such a comprehensive fashion.

How to present a true narrative was a particularly daunting task. Card sets do not come in order—tracking down all the cards is half the fun. "We were shooting for something a little high concept," Daley admits. The story line Doug Moench developed offered the perfect solution: after Batman's apparent demise, everybody in Gotham City, and especially the Dark Knight's perennial foe, the Joker, give their own takes on the legendary crime fighter.

Moench—who had been the premier Batman writer for over 15 years—was up for the challenge. In fact, he had once proposed a similar idea to Bruning. "He really gets into the heads of these characters," says Daley, "and what he pulls out is wonderful." Moench devised "story beats," which were then assigned to four painters: Scott Hampton worked on the more narrative sections; Carl Critchlow took on the Joker cards that punctuate each beat; Dermot Power put his twist on the villains who haunt Batman's nights; and Duncan Fegredo illustrated a series of fantastical scenarios sprung from the Joker's feverish imagination. The artists relied not only on inspiration from the story, but on an art concept and art directions (reproduced here for the first time) supplied by Doug Moench, as well as on input from the DC Comics editors.

Daley recalls that the editorial and creative teams "wanted everyone to be thinking about the Batman, and everyone reflecting on what the Batman meant to them." Even the chase cards (special cards, often with custom printing, inserted randomly into packs, which are harder for collectors to find than cards in the sequential set) were designed to fit in with the overall concept. In the trading card series, and now in *Batman Masterpieces,* a composite portrait of one of popular culture's most enduring icons gradually emerges.

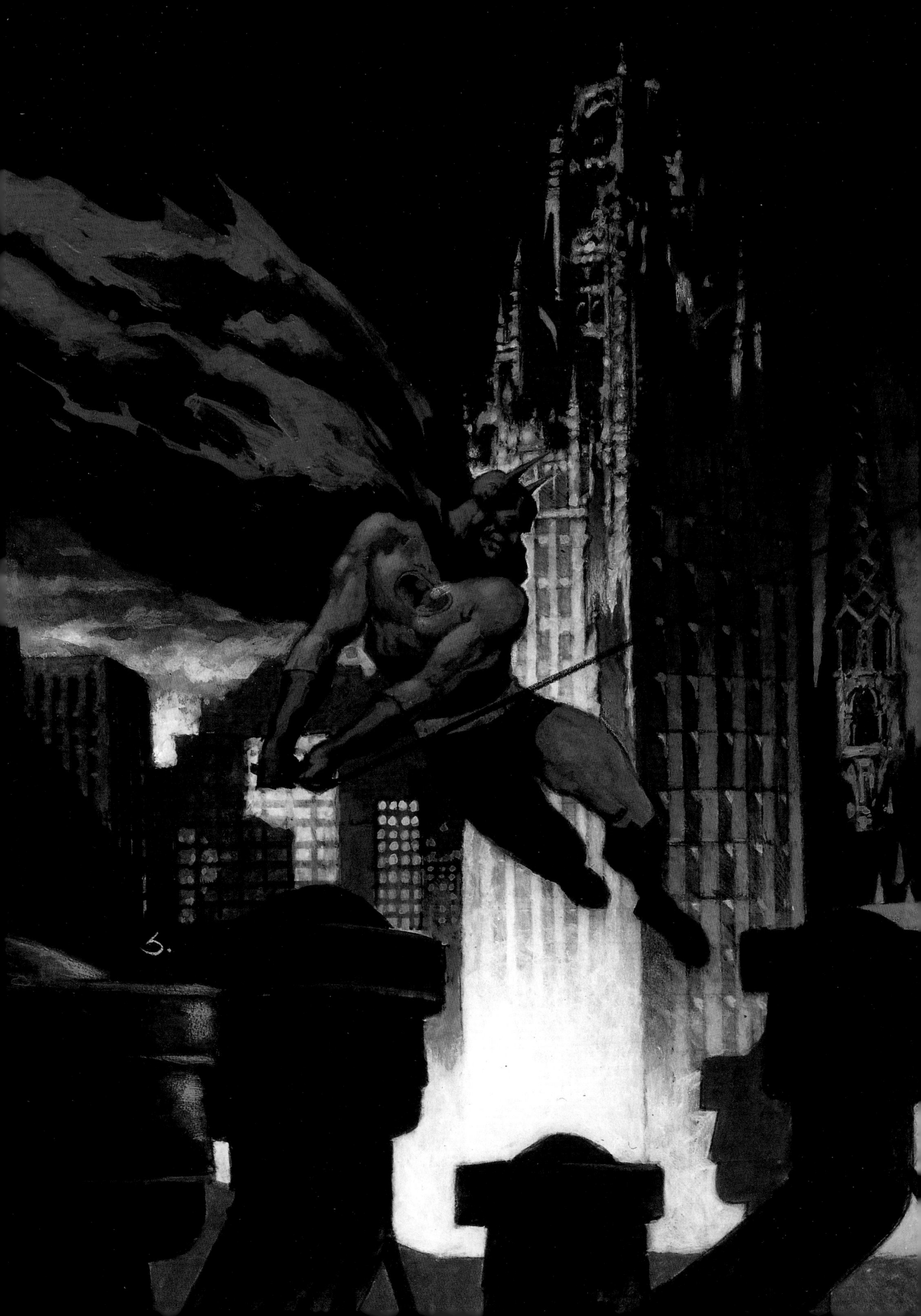

GOTHAM

Shadows and sounds. The spitting snarl of a greasy cat. Chattering trash cans. Snap of chain, smash of glass. A long shriek cut short. A tugboat's moan floating on fog. Pounding footsteps. Sirens. And a black swooping hiss slashing the night. . . .

Gotham: A nether-realm of evil sealed in every stone, so dark that its only savior is the *Batman.*

ART CONCEPT

Batman as a giant shadow-presence only, looming over darkly dangerous & atmospheric Gotham a la Anton Furst.

SCOTT HAMPTON'S SOLUTION

"My initial thought was to do something cute. I wanted to have an image of a bat catching a fish—the bat symbolizing Batman and the fish symbolizing the Joker.

"I decided to go for something more iconic. I did a shot of Batman zooming through an alleyway, swinging through the city. I was asked to change the angle to a worm's-eye view (looking up at Batman), but instead I just put him up at the level of the rooftop."

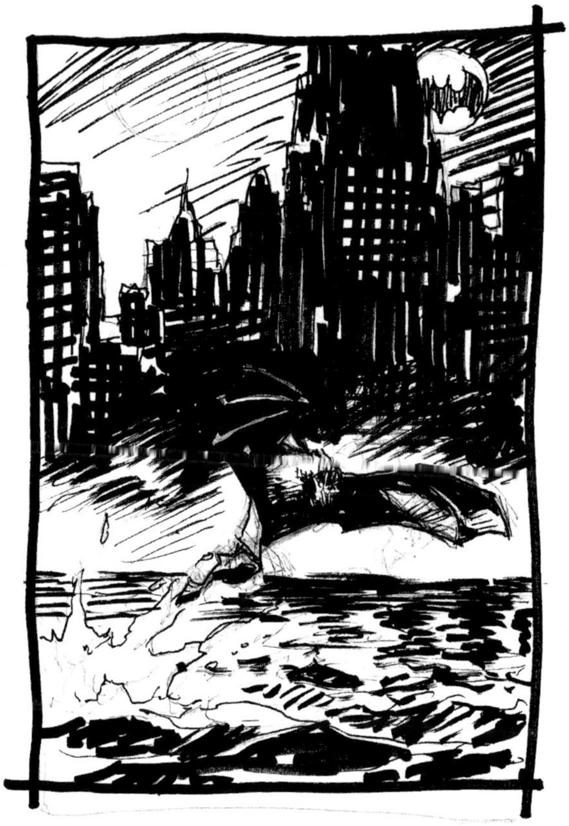

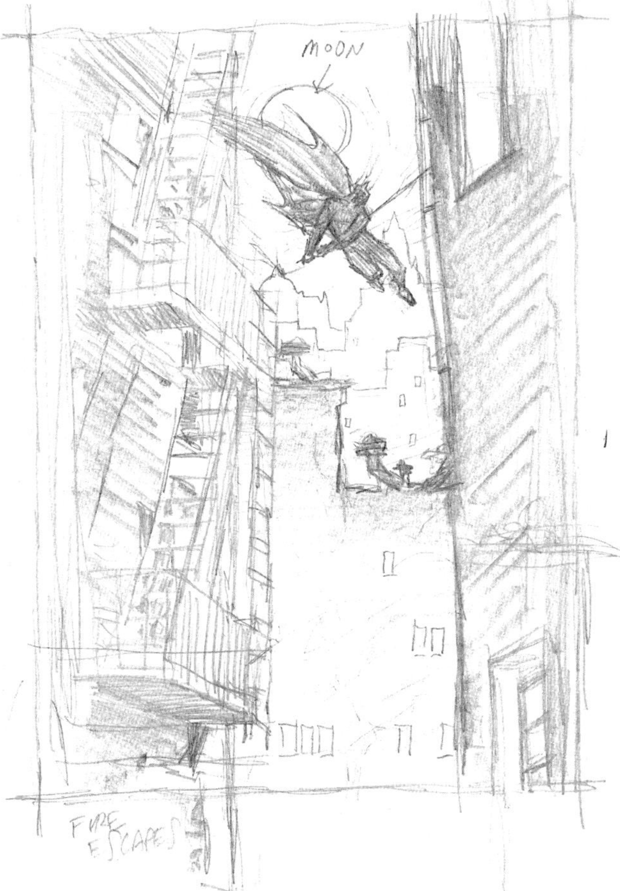
MOON
FIRE ESCAPES

Finally, Hampton settled on Batman patrolling Gotham. "It set up Batman, but it also set up Gotham—a place of grandeur and beauty, but also a place of darkness and mystery."

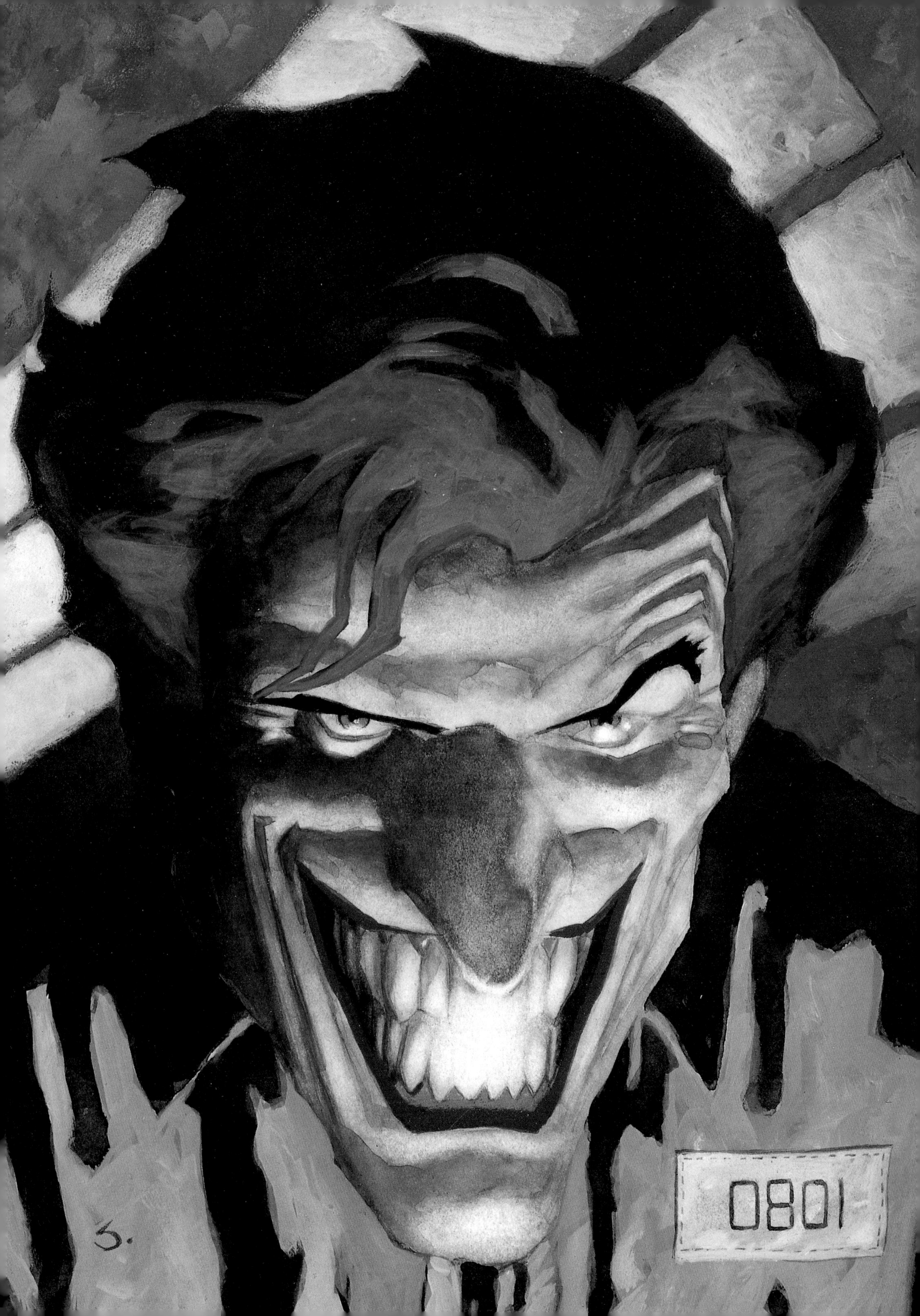
0801

ARKHAM ASYLUM FOR THE CRIMINALLY INSANE

Within the Madman's mind: "The mind is a prison holding Madness captive but mind shattered so Madness free even with another prison called Arkham (reminder: *Kill Bats!*) holding the prison of body holding Madness captive or so they *think!*

"Plan: Shatter Arkham with teeth and enjoy last explosive laugh plus Crime or Chaos or Death with Madness free for all three.

"*Wheeeeee!*"

ART CONCEPT

A portrait of the Joker, or just a head shot.

SCOTT HAMPTON'S SOLUTION

"Originally, there was just going to be one shot—the Joker breaking out of the asylum—but Larry Daley, the editor, had the idea to introduce the Joker with a portrait, to have him just staring at you. We split this card up, so that first you meet the character, the Joker, and then you see him doing something."

Hampton had no complaints about doing an additional card. "This card actually ties into the ending, where I close out the set with a portrait of Batman. So these two images more or less book-end the set."

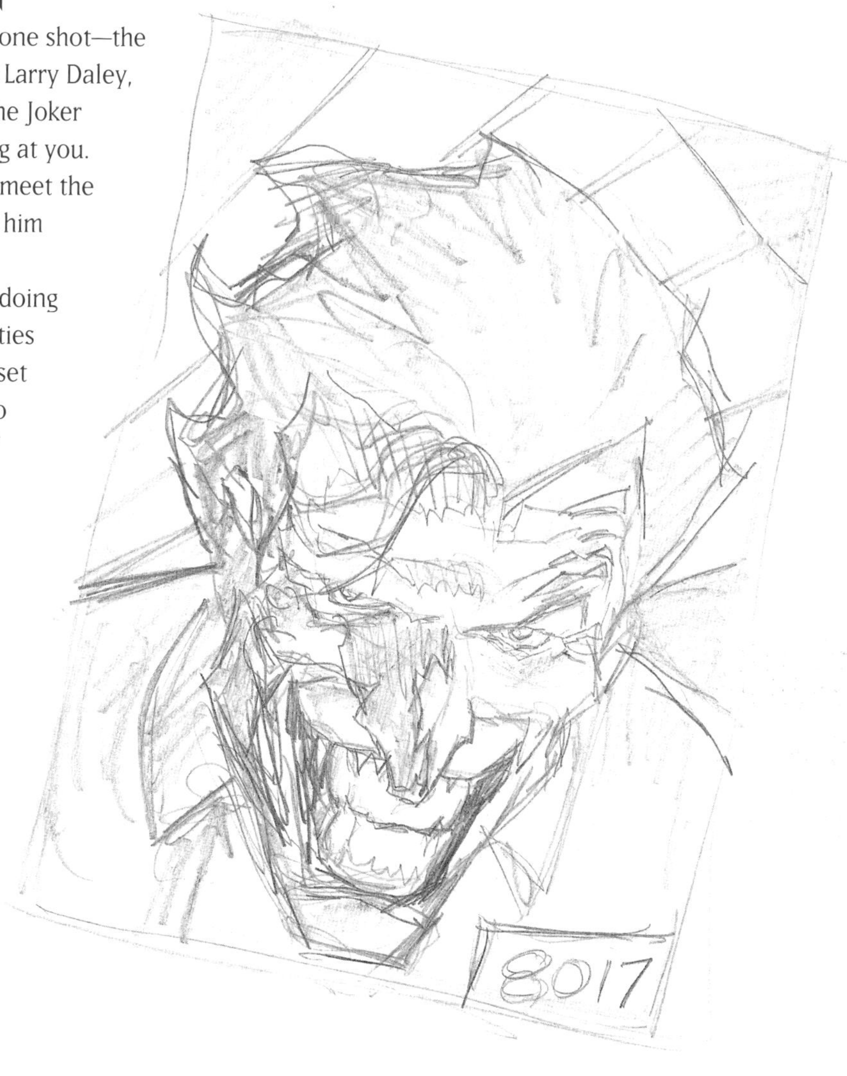
8017

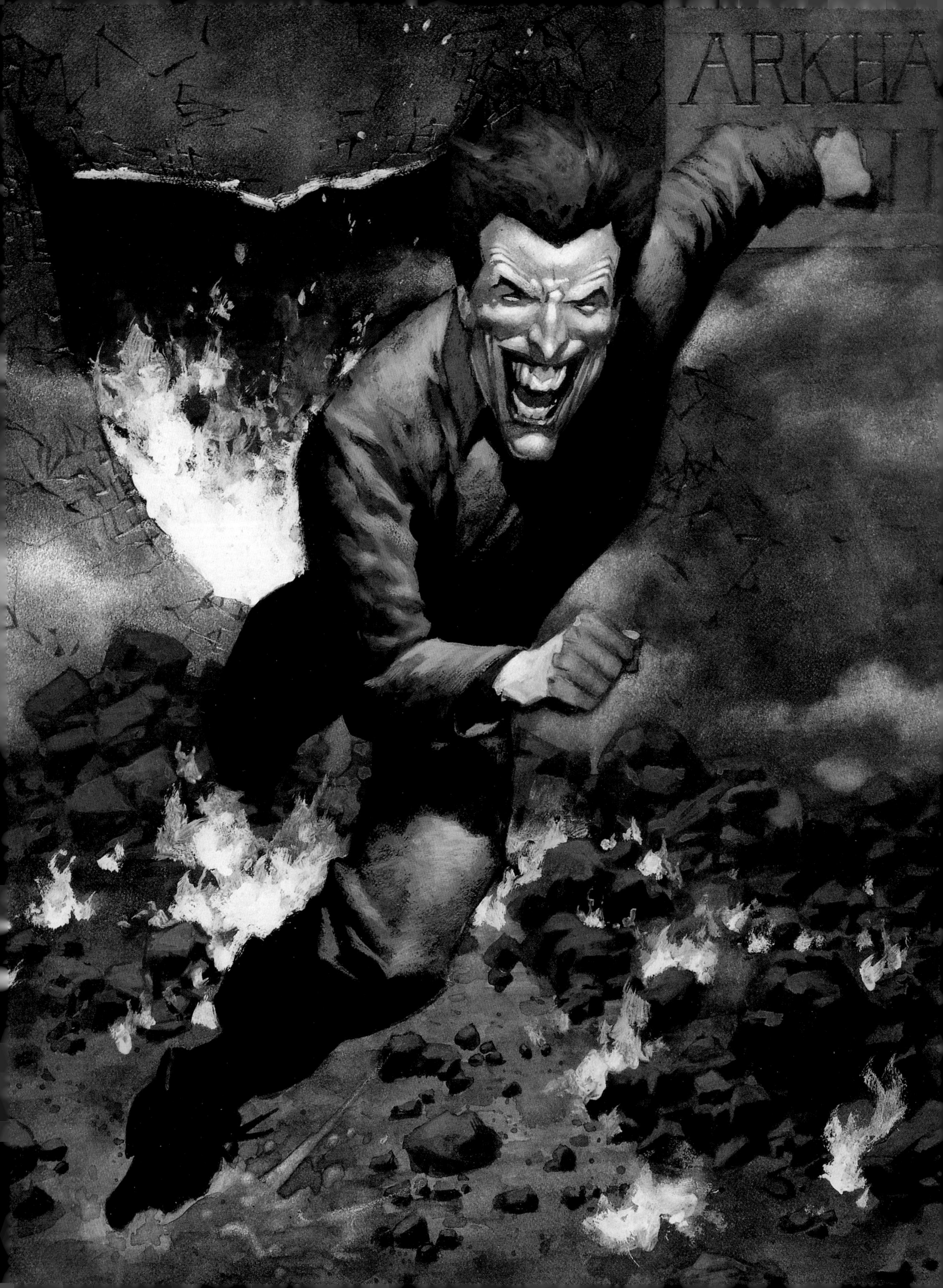
ARKHA

BULLETIN

"Police are now convinced the Joker entered Arkham last November with a set of *false wisdom teeth* containing concentrated *liquid explosive*—applied three nights ago to the inner side of his cell wall, in the shape of his own grotesquely grinning mouth.

"Meanwhile, the Bat-Signal continues to blaze, apparently unanswered for the third straight night—with Commissioner Gordon having *no comment.*"

ART CONCEPT

Maniacally laughing Joker in foreground, coming at us, wearing asylum-inmate coveralls; beyond him in background is a still-smoking hole blown thru stone wall of Arkham Asylum, and the hole is in the shape of a huge Joker-mouth leering grin. **Overall image:** Joker has just escaped thru this Joker-mouth-shaped hole he has blown thru wall.

SCOTT HAMPTON'S SOLUTION

"When I approached this piece, I was primarily interested in focusing on the Joker. Doug had written in that the explosion causes the hole in the wall to resemble the Joker's smile, and I suggested it somewhat, but I did not overemphasize it. Now I wonder if it's a little more subtle than it should be. . . .

BAT SIGNAL
GOTHAM IN DISTANCE
SMOKE
FOG
SMOKE
JOKER DISAPPEARING INTO FOG
RUBBLE
RUBBLE
JOKER ESCAPE. SEEN THRU GAPING JOKER GRIN IN WALL.

SMOKE
SMOKE
RUBBLE
RAIN PUDDLE

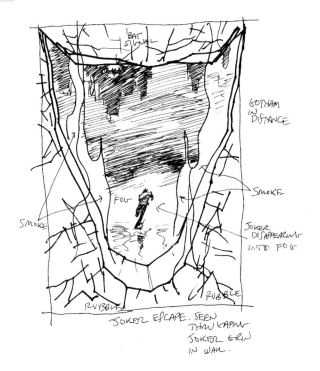

"My main goal was to establish the grimness and grayness of Arkham Asylum. While doing that, though, I still wanted to make the fire behind the Joker bright without outshining him. That's why the fire's colors look so muted."

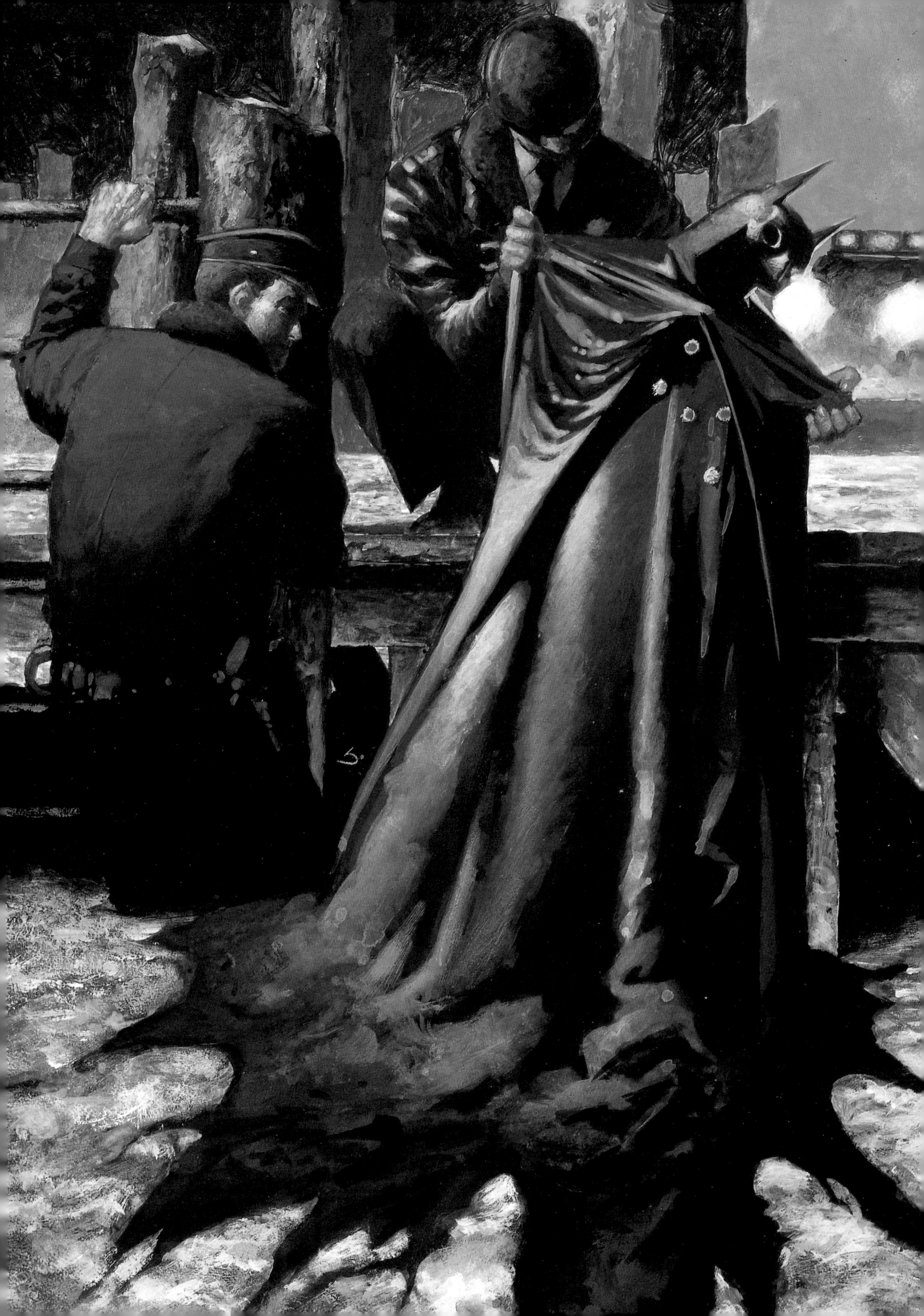

PIER 13

Two cops on the pier, after finding the cowl:

"The Commish ain't gonna like *this. . . .*"

"Ask *me,* he relied on the Batman too much anyway."

"Not anymore he won't . . . but this sure is hard to believe . . . the Batman *gunned down,* I mean."

"With the *Joker* at large, *nothin's* hard to believe. Go against *that* maniac enough times, sooner or later you *gotta* croak—even a *vampire* bat."

ART CONCEPT

Spooky fog snaking thru entire image; strip of yellow crime-scene tape stretching across bottom foreground (GOTHAM P.D. CRIME SCENE DO NOT CROSS) to seal off the end of a sagging, weather-beaten pier; just beyond the yellow crime-scene tape, two uniformed Gotham cops are standing at the end of the pier, holding up their shocking find between them: Batman's tattered & bullet-riddled cape & cowl/mask.

Five or six large-caliber bullet holes, suggesting Batman has been repeatedly shot in the back.

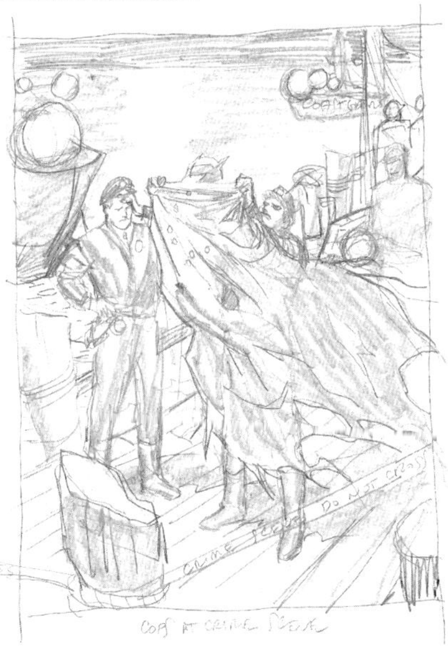

SCOTT HAMPTON'S SOLUTION

"We went through a number of stages with this card. It took a long time to get it, but it's one of my favorite images. It really gave me an opportunity to play with the paint and texture. It was one of the first cards that I did, and it established an approach (to some extent) to a lot of the other cards.

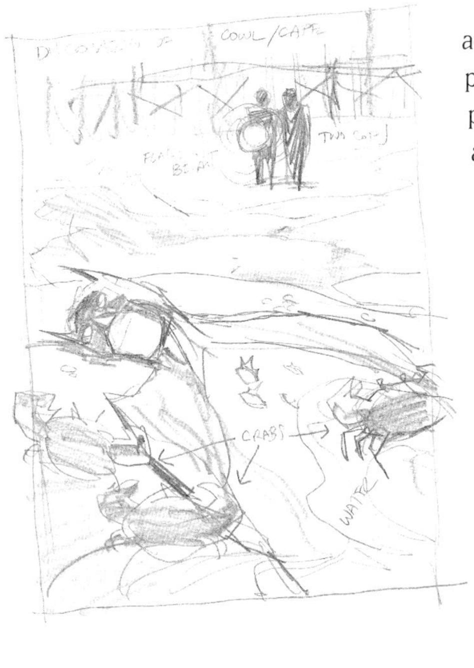
COWL/CAPE
CRABS
WATER

"Prior to this card set, I hadn't used too much acrylic. I think this was the first entirely acrylic painting that I had done. I wanted to make this piece work as if it was just being shot for black and white. The way I see color initially is just as a grayscale from very high lights to darks.

"There are two things I'm after—smoothness and roughness. That's what this card gave me to play with. The cape was smooth, the lumber of the dock was rough. I also got to experiment playing with the water. I wanted craggy water, which isn't realistic, but does have an edge. I didn't want to lose the tension or drama that was implicit for the card. So no smooth cape in smooth water."

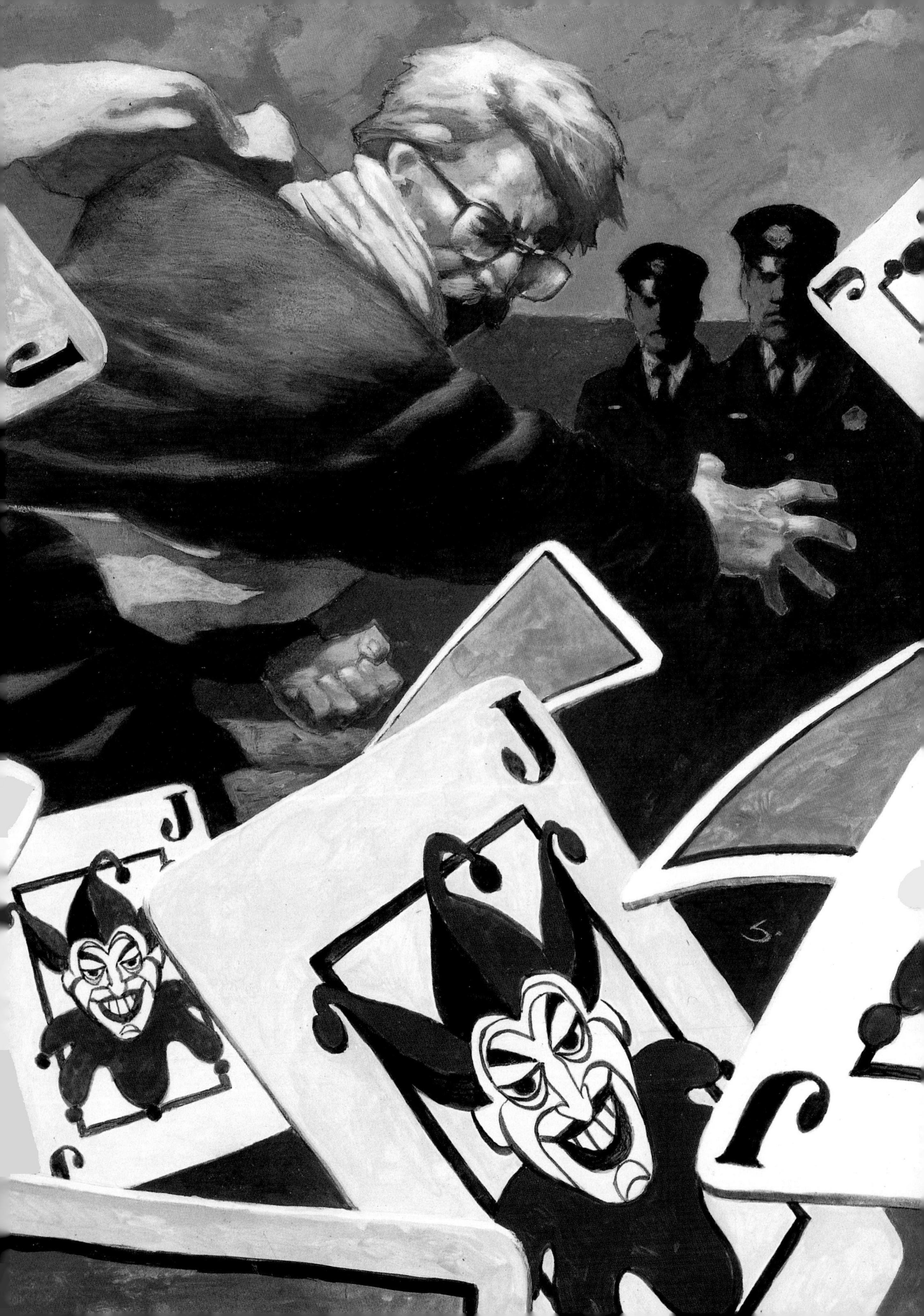

STACKED DECK

Badgered by reporters, Police Commissioner James Gordon momentarily snaps:

"No, we have *not* recovered a body . . . but fifty-two of *these* have now washed ashore—an entire deck, *all Jokers*—making the preliminary evidence *unanimous*. Shot by a large-caliber weapon of the type favored by the Joker, the Batman is missing and *presumed dead*. Now please *back off* and let us *work!*"

ART CONCEPT

Grim Gordon holding several soggy (and maybe oversized?) Joker playing cards, extending them toward us—into foreground. Reaching into both sides and bottom of image are various hands holding microphones and maybe a camera or two. **Overall image:** Surrounded by reporters, Gordon is making a statement as he holds out the Joker cards.

SCOTT HAMPTON'S SOLUTION

"They had sent me the classic Bob Kane Joker playing card, and I used that as the basis for these. I didn't want them to be flat; I wanted to suggest the tilt, the action. So I took the image, photocopied it up, mounted it on a piece of cardboard, and put that into an Art-O-Graph, a machine that projects images onto a flat surface so that you can trace them off. I put it in there at a slant, but as I put it further into the machine, trying to get the angle that I wanted, I burnt my hand . . . but I got the tilt that I wanted.

"Of course, if I were more computer oriented, I could have painted the playing card separately, and asked that it be scanned and introduced at some sort of wonky angle into the painting. But I always prefer, if possible, to have an original painting that looks like the published piece."

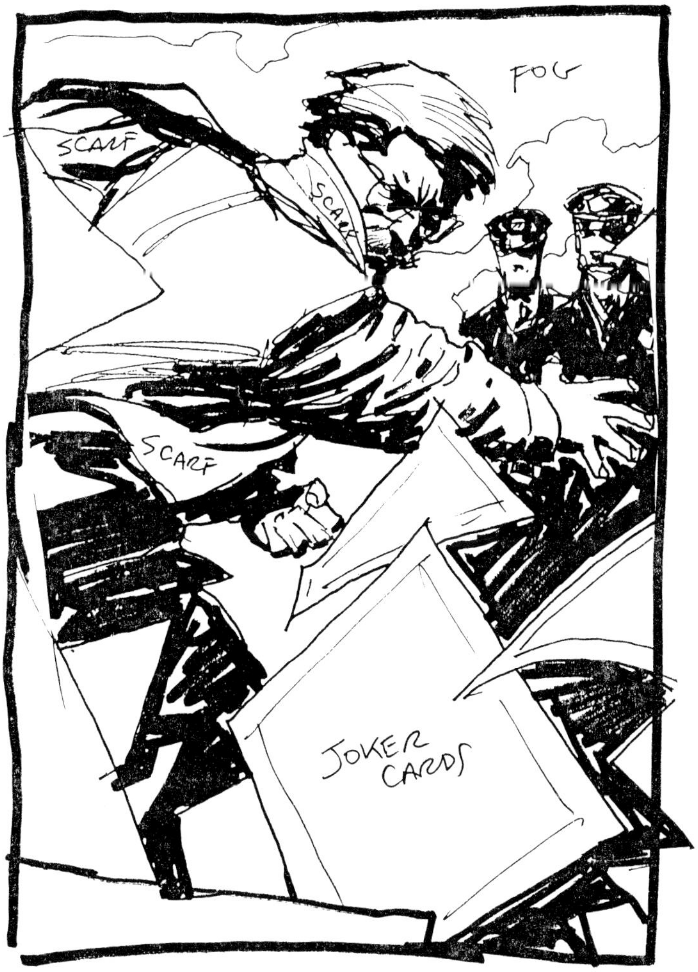
FOG
SCARF
SCARF
SCARF
JOKER CARDS

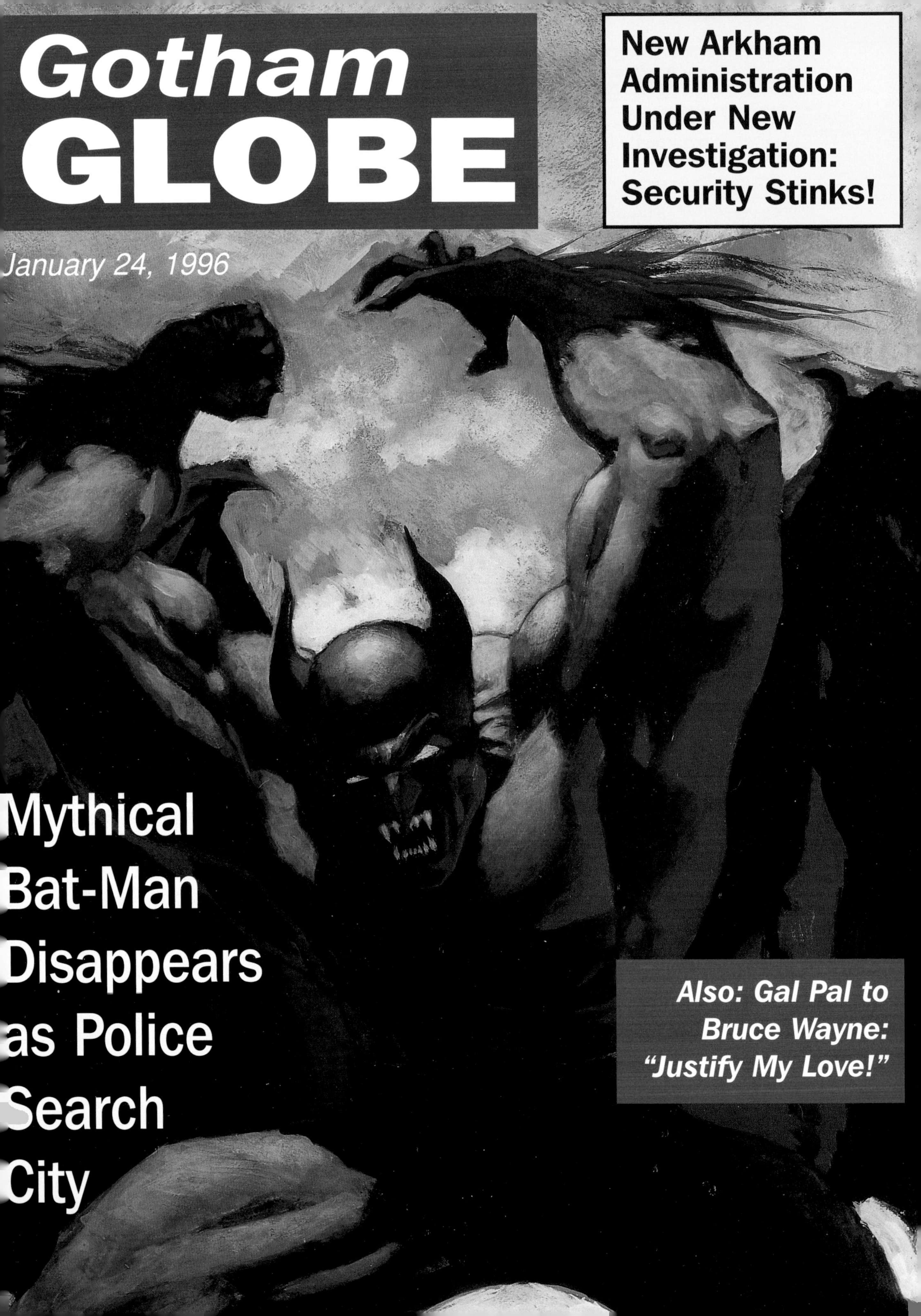
Gotham GLOBE
New Arkham Administration Under New Investigation: Security Stinks!
January 24, 1996
Mythical Bat-Man Disappears as Police Search City
Also: Gal Pal to Bruce Wayne: "Justify My Love!"

GHOST OF A GHOST

Editorial by Gotham Talk Radio general manager Kyle Stevens:

"They tell us he's *dead,* but did he ever *live?* For years we've heard about the exploits of a near-mystical 'Guardian of Gotham,' a Dark Angel wrapped in the intimidating image of nothing less than a *bat.* More like the *boogeyman.* Now he's fallen, and if and when he is resurrected the Urban Myth will be complete, ready to join the ranks of ghosts, alien abductors, and sewer farms of albino alligators."

ART CONCEPT

Cover of picture newsmagazine with logo and one of the few actual photos of Batman in existence. It is, however, taken from long range and shows him even darker & more mysterious than in his "Creature of the Night" mode, maybe one arm holding his cape up to shield already-masked face, Dracula fashion, as if sensing he's being photographed even from afar.

The overall effect is akin to those tantalizing but maddeningly inconclusive Bigfoot or UFO photos. Magazine cover copy at or near bottom: BATMAN R.I.P.

The "Bat-Man" image is the first of our "alternate takes"—vaguely recognizable & resembling Batman in certain respects but almost all wrong and even bizarrely so; nevertheless, no reason it can't be a strikingly super-cool misrepresentation.

SCOTT HAMPTON'S SOLUTION

"Initially, the image was going to be inset into a newspaper headline, so what I did was a horizontal painting. There's a lot more to this image than you see on the card. The figure is complete, the wings are complete.

"In production, they opted to go for more of a cover image, to keep the news feel, but changed from a newspaper to a magazine, with a photo cover. The picture ends up looking like a photo that someone just got, rather than the composed piece that it is—which works for this instance. But if I had known that it was going to be cropped this closely, I probably would not have done it the way I did."

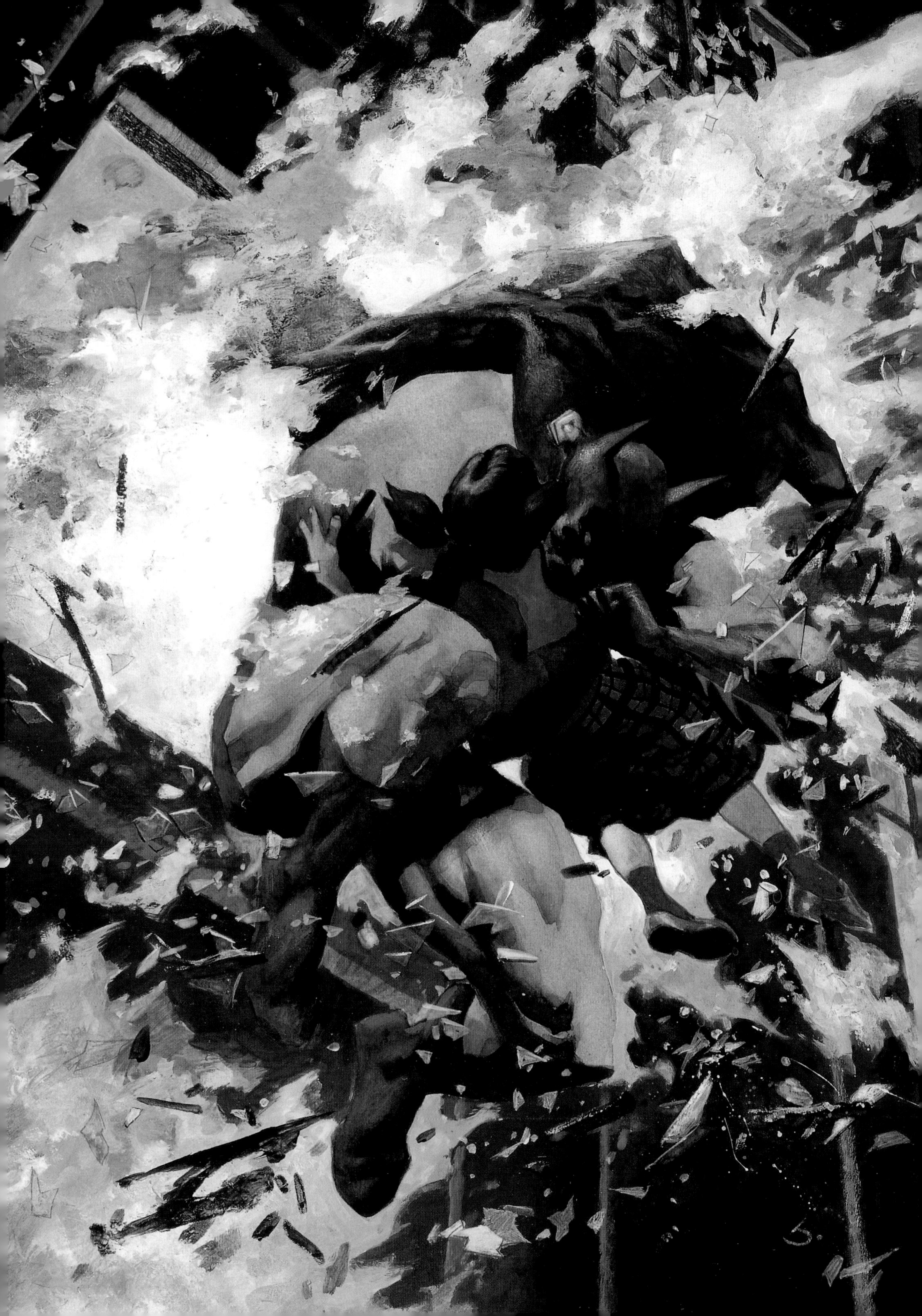

HE WAS REAL!

"I saw him! The firemen couldn't reach me. I heard my mom screaming. It got *real hot*. Then there was this big noise of sparks flying and a whole humongous piece of the wall crashed down. It was the *Batman* and he was flying in. Then I was outside safe and he was *gone*. It was like he *wasn't* real but I *know he was.*"

ART CONCEPT

Heroic Batman bursting or surging from a burning building (or simply coming thru flames), protectively holding an 8-year-old.

This should be an essentially accurate version of Batman, but in his larger-than-life "brighter-hero" mode—not as "Creature of the Night."

TV screen is showing a close-up of the kid being interviewed. Copy can be around, below, or superimposed over image.

SCOTT HAMPTON'S SOLUTION

"The editor asked me repeatedly that I paint Batman as a '500-pound gorilla.'"

What does a 500-pound gorilla do?

"Anything he wants," laughs Hampton. This image was the first in a series portraying Batman as larger than life. "Those cards have to do with how Batman is perceived by people when they only get glimpses of him but experience what power he wields.

"This was one of the rare chances in the set that I had to play with more color and a little more light than normal.

"In some ways, this was a difficult card to achieve. I had to suggest the angle of the building, the explosion, the glass, the rest of it, as well as the figures."

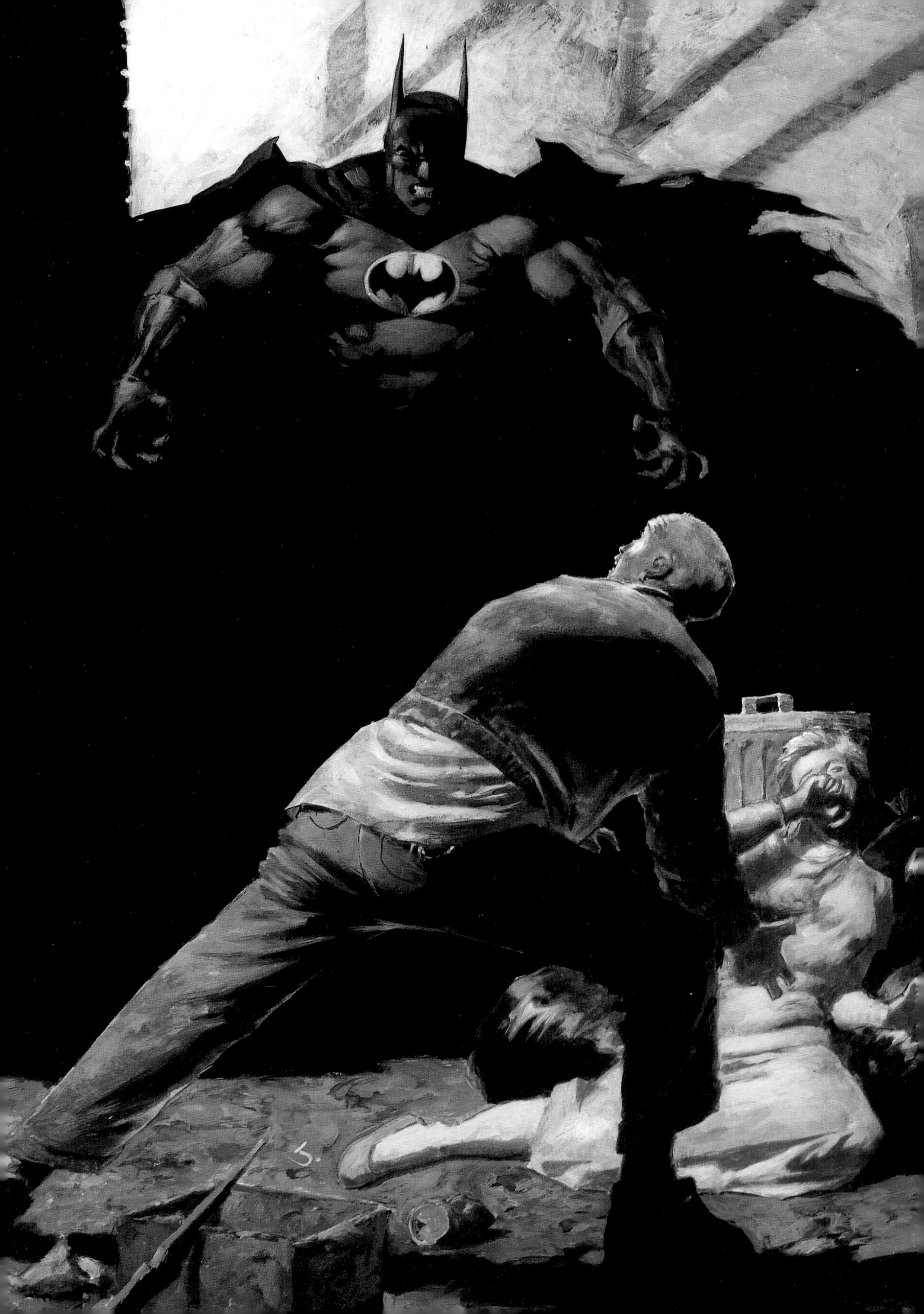

DEATH OF A DARK LEGEND

"How can the radio say he wasn't real? I was there. Dragged into that awful alley. Listening to that horrible voice describe what would happen to me before I died. Then the blackness. The sound of that huge cape. And I was free. He saved me. Now he's dead and they're trying to say he never existed. It's not fair. I owe my life to him and they're trying to kill him *twice*."

ART CONCEPT

Although the mugger is central to the image, neither the villain, the victim, or the viewer doubt who's in charge.

SCOTT HAMPTON'S SOLUTION

"This is another of the '500-pounder' shots. Batman is beefed up, much bigger than he normally is.

"Still, I didn't mean for the mugger's shoe to be so close to the right edge of the card, but the intention was to get close to the action.

"This piece and Pier 13 [page 13] really crystallized the approach I wanted to take. I tried to get some texture in the piece, even though some of the spaces were supposed to be fairly flat. I like layering my paint, thin to thick. I start with transparent colors, and then get thicker and thicker. I scrubbed a sienna-based color in, and then worked it up. I think it adds a feel to it that you can't always achieve with acrylics."

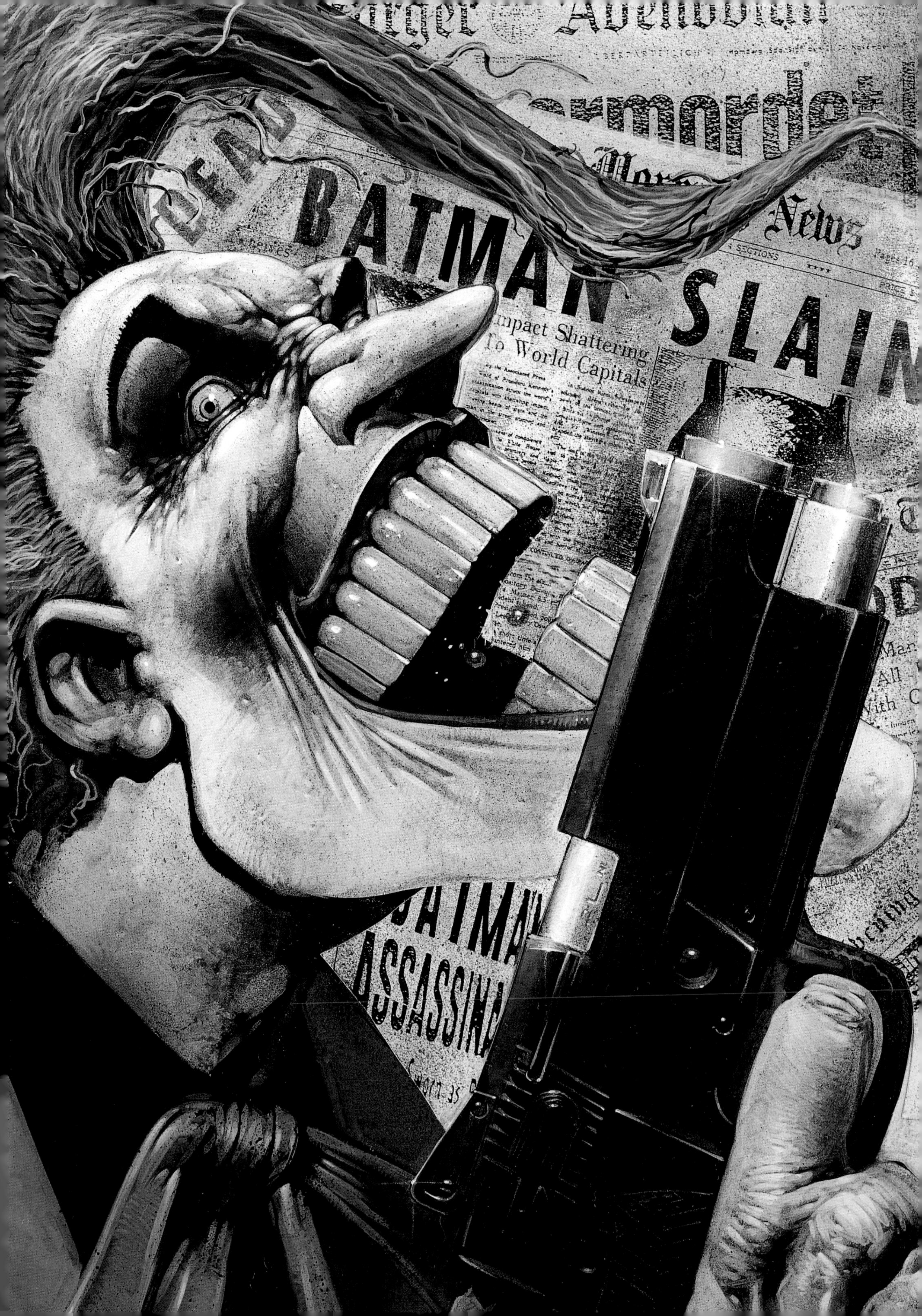
BATMAN SLAIN
Impact Shattering
To World Capitals
News
ASSASSINA

I DID IT!

"I clipped his dark wings forever! I *killed the Batman! HYAHAHAHAHAAA!* Or . . . *did* I? The deck of calling cards *seems* like me, but I haven't even *seen* Bats since blowing Arkham . . . or *have* I? But if I *didn't* kill him, *who did?* And even if I *did* kill him, he *can't* be dead—heh heh hyee—because *I forgot to enjoy it! HYEEHAHAHAAAA!"*

ART CONCEPT

Maniacally laughing Joker holding his .45 automatic, maybe twirling it with his finger thru the trigger-guard; he is now wearing his familiar purple suit; background is a crazily overlapping patchwork montage of newspapers, magazines, & TV screens, all blaring a similar message:
BATMAN DEAD! WHO KILLED THE BAT? BATMAN R.I.P.
JINXED BY THE JOKER DEATH OF A DARK KNIGHT
VIGILANTE VICTIM OF VIOLENCE BYE-BYE BAT
FALL OF THE BAT

CARL CRITCHLOW'S SOLUTION

"I was trying to get a big Joker onto each of my cards—that was my plan. I knew my cards would be spaced through the set, and a common element (a big head) would link them together.

"I wouldn't have done it if, say, I was painting cards 1 through 9. Then you'd end up with a big line of faces, which wouldn't work so well."

When given the task of painting how the news media respond to the death of a super hero, Critchlow looked to history.

"I went out and bought a book which was all about the assassination of President Kennedy. It had newspapers in it, and the headline 'Kennedy Slain: Impact Shattering the World Capitals . . . ' seemed appropriate.

"I photocopied them, and pasted 'Batman' over 'Kennedy.' I stuck them on the back [of the illustration board] and painted around them."

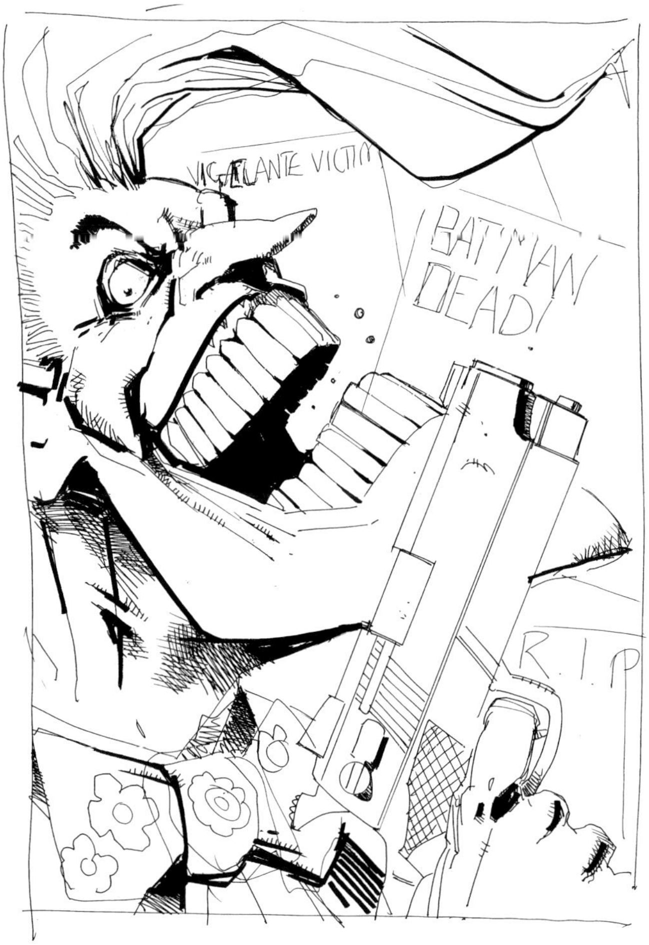
VIGILANTE VICTIM
BATMAN DEAD!
R.I.P

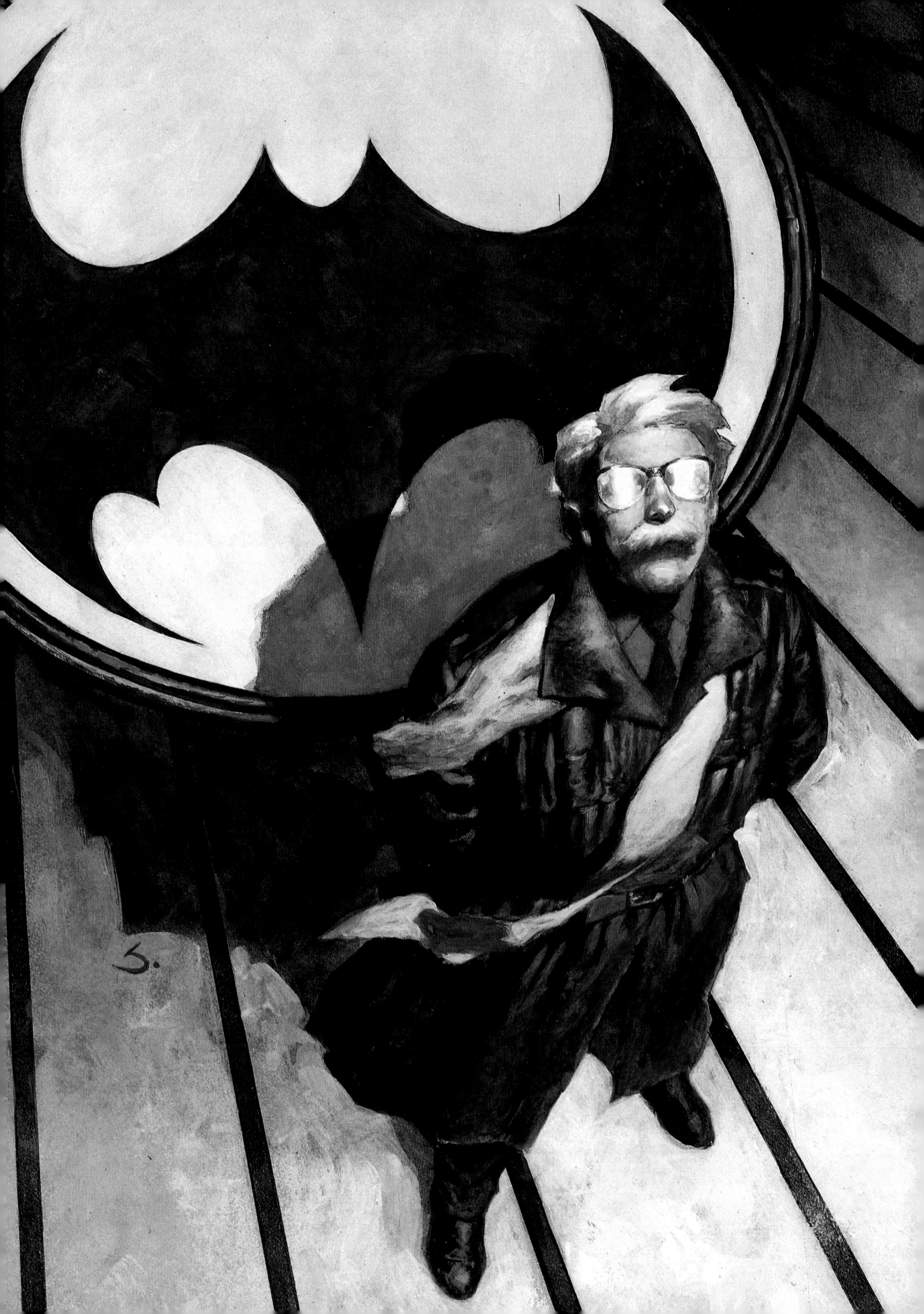

HEADQUARTERS

Below, the station bustles with a normal nightwatch in Gotham. Phones ring and radios crackle. Suspects are booked, printed, and jailed. A stubborn coffee machine is kicked and pounded. Cops trade war stories with gallows humor. And the pizza boy searches for Bullock. . . .

But up here on the roof all is darkness, the stars occluded by smog and a signal, never answered, finally cut dead.

ART CONCEPT

Police Commissioner James Gordon (in trench coat) on the roof of Police Headquarters, looking grimly somber as he stands next to the Bat-Signal beacon; the beacon has been turned off and is dark—but we can nevertheless still clearly see the Bat Emblem painted on beacon's glass.

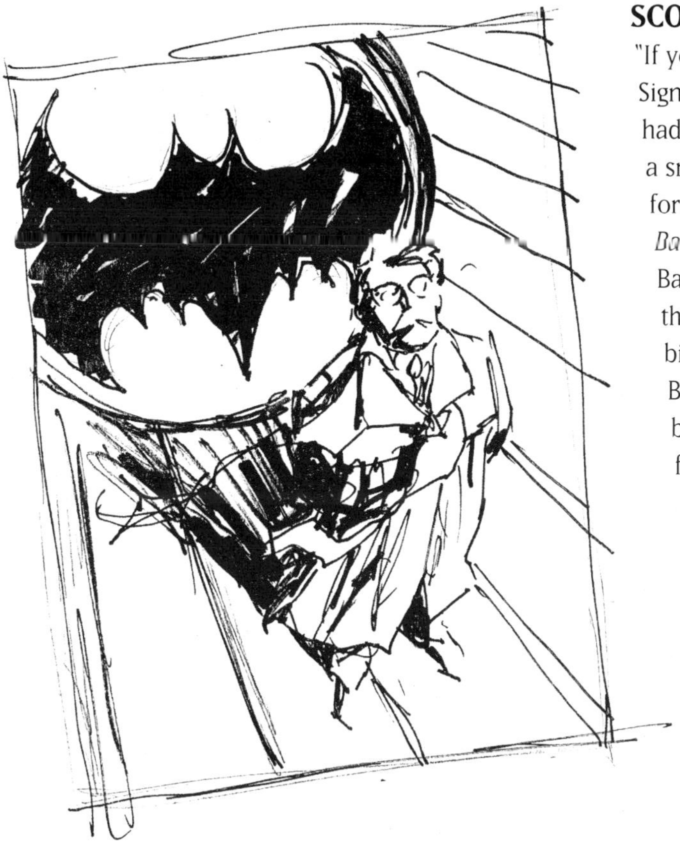

SCOTT HAMPTON'S SOLUTION

"If you look through the sketches, the Bat-Signal is small, and then it becomes bigger. I had initially conceived the Bat-Signal as being a smallish thing, but that really didn't work for me. Then I saw the Seal video from the *Batman Forever* movie. Seal makes use of a Bat-Signal that is just gigantic, and I thought, 'ah, cool!' I felt freed up to use a bigger one; with the round shape of the Bat-Signal and the vertical of Gordon beside it, the composition really worked for me.

"I also thought this was a nice moment. Commissioner Gordon is not sending out a signal for Batman to meet him; the Bat-Signal is off. Instead, he's contemplating."

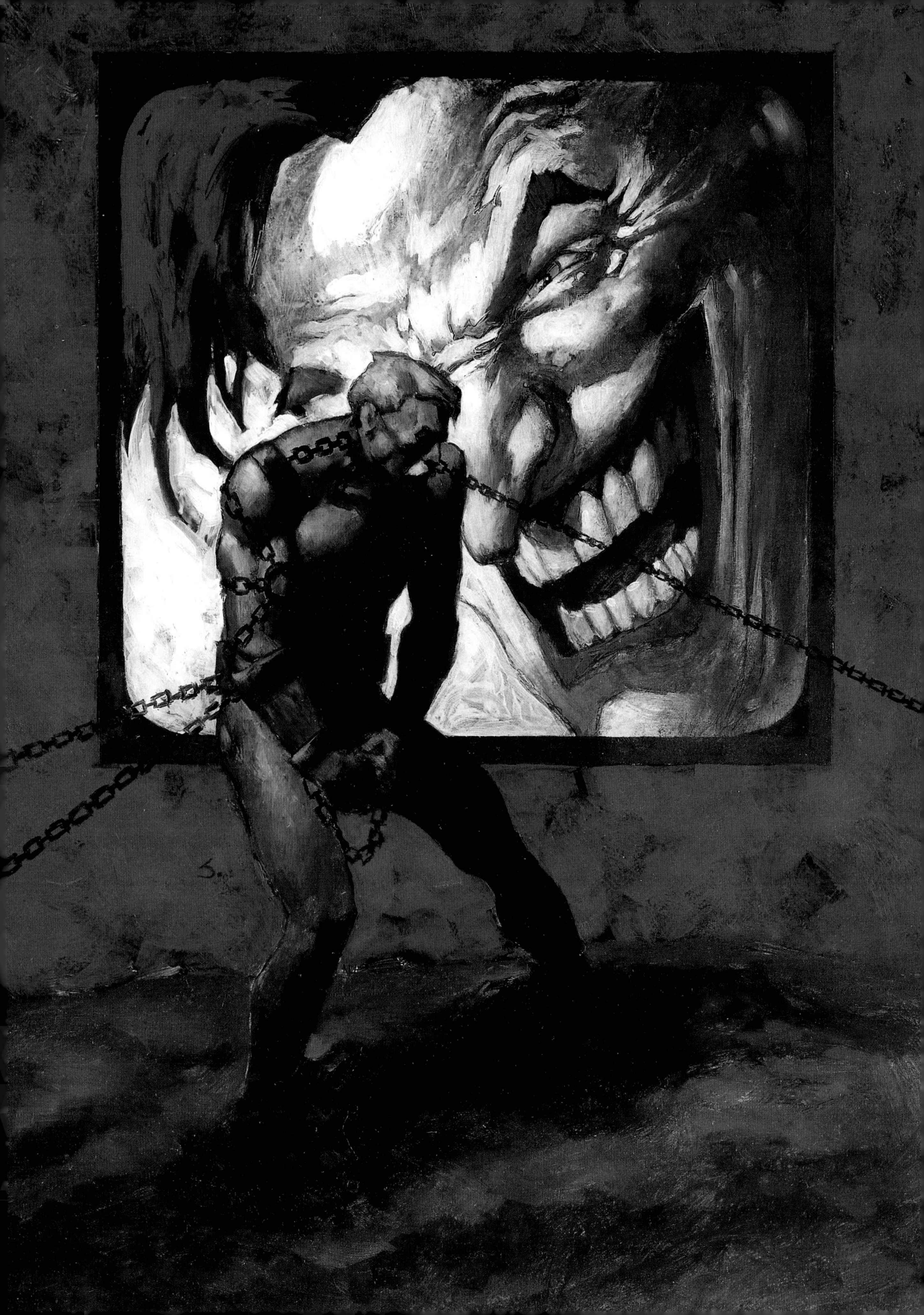

THE LOG OF COMMISSIONER GORDON

"He's faced the Joker a dozen times, staring insanity right in its leering face, emerging whole and victorious every time . . . until now.

"Again and again he has saved countless lives, including mine, from the Joker's maniacal schemes.

"Always, he has prevented death and locked down the mad death-bringer himself . . . until now.

"So *now* . . . who will stop *the Joker?*"

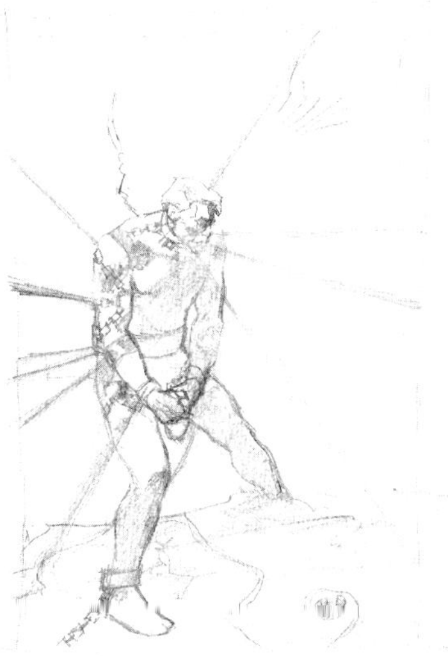

ART CONCEPT

From graphic novel *The Killing Joke:* Gordon menaced by the Joker, maybe in the amusement park—and maybe with the looming shadow of the Bat, about to strike. **Alternative:** Bound Gordon watching as Batman and Joker battle/struggle.

SCOTT HAMPTON'S SOLUTION

This was the first of the images in the set that were "a different kind of difficult." The card retells a scene from *The Killing Joke:* Gordon has been kidnapped, stripped naked, and bound in chains, and is being menaced by the Joker while surrounded by the villain's midget henchmen."

"This painting is actually much bigger than the card showed. In the actual painting, Gordon is full figure, Joker is full figure, on a television set. But the full image was thought to be 'too much' for an all-ages card set. They decided to crop in on it, to the point where you can't see his knees. They also canted it about 20 degrees. In the painting, the Joker is the one who's looming in at an angle, instead of being straight up and down, which is what he's doing in this card. I think that it de-emphasizes the fact that the Joker is humiliating Gordon.

"I think it's more effective the way that I painted it, but then," Hampton laughs, "I would."

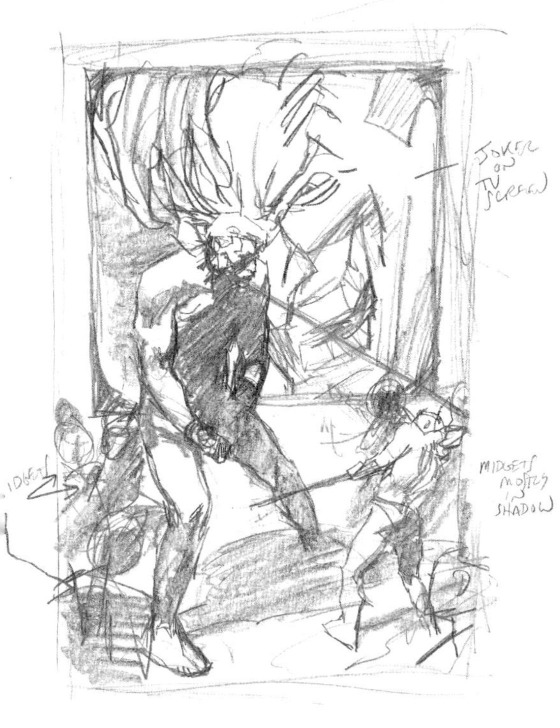
JOKER ON TV SCREEN
MIDGETS MOSTLY IN SHADOW

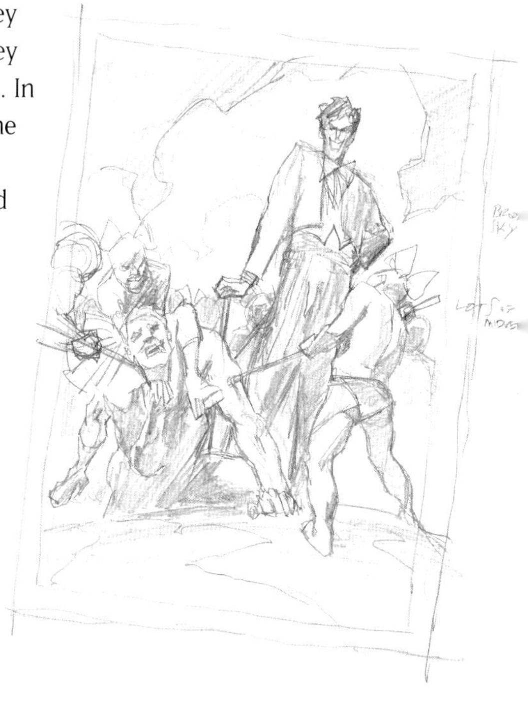

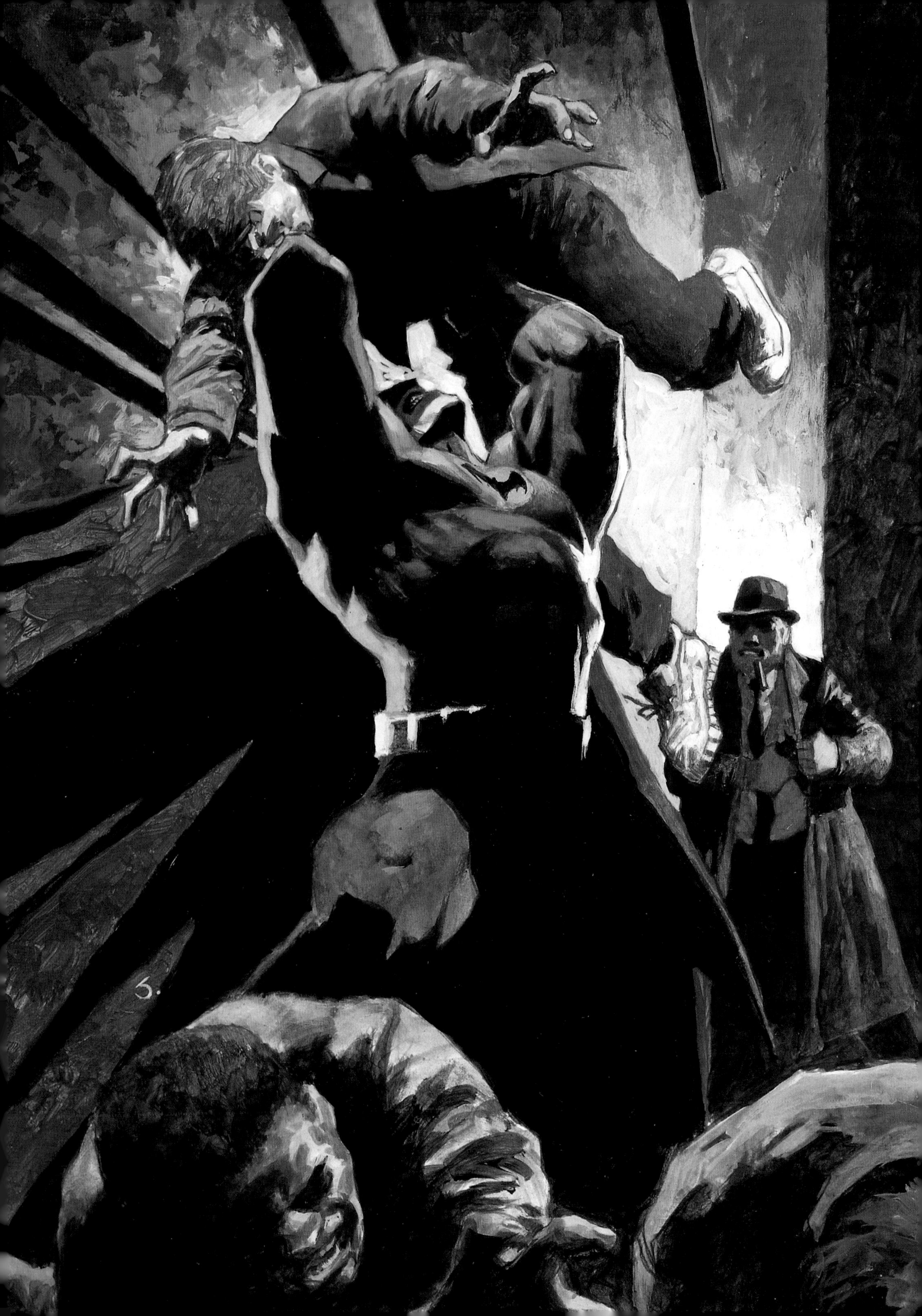

SGT. HARVEY BULLOCK

"I tell ya, Montoya, it's hard ta *believe*. All's I can remember is the first time I ever seen that freak thump some thug butt in that alley. Talk about yer scary force o' nature. I mean, gettin' blown away by that nutcase Joker *kinda* makes sense, but it's still hard ta believe the Bat could ever kick the big can . . . ya *know?*"

ART CONCEPT

Beefy rumpled-slob bull-in-a-china-shop Harvey Bullock is for once awed as he watches (from background would be fine) Batman in furious alley action, brutally efficient as he puts down several thugs—or puts down one thug with several others already sprawled/felled. **Overall image:** Bullock's "vision" of Batman is that of a frightening fighting machine—a force of awesome action and someone not to be messed with.

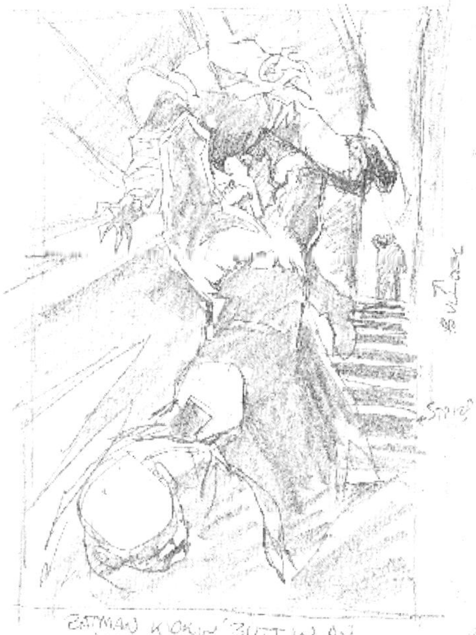
BATMAN KICKIN' BUTT IN AN
ALLEY

SCOTT HAMPTON'S SOLUTION

"I came to know more and more about these characters as I did this set. I went through a ton of reference material to get a feel for them. I found that Bullock was a really interesting guy.

"He wears a crumpled trench coat and smokes a stogie while criticizing Michael Stipe from REM. There's a neat dichotomy to the character: he seems sensitive, he seems to have a nice duality to him. He looks like a classic flatfoot, like the kind that would play in a *Dirty Harry* movie to make [Clint] Eastwood look good.

"This is how he sees Batman. . . . It's another one of the 500-pounder images. I wanted to give the impression that many people see Batman as this gigantically huge thing.

"I think that comes across better here than with some of the other images."

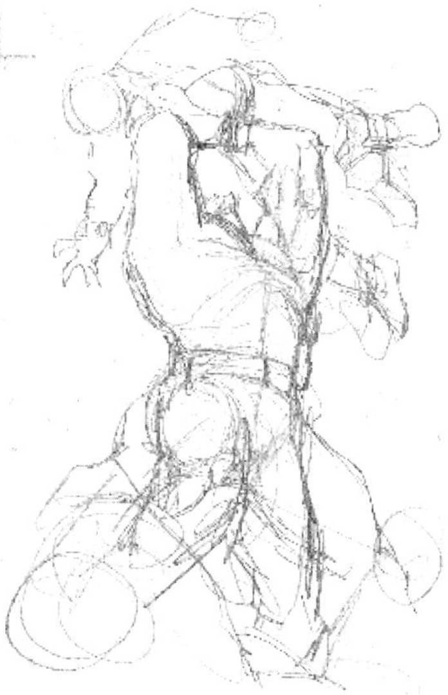

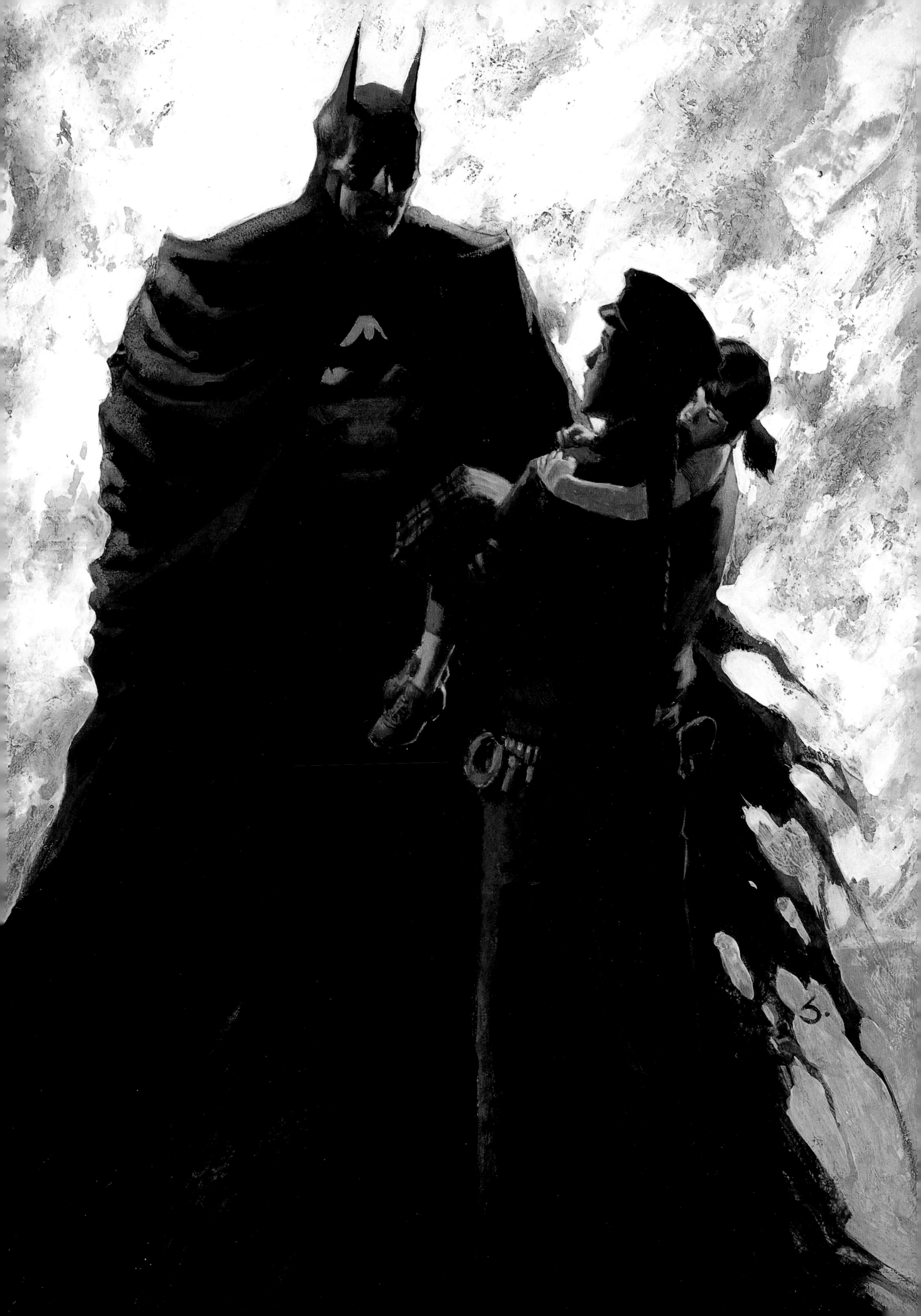

OFFICER RENEE MONTOYA

"He was *more* than scary, Harv. He was everything a good *cop* should be, and *more.* Risking his life at every opportunity, never hesitating and never even drawing pay. He was the living definition of a *true hero*—and everything I've ever wanted to be. But you're right about one thing . . . it's *impossible* to believe he's gone."

ART CONCEPT

Montoya (in her police uniform) regarding Batman with respect and admiration as he extends (to her) the 8-year-old kid he has just rescued from burning building—same kid seen on the He Was Real! card [page 19]. Background is the burning building or at least flames. **Overall image:** Montoya's "vision" of Batman is that of a Dark Angel savior.

SCOTT HAMPTON'S SOLUTION

Renee Montoya has been recently promoted and partnered with Harvey Bullock. She's said to be intelligent, compassionate, and patient—which helps with dealing with Bullock.

"This is a very simple card. This is a follow-up to Batman crashing out of the window with the little girl. With both cards, I made the conscious choice not to make the fire the light source. I felt that too much information would be lost if I did that, so I left him with just blues set against the warms. For the purposes of good storytelling, I wanted to make the figures clear."

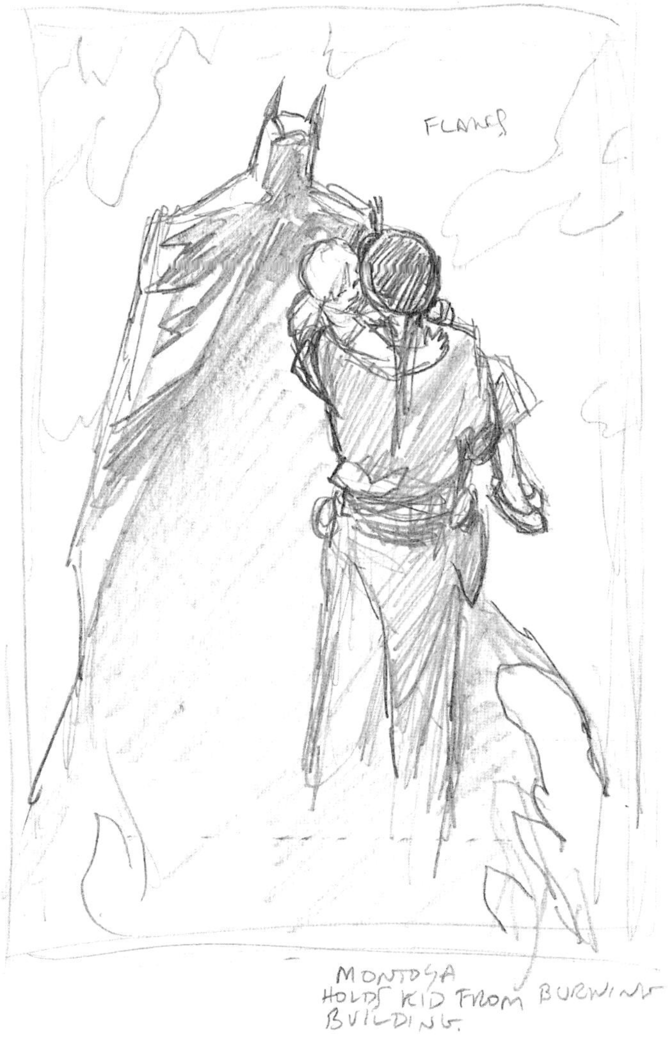
FLAMES
MONTOYA
HOLDS KID FROM BURNING
BUILDING.

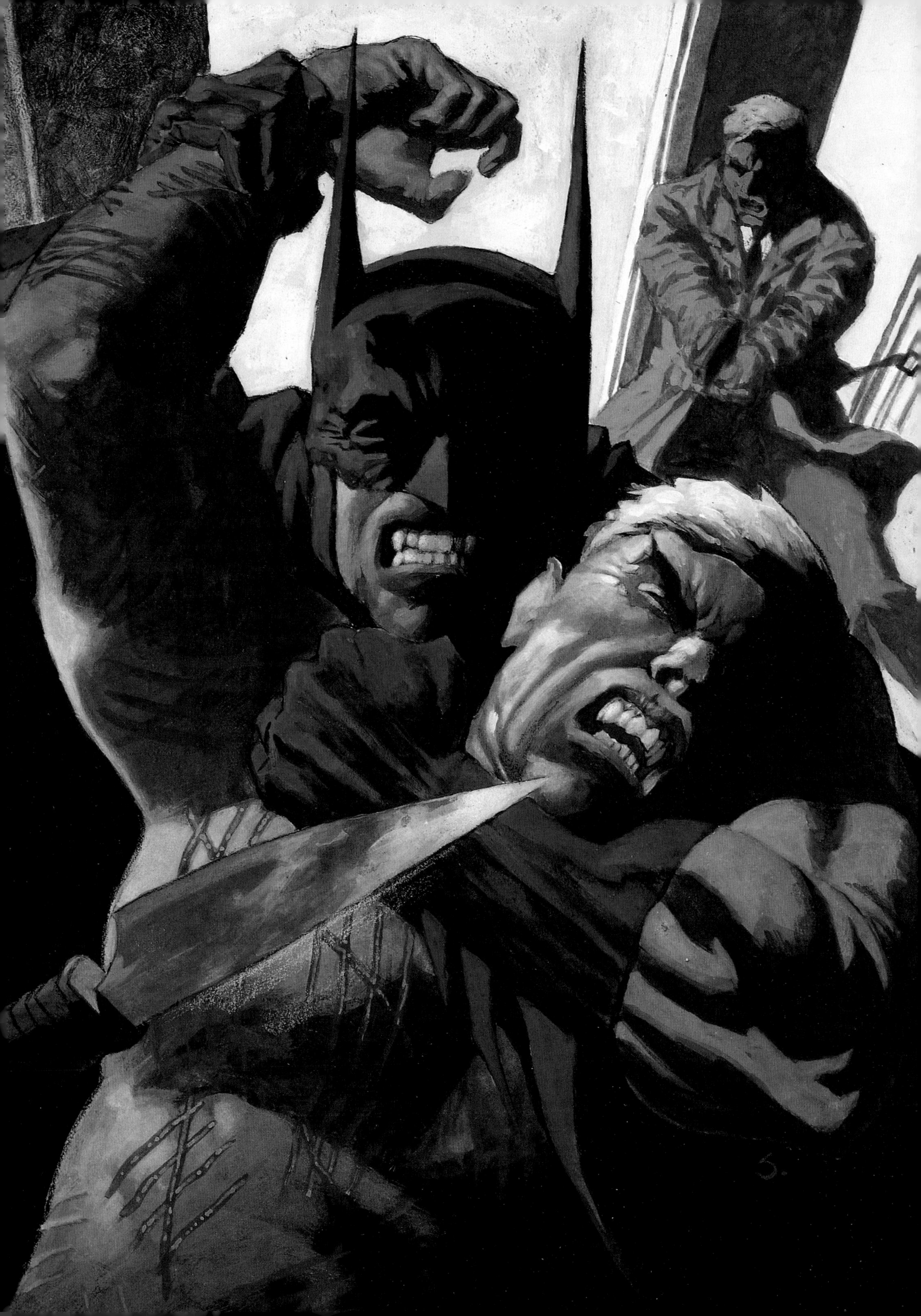

LIEUTENANT LAWRENCE KITCH

"I've got a different take. You all know I'm strictly by-the-book. And to me the book is *sacred*. Rules have *reasons*. The Batman *broke* the rules left, right, and center. He was a *vigilante*, not a cop. But yes, he got *results*. Saved *lives*. If anarchy *can* be good, I suppose he was one of the good guys. Am I right, Bock?"

ART CONCEPT

Plainclothes homicide detective Lt. Kitch (the blond guy) showing grudging (very grudging) respect as he faces "Grim Avenger" Batman over the fallen body of serial killer Mr. Zsasz—the guy who wears nothing but shorts and whose body & face are covered with "tally scars," each self-inflicted scar marking another of his victims. **Alternative:** Batman could be holding limp/unconscious Zsasz by the neck, turning him over to Kitch.

SCOTT HAMPTON'S SOLUTION

Kitch is perhaps the one cop on the Gotham City Police Department that would have met Batman socially—as Bruce Wayne. He's young and idealistic, a "society" lawyer who wanted to do more for society. Luckily he's currently partnered with street-smart and realistic Detective Caz Sallucci.

"Keeping Batman in action with these cards, or having to relate to these different detectives. . . . It was difficult to have to find new ways for them to be around. I wanted to make sure that this painting was a little off-balance, a little bit off-kilter. There's a little bit of a spray with the lines, they're not just all up and down. . . .

"This is one of those instances where the sketch is more effective than the painting, unfortunately. The sketch has so much more life than the painting does. Sometimes, the energy of the sketch gets lost in the finished piece."

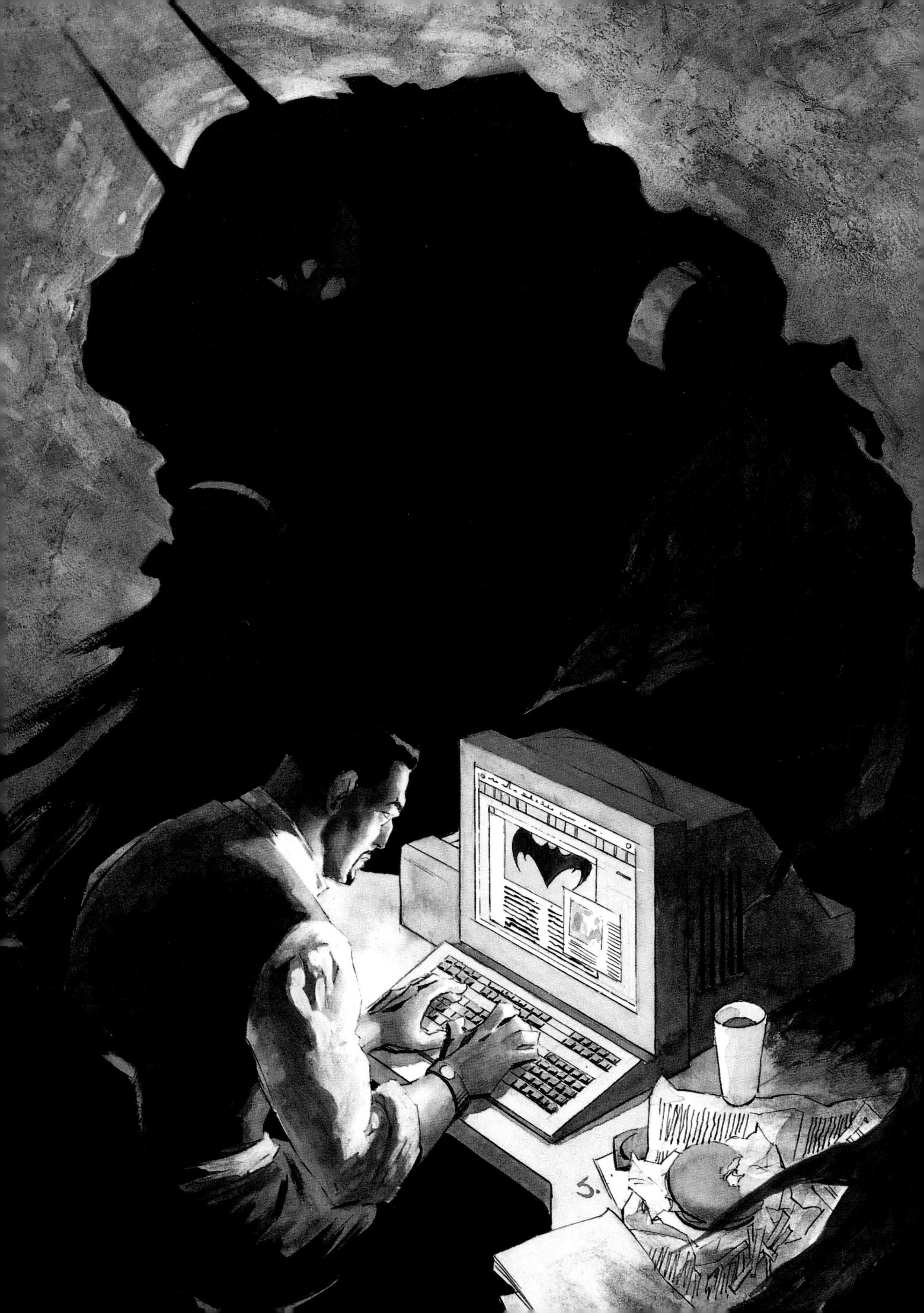

SGT. MACKENZIE "HARDBACK" BOCK

"Until I was transferred to Gotham, I didn't believe there *was* a Batman. I figured he was some disinformation myth you people floated as a psychological secret weapon. Now that I've done *reading* on the subject . . . press accounts, department files, witness statements . . . he's *still* vague in my mind, still a *myth*, some secret part of the night, and maybe even a living shred of the darkness within our souls."

ART CONCEPT

Close-up MacKenzie Bock [recent continuing character—plainclothes cop with the nickname "Hardback"] in lower foreground left; beyond is a "vague" and shadowy/mysterious full-figure image of the Batman.

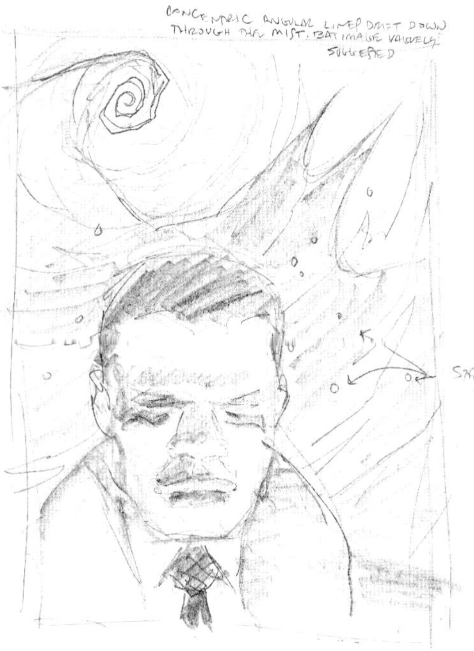
CONCENTRIC ANGULAR LINES DRIFT DOWN
THROUGH THE MIST. BAT IMAGE VAGUELY
SUGGESTED

SCOTT HAMPTON'S SOLUTION

The nickname "Hardback" was a gift from Bullock—given for Bock's passion for reading, research, and reports. There's little he doesn't know (save, perhaps, for Batman's secret identity).

"This painting turned out a little bit more darkly than I expected, but I'd rather an image go darker than lighter. It wasn't particularly evocative, so I tried to put some detail and subtleties into the image.

"This painting establishes Batman as a symbolic, almost spiritual entity in Gotham rather than as just a man. Here, Bock is surrounded by the 'cave' created by Batman's cloak, suggesting that Batman is almost mythical in his presence.

"This was one of the few paintings [the other was Killing Joke (page 53)] in which I applied acrylic initially, and then spread fine charcoal into the shadowed areas. Again, it has a uniform sort of coating, but it gives a certain amount of grit to the paintings. My only problem with charcoal is that it's messy. The results are interesting, especially with the crevices created by the acrylics. I liked the way it reproduced."

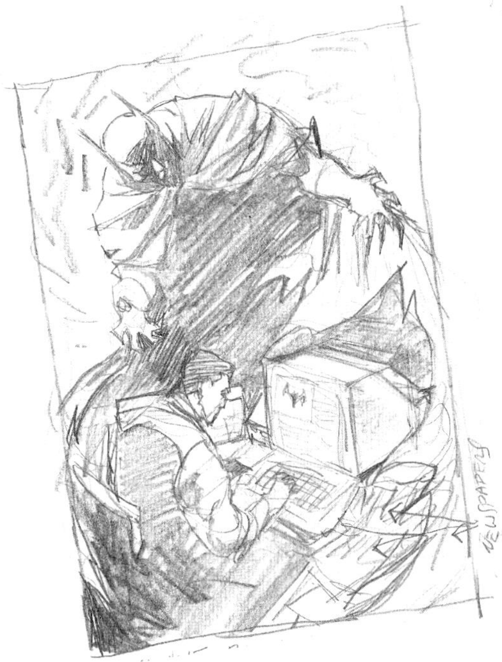
NEWSPAPERS

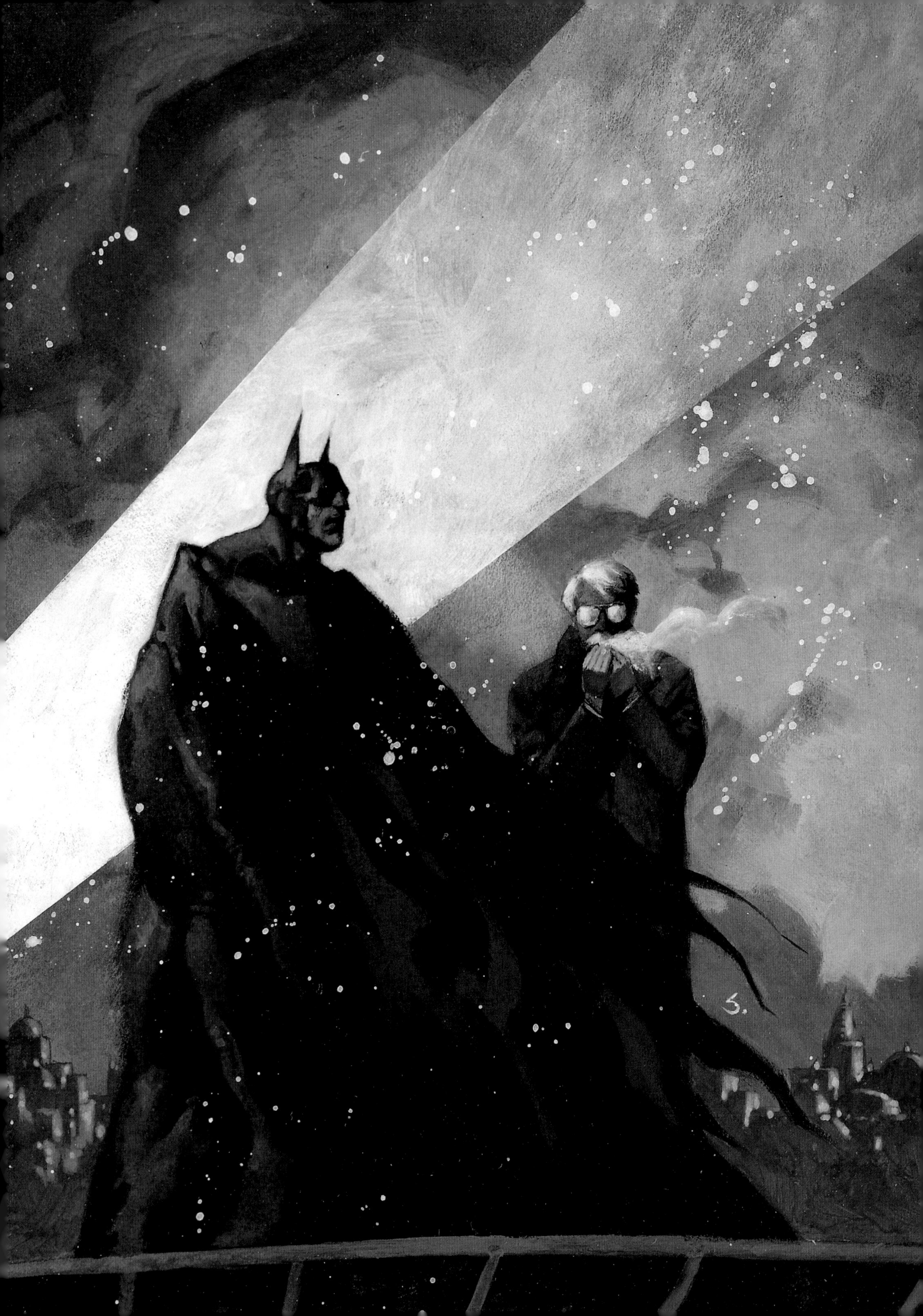

"FRIENDS"

"That's what we were, I suppose, although never in the traditional sense. He wasn't a cop, but he was the finest and best crime fighter who ever lived. It was a huge and dangerous choice I took, sharing police confidence with a 'vigilante,' but no man ever earned more of my trust and respect.

"May his dark and indomitable soul rest in peace."

ART CONCEPT

A Gordon "vision" of Batman from the past—the two meeting as trusted confidants on Police HQ roof (maybe Gordon extending police report file folders to Batman)—with the now/then-blazing Bat-Signal beacon seen between and/or beyond them, stabbing its bright beam diagonally upward off-image.

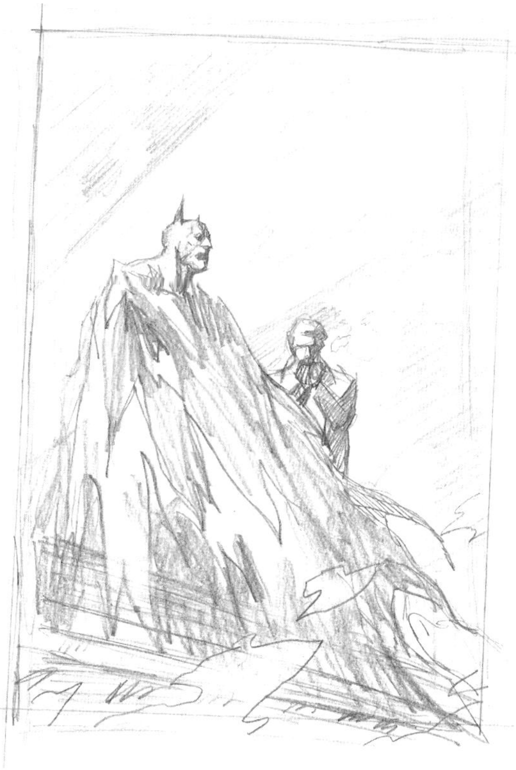

SCOTT HAMPTON'S SOLUTION

Before joining the Gotham City Police Department, Police Commissioner James Gordon served in the military and on the Chicago police force. When Batman first appeared in Gotham, Gordon, a tough and honest cop, was assigned to the task force charged with bringing the Batman down. In time, they became allies, and finally, friends.

"Emotionally, this was the card I was the most responsive to. I like the idea of Batman and Gordon hammering out ideas on top of police headquarters.

"I had Gordon lighting his pipe. But Gordon doesn't smoke anymore, and we didn't want to tell kids that they need to smoke, so I changed the image so Gordon is holding his hands in front of his mouth as if it's cold and he's blowing on them to keep them warm."

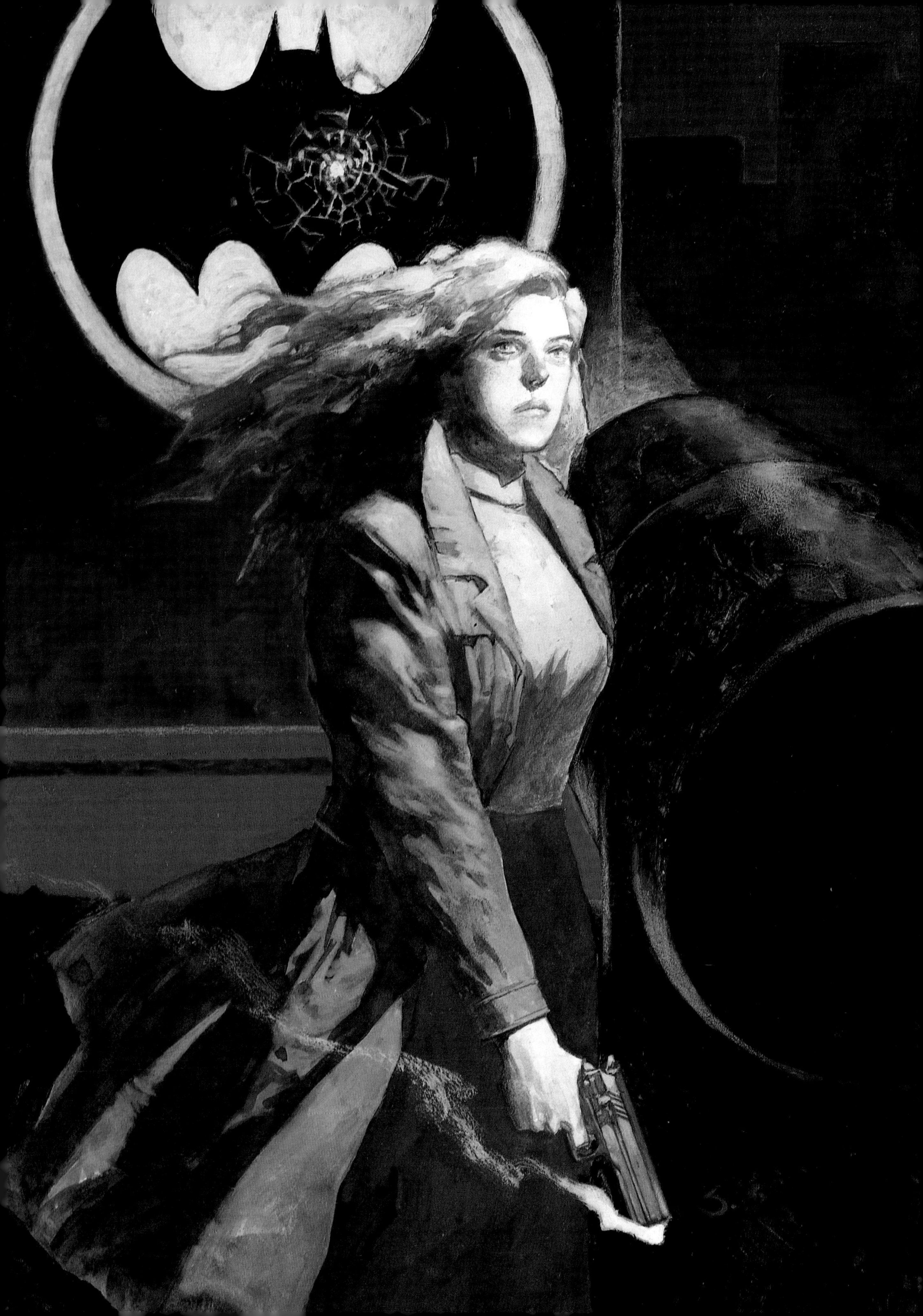

LT. SARAH ESSEN GORDON

Commissioner Gordon:

"My wife, one of the best cops I've ever known, always insisted I was wrong about him. She resented the Batman as a symbol of police failure. Even more so, she resented my 'dependency' on him. In her eyes, I should have been strong enough to need no help—other than hers.

"And yet, just an hour ago . . . she wept at the news."

ART CONCEPT

Slightly low-angle shot on plainclothes Sarah Essen Gordon on roof in foreground with hard eyes and still-smoking service revolver in hand; looking upward & beyond her, we see the Bat-Signal projected on clouds—riven with jagged cracks radiating outward from a hole in the center of the black Bat Emblem. **Overall image:** She has just pumped a bullet into the beacon's glass, although no need to show the beacon itself—just the shattered/cracked emblem/signal projected up in sky.

SCOTT HAMPTON'S SOLUTION

Sarah, Gordon's second wife, has been used as a pawn in power games between Gordon and the mayor of Gotham, culminating in her appointment as Gotham City Police Commissioner. Currently, she helms the G.C.P.D.'s Major Crimes Unit.

"Everything in this card, except for the flesh tones, is done in acrylic. For the flesh tones I wanted clarity and lightness, and a subtlety of brush tones. I wanted a gentleness and a fragility in the face, to suggest the emotions Sarah might be feeling. Rather than using opaque acrylics and playing with them to achieve the effect I wanted, I just used watercolors."

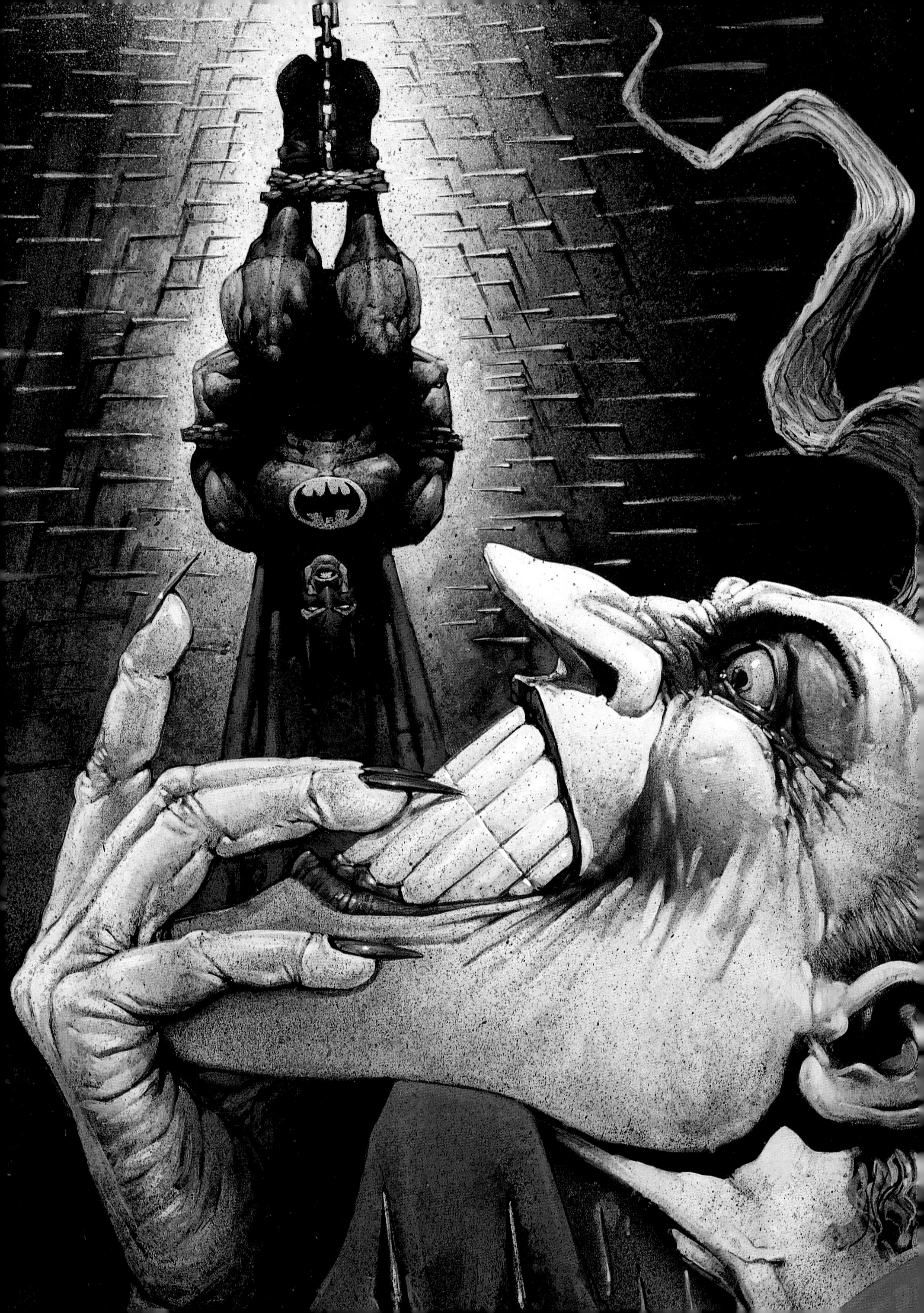

DEATHTRAP

"It makes *no sense*—usually a *good* thing, but this time I don't *like* it! If I couldn't kill Bats with my ingenious shrinking *Room of Doom,* how did I manage it with a few measly *bullets?!* But on the *other* hand, I *had* to do it—because if *I* couldn't kill him, *no one* could! Yi-yi-*YAI!* The whole thing's enough to drive me *Batty!*"

ART CONCEPT

Bound at wrists & ankles, Batman dangles upside-down in a room utterly barren except for the nasty spikes bristling from floor, ceiling, and closing walls. A classic deathtrap from which there should be no possible escape. Joker should be seen either peering thru a window in background (as part of scene) or (symbolically) as a superimposed close-up in extreme foreground.

CARL CRITCHLOW'S SOLUTION

"I was quite pleased, because this was one that I could sort of picture before I started. It came out more or less as I imagined it, which is a bit of a bonus. Again, it's a big Joker head, but this time, the Batman's in the picture.

Critchlow prefers painting with acrylics and "a bit of ink."

"Acrylics go on quickly, dry quickly, and you get nice bright colors. The only other alternative, for the sort of effects that I'm after, is to use oil paints, which take years and years to dry. And then you can't work back into it in the end, and they look like a right mess and take too long.

"So acrylics are just the best things for me, really."

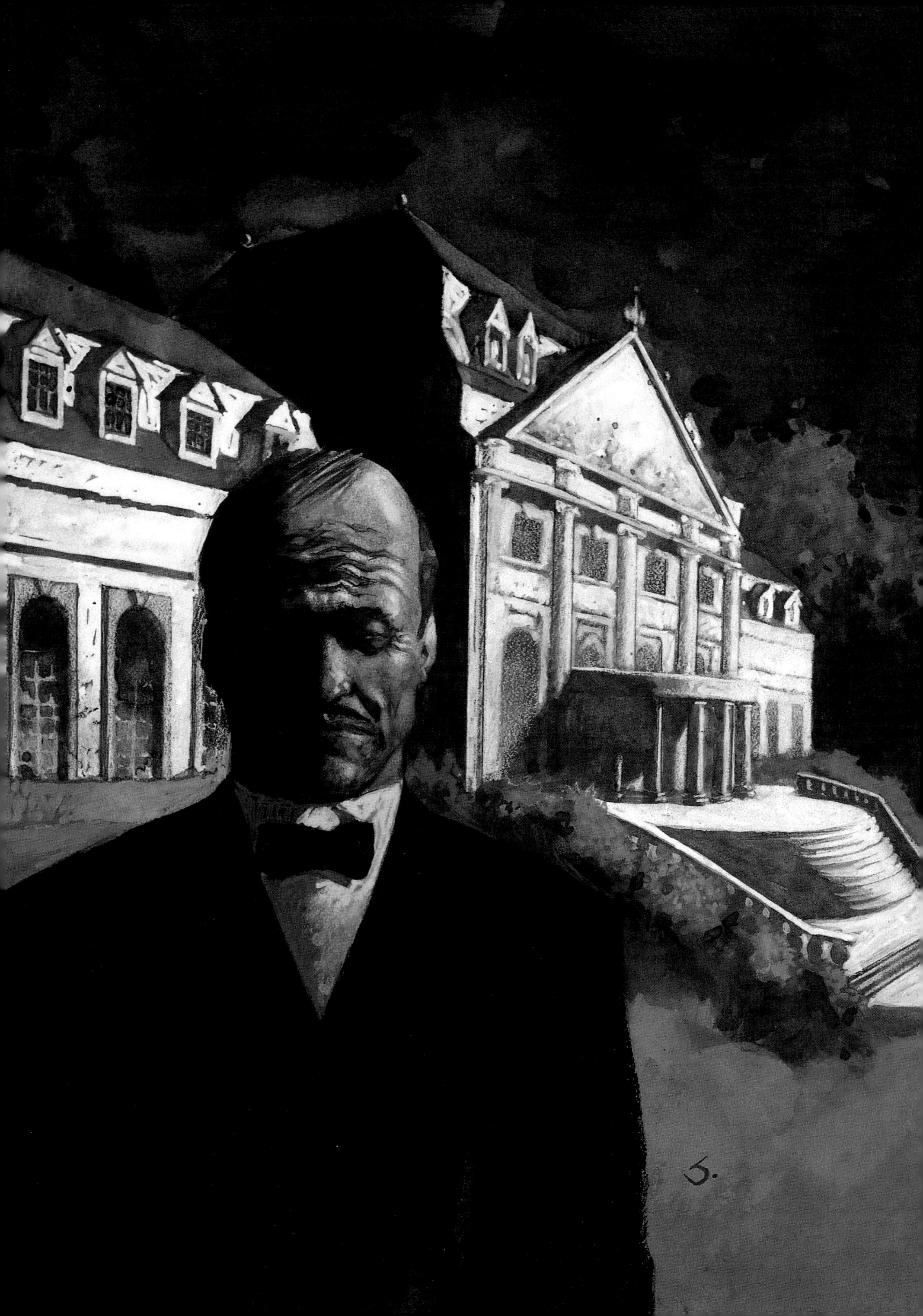

WAYNE MANOR

Its windows are dark, lavish rooms and long halls empty. The only sounds are the creak of old wood, the ticking of a stately grandfather clock. Then the house itself seems to sigh, and the clock tolls the death of another hour, heard by no one. Outside, knowing his master will never return, a faithful man waits. He sighs once over a thousand memories. Then he silently weeps.

ART CONCEPT

Quietly weeping Alfred in foreground, one tear sliding down his cheek as he tries (and fails) to be brave; beyond him is an establishing shot of Wayne Manor, looking dark & desolate. **Overall image:** As if Alfred has come outside to wait in vain. **Optional:** Ghostly image of Bruce Wayne looming above the manor.

SCOTT HAMPTON'S SOLUTION

"I always thought of Batman as a rather distant character. Many felt they knew Batman (and Bruce Wayne), but obviously, none knew him that well.

"I like to think of Alfred as the guy that Bruce really relies on, that Batman doesn't hold back from him. If he holds back anything from Alfred, he's probably holding it back from himself, as well.

"It's almost as though Batman only gets so close to people because there's only so much that's there. He's not a complex character, really—everything is good or evil, right or wrong. As the surrogate father to both, Alfred sees two sides of the character, Bruce Wayne and Batman. Alfred's not intrusive, he tries to guide, but he knows that Batman/Bruce is going to do what he thinks is best, whatever Alfred says."

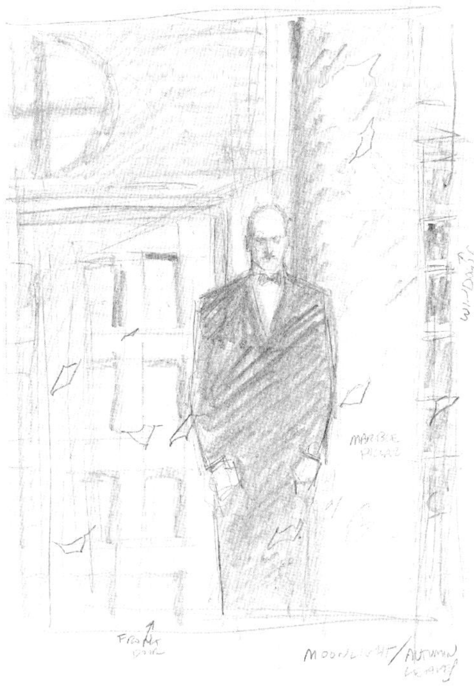

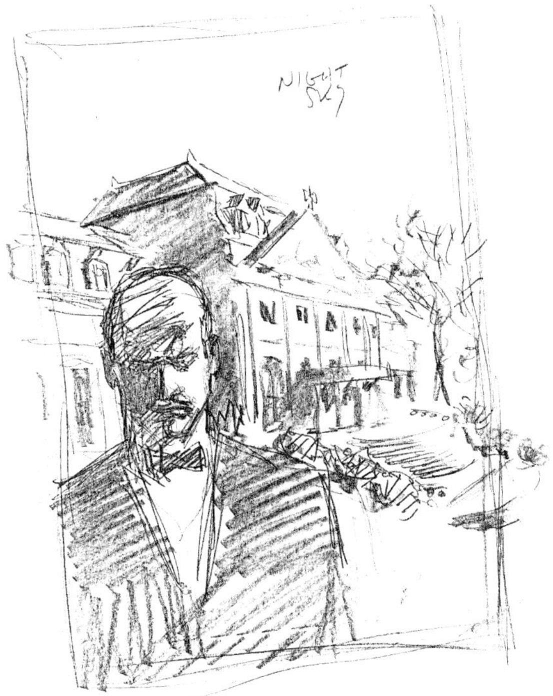
NIGHT SKY

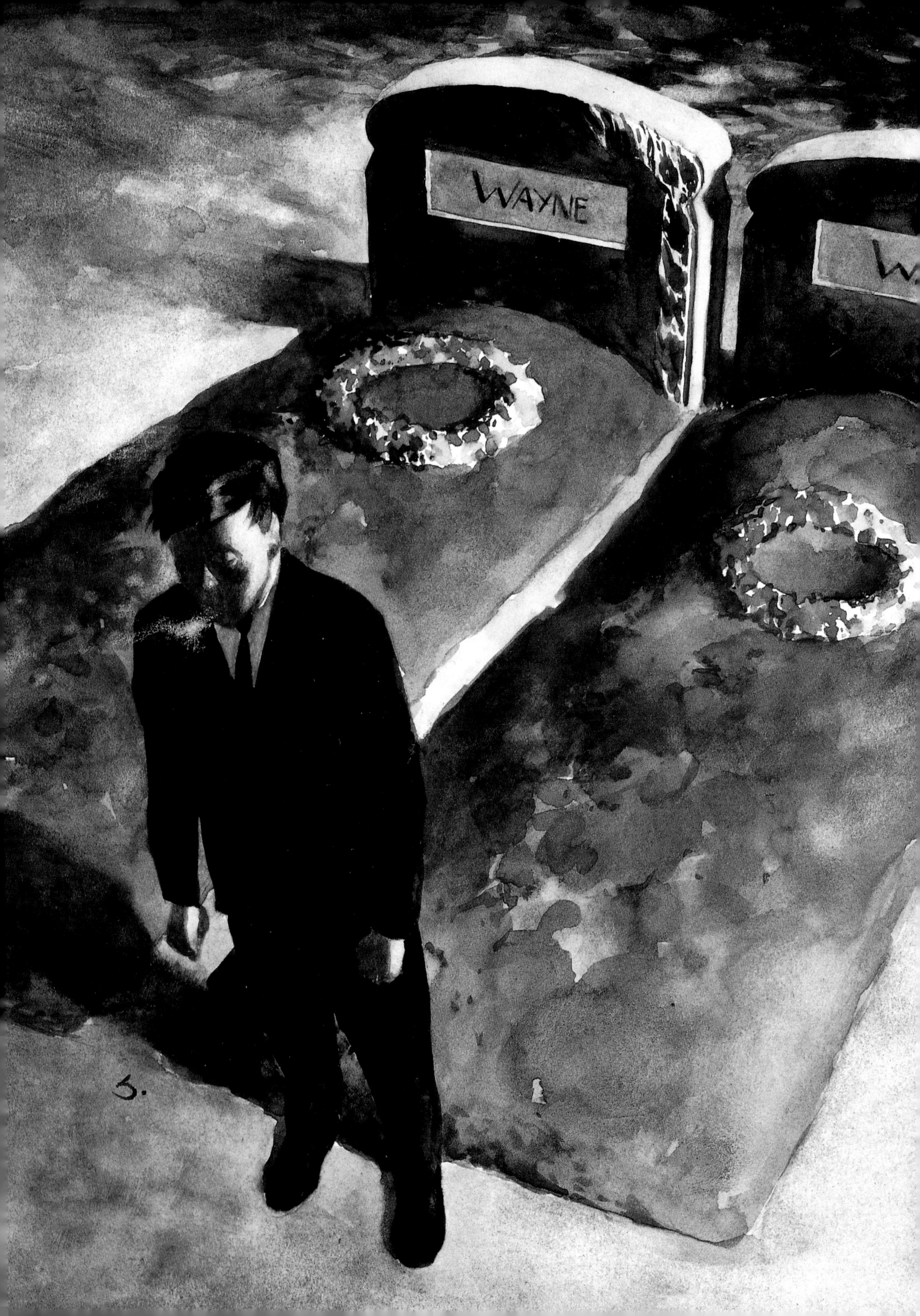
WAYNE

THE JOURNAL OF ALFRED PENNYWORTH

"What began with tragedy now ends with the same, a closed circle of murder most foul. But what was it like for the boy? Was the night chill or warm, bright or moonless? What was it like to witness the destruction of his world, helpless before something so unutterably dark and alien rushing in to fill his young soul? What was it like to suffer the ultimate horror?"

ART CONCEPT

Classic origin shot; young Bruce watching in horror as The Man With The Gun shoots his parents dead. (Actually, no need to see the entire killer; cropped hand & gun would suffice.)

SCOTT HAMPTON'S SOLUTION

"That one was tough, I had to really work to come up with an image. We started with some shots of the deaths of the parents. I went through sketch after sketch on this thing.

"Initially, I had shots of the parents being killed. And then, there were shots of Alfred sitting by the bedside of Bruce as he was being tortured by nightmares. Ultimately, I came up with this shot, which works in its way.

"I limited the palette to be very gray-brown, so that it would suggest winter. I didn't want a lot of color in the piece, nor did I want to romanticize it by making it silvery gray or raining. I wanted, in a way, to make it ugly, so that it wouldn't be seen as any less than a devastating horribleness. I wanted to suggest the fragility of his mental state by letting this be the only card in the set that was a watercolor, pure watercolor."

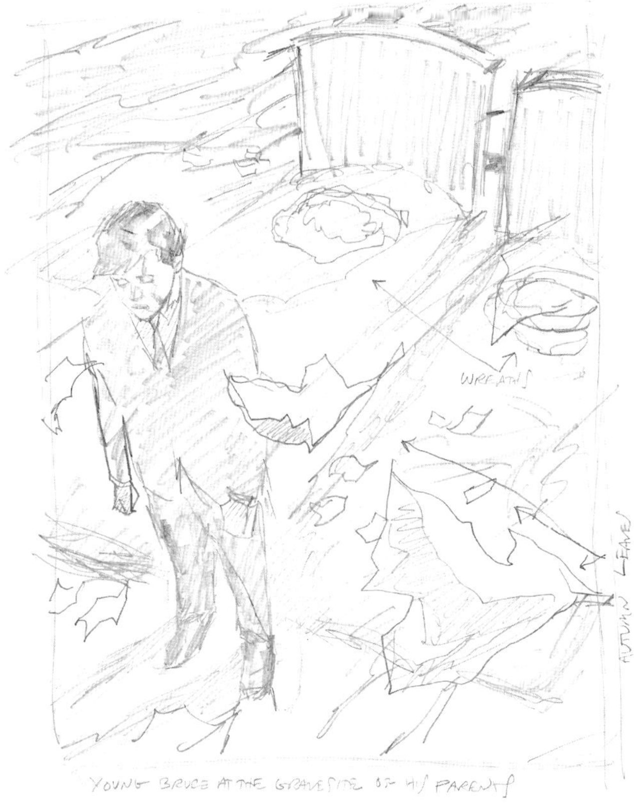
WREATHS
AUTUMN LEAVES
YOUNG BRUCE AT THE GRAVESITE OF HIS PARENTS

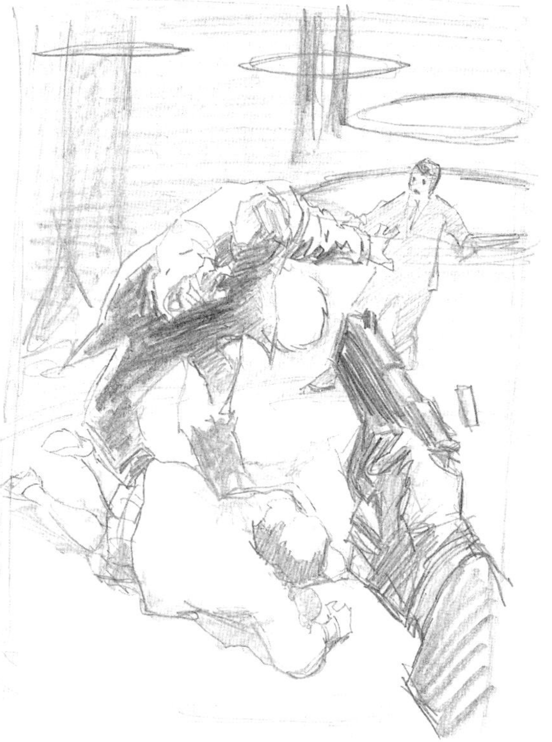

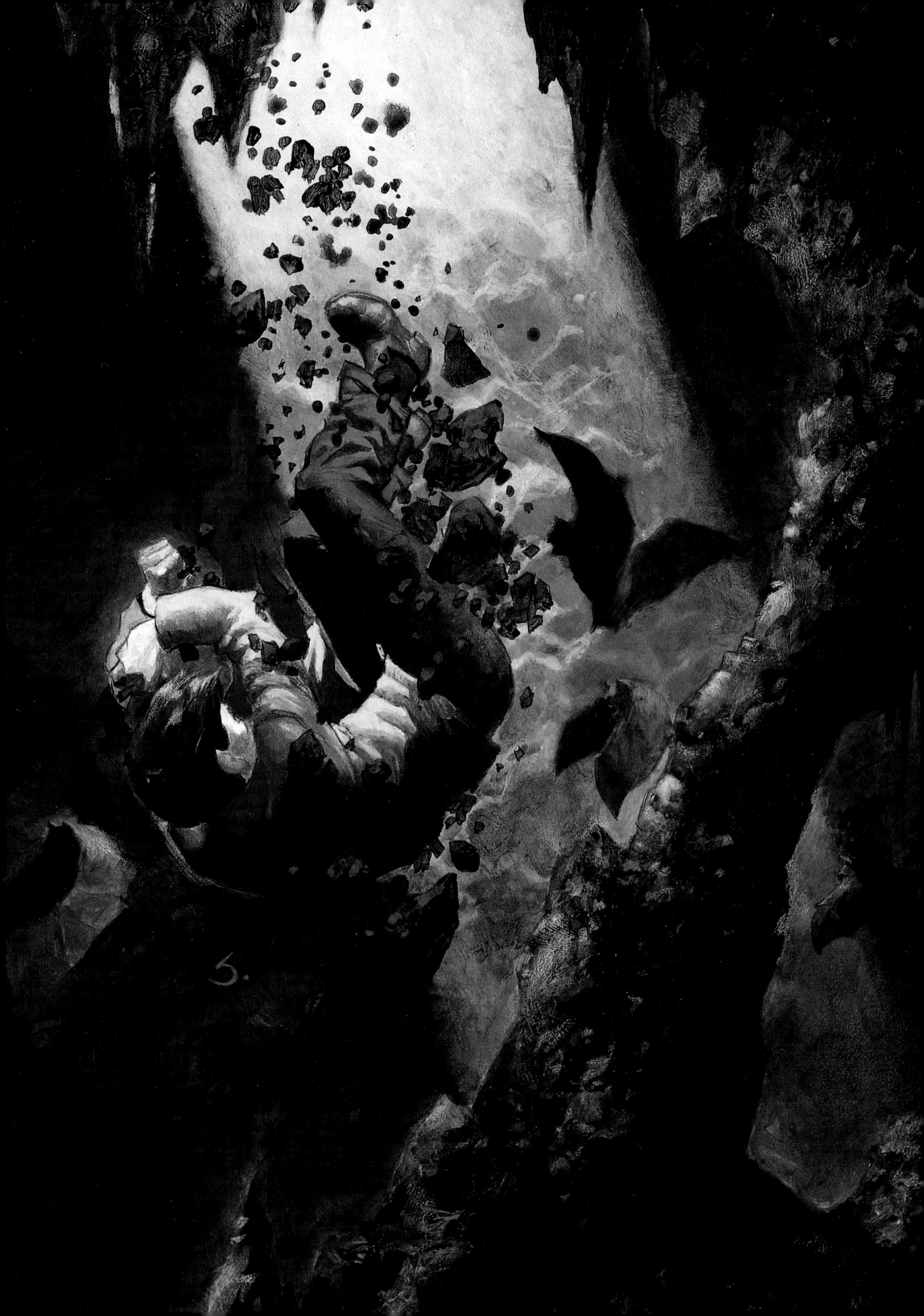

DESTINY

From the journal of Alfred Pennyworth:

"Master Bruce once told me that the only nightmare he ever had before his parents were murdered was something which actually happened. The very ground fell away and he was plunged into a place of chill dank echoes, where blackness ripped apart in tattered shreds and attacked him. As a boy, he found fear down in that darkness. As a man, he would *use* it."

ART CONCEPT

Interior virgin/natural cave; the ground above has just collapsed under 10-year-old Bruce Wayne, dumping him down here into a gloom of stalactites & stalagmites; dirt & pebbles still sifting down on him—and he has his hands up in terror, to ward off the flurry of bats he has just disturbed & which are swooping past him. Bats should be nasty & scary.

SCOTT HAMPTON'S SOLUTION

"Painting this was much more enjoyable than painting the last card.

"I didn't want to show young Bruce exploring the cave. . . . I wanted to have him in mid-air and off-balance. I think that it's very symbolic in the Batman myth that to find his eventual headquarters, Bruce had to fall into darkness and out of the light. . . . The suggestion of the rocks behind the light, painting that was a lot of fun. I underpainted the rocks a bit darker, not quite as dark as the background, but dark. Then I scumbled white paint up top fairly thick, and then I started using water to dilute it as I went down further and further so that it became less opaque and showed the rocks more and more. After that, I just hit some of the rocks with highlights, to punch them out some more. Then I added all the rocks that are falling in front of the light, with young Bruce falling, and made them pop out. I didn't want them to be swallowed [up] by all those opaques."

Note: To *scumble* is to make less brilliant by covering with a thin coat of opaque or semiopaque color.

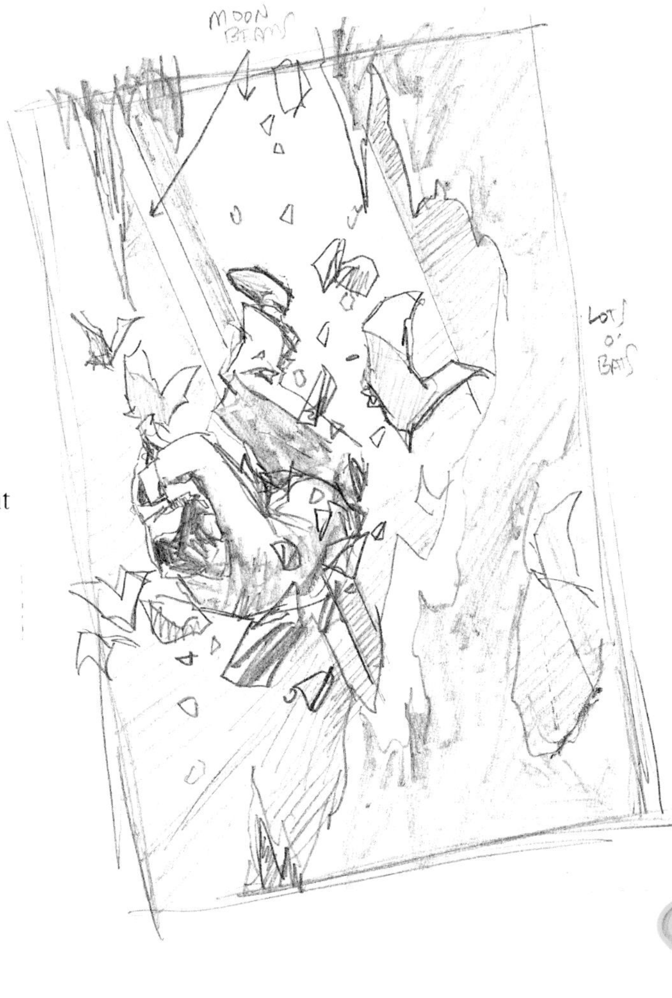
MOON BEAMS
LOTS O' BATS

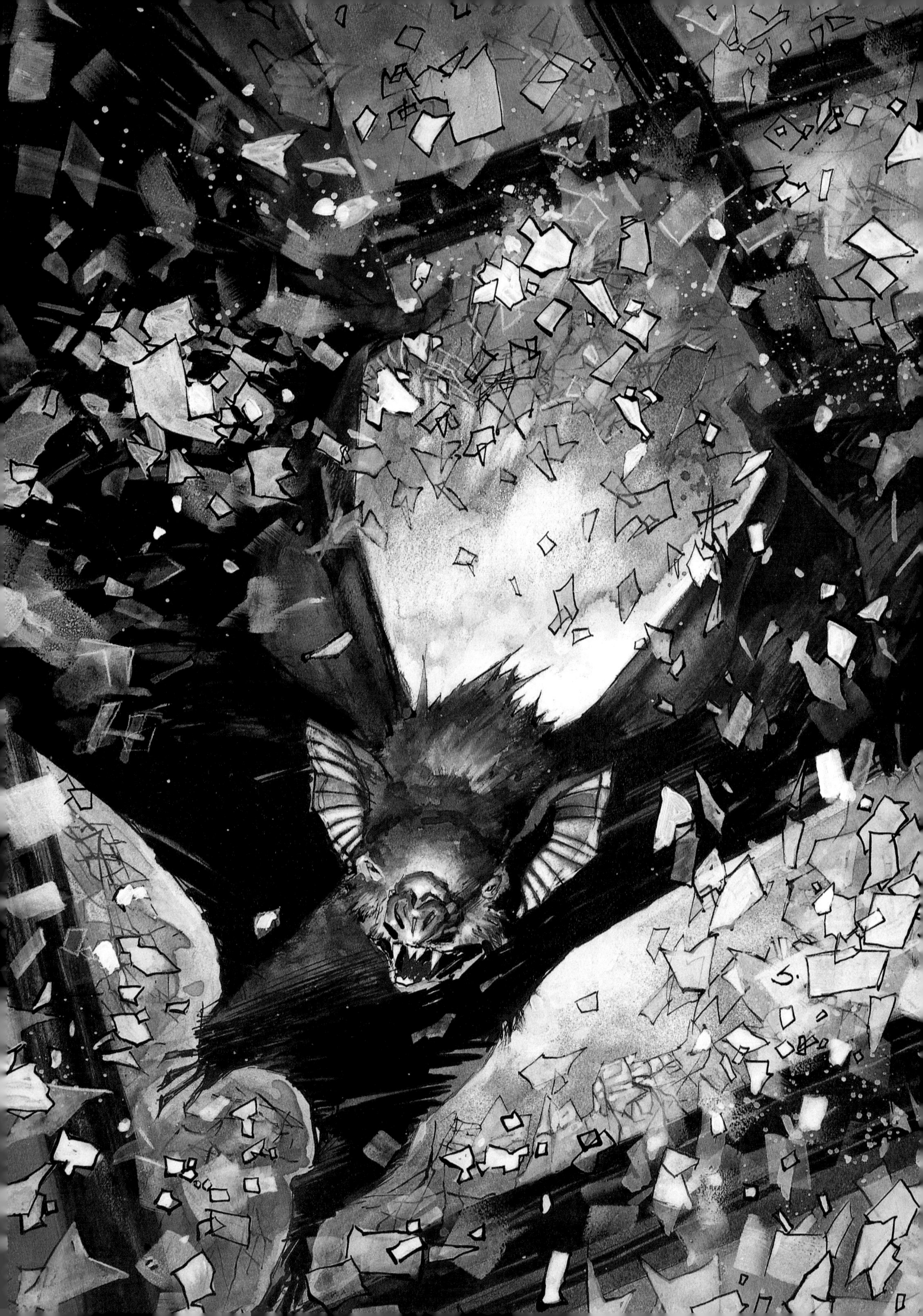

INSPIRATION

From the journal of Alfred Pennyworth:

"In his waking moments Master Bruce gave the bats no further thought, until that night when all his long training was complete but he still was not. He knew something was missing, and the lone creature of the night was a sign, he said, of the fear which could be used against cowardly, superstitious criminals. And in that moment, with 'Bruce Wayne' long dead, he finally knew who he *was*."

ART CONCEPT

Interior manor's gloomy library; fully grown (i.e., a young man) Bruce Wayne in chair, startled as a single bat crashes in thru the tall, many-paned window. (See graphic novel *Year One*.)

SCOTT HAMPTON'S SOLUTION

An accomplished storyteller, Hampton knows that sometimes typical super hero action isn't the right focus.

"I had to argue to make this happen. They wanted a classic shot—Bruce sitting there, and the bat crashing through, both in the frame. I wanted to just focus on the bat.

"Ultimately, they agreed, and I was glad. I enjoyed the idea of this piece, and it was fun to draw the goofy bat. It gave me a chance to draw something other than Batman or the main characters doing things. This was a storytelling panel, to me.

"Too many times, I think, card sets are full of these representative shots. Too representative! You *have* to see the full figure of Batman and the full figure of the thug, and blah blah blah. It's often so action-oriented.

"This was a shot that the storyteller side of me wanted to see done. I wanted to make it more than just a good card."

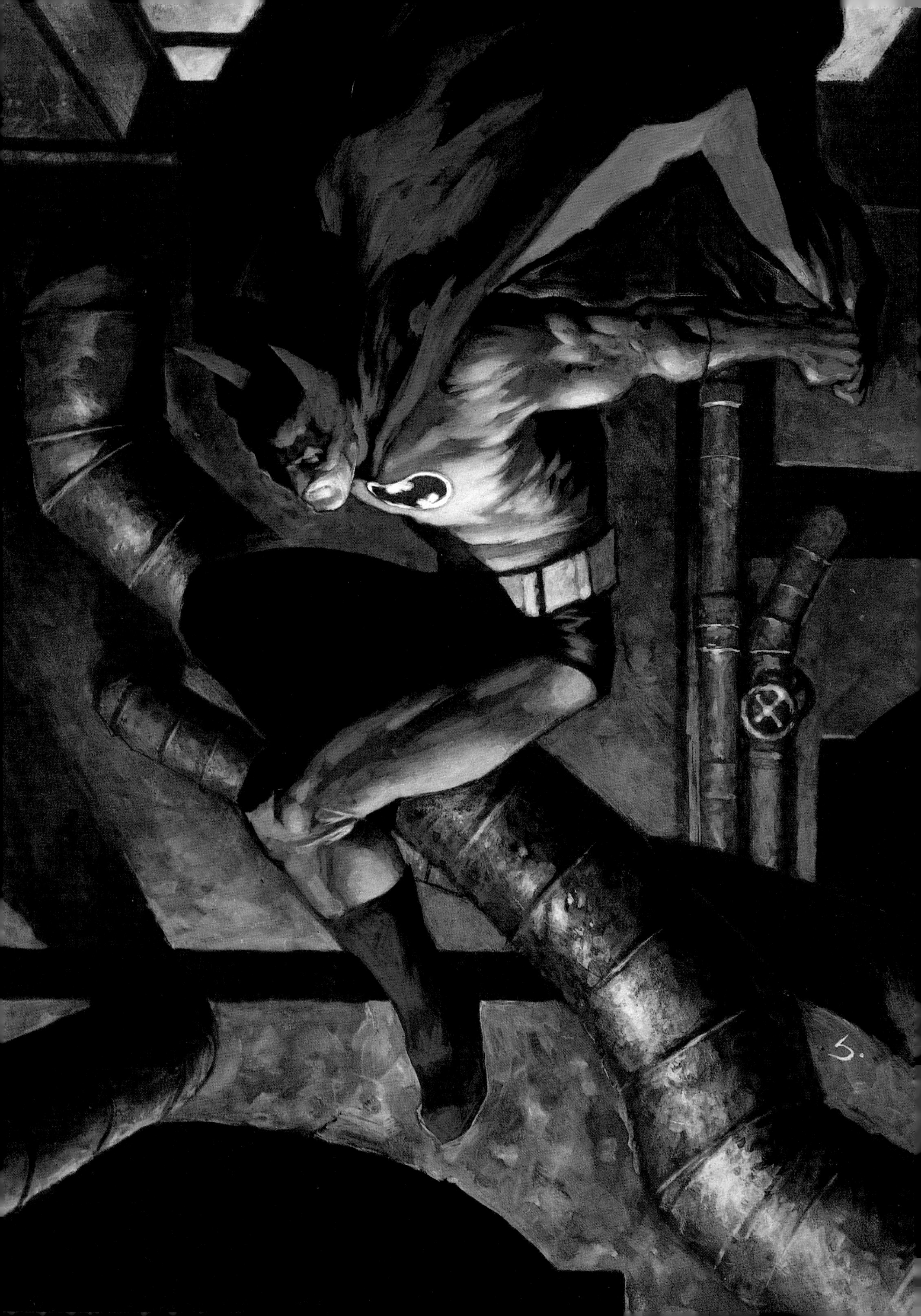

YEAR ONE

From the journal of Alfred Pennyworth:

"I have always preferred seeing him as Bruce Wayne, a normal man who donned a mask to impersonate a dark myth, but the myth became the man in that very first year. The true mask was Bruce Wayne, a mere role forced upon the Batman to ensure his existence.

"Now, the death of either is almost impossible to accept."

ART CONCEPT

By a full-length mirror in manor's master bedroom, Batman Year One Version (short ears, bulky utility belt, no yellow circle around oversized chest Bat Emblem, etc.) pulls the cowl down over his face, completing the change from Bruce Wayne to early Batman. Butler/manservant Alfred (younger) stands next to him, with Bruce Wayne's clothes draped over one arm, further signifying the change which has just been made.

SCOTT HAMPTON'S SOLUTION

"I went to the Tower of Terror [in Walt Disney World] with friends, and fell in love with that ride. It's much more than a bad elevator ride: It's all the stuff leading up to it. One of the rooms is a basement with lots of furnaces and boilers and 1930s-style ducts. I shot all kinds of reference pictures.

"Doug [Moench] had wanted a picture of Bruce about to put on his costume, ready to go out into the action. I did do some sketches of that, but they didn't quite make it. I kept trying to come up with something else that might work. Finally, I had the idea of just showing him in action.

"It's not obvious in the finished painting, but in my initial sketch for this piece, I had Batman crashing through a skylight. But I decided that it wouldn't work, as I had just had a bat crashing through the window. Instead, we've got Batman jumping through some subterranean part of the sewer system, from one level to the next."

Why the sewer system?

"Because of all those fun ducts and things. I'm a big fan of industrial photography and, whenever possible, I enjoy incorporating this sort of imagery into my paintings."

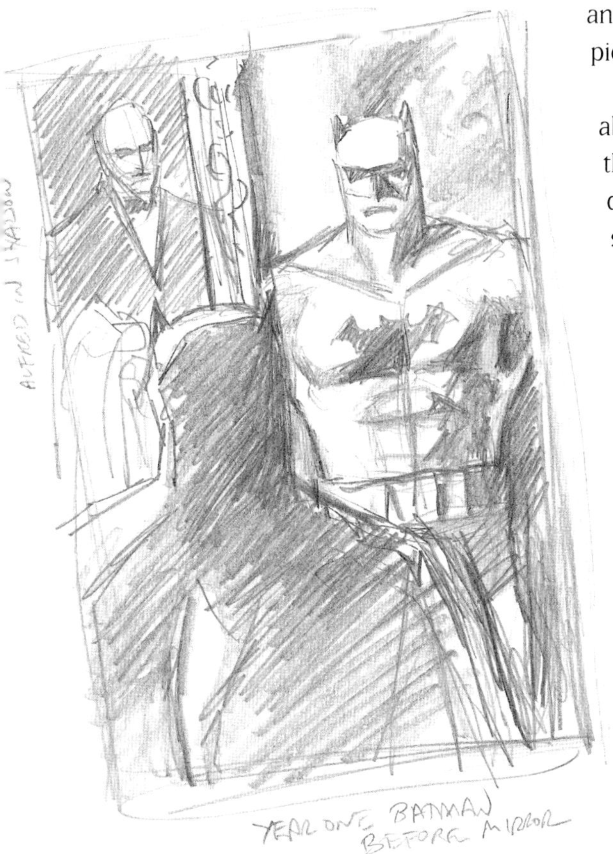
ALFRED IN SHADOW
YEAR ONE BATMAN
BEFORE MIRROR

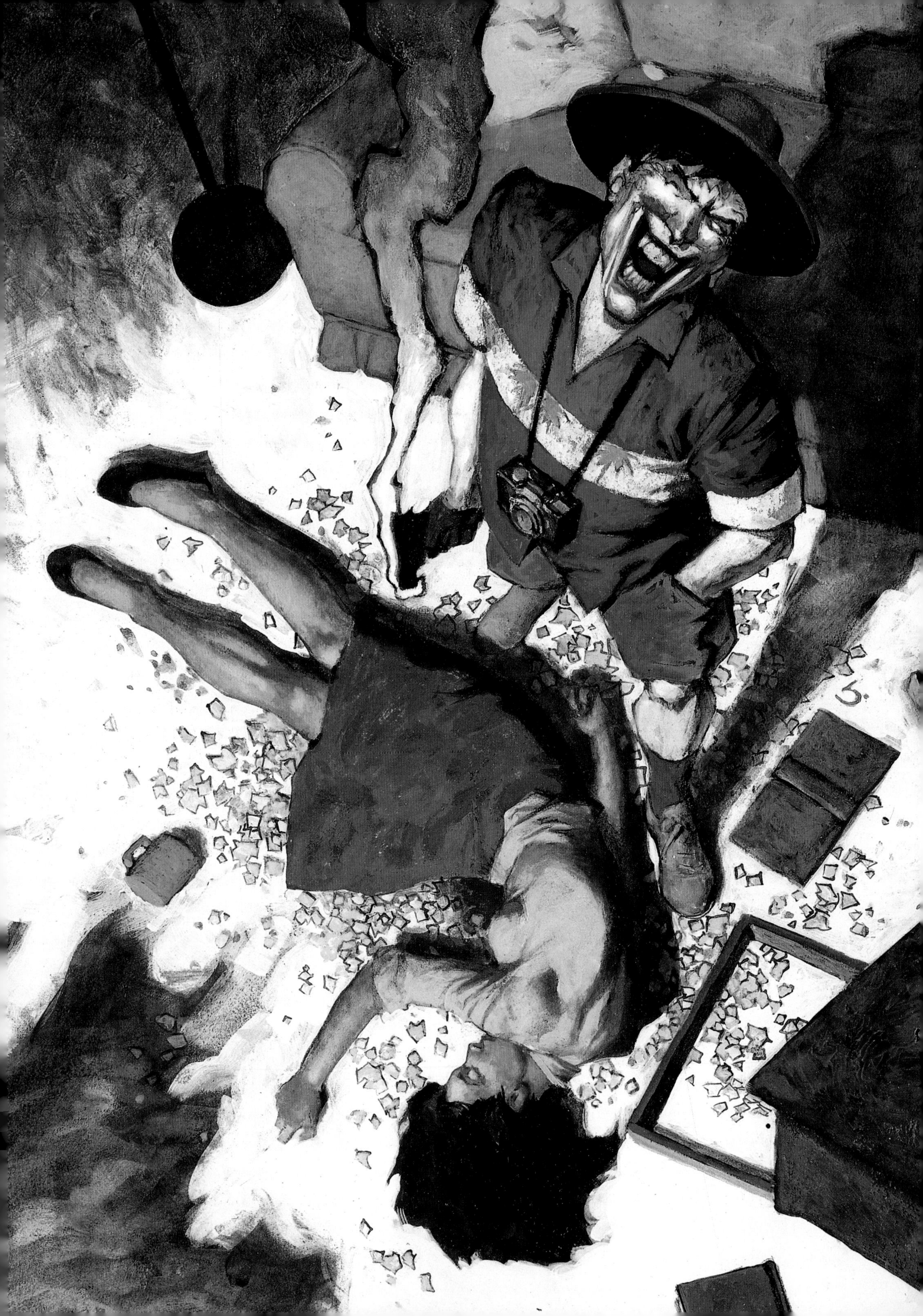

KILLING JOKE

From the journal of Alfred Pennyworth:

"The Joker was the first of his 'weird foes,' the inaugural entrant in a Rogues Gallery of grotesqueries. Always the Master's prime nemesis, no one did more damage than the laughing madman. Barbara Gordon, Jason Todd . . . the Master himself.

"First of the weird foes . . . and now, curse his dark demented soul, the last as well."

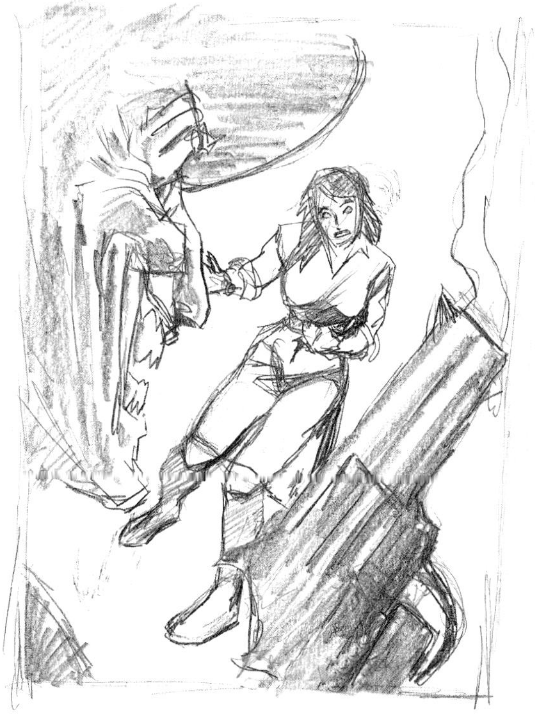

ART CONCEPT

Joker shooting Barbara Gordon, and laughing about it—from *The Killing Joke.*

SCOTT HAMPTON'S SOLUTION

"Another difficult image was the first from *The Killing Joke,* where Barbara Gordon was paralyzed by the Joker. But this was a different kind of difficult.

"This image, where the Joker has shot Barbara Gordon in the stomach, incurring spinal damage and causing her to be wheelchair-bound for the rest of her life, is a pretty strong and disturbing one in the middle of a set that basically isn't particularly grim.

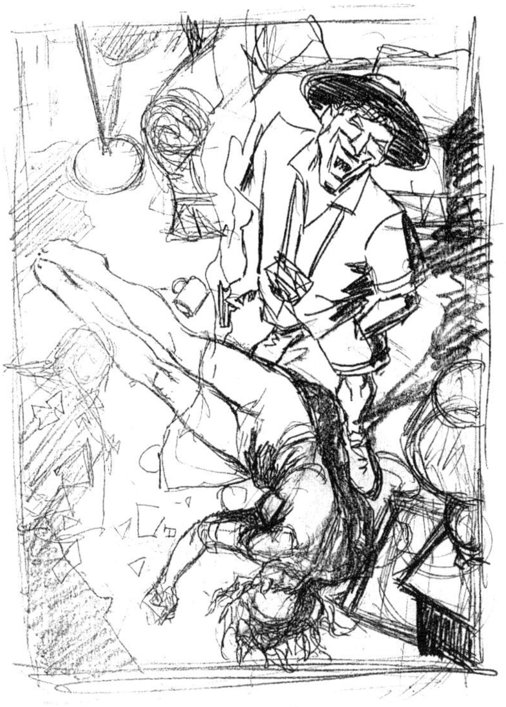

"The first sketch I did shows the Joker from behind, still with the gun and shooting Barbara. I really liked the drawing of the first one. I'm not the kind to turn in three sketches and let the editor choose. I'll submit the one I like, and I'll argue for the one I like.

"But the editor felt my original sketch was too similar to another image already in the set. And you can't argue with that."

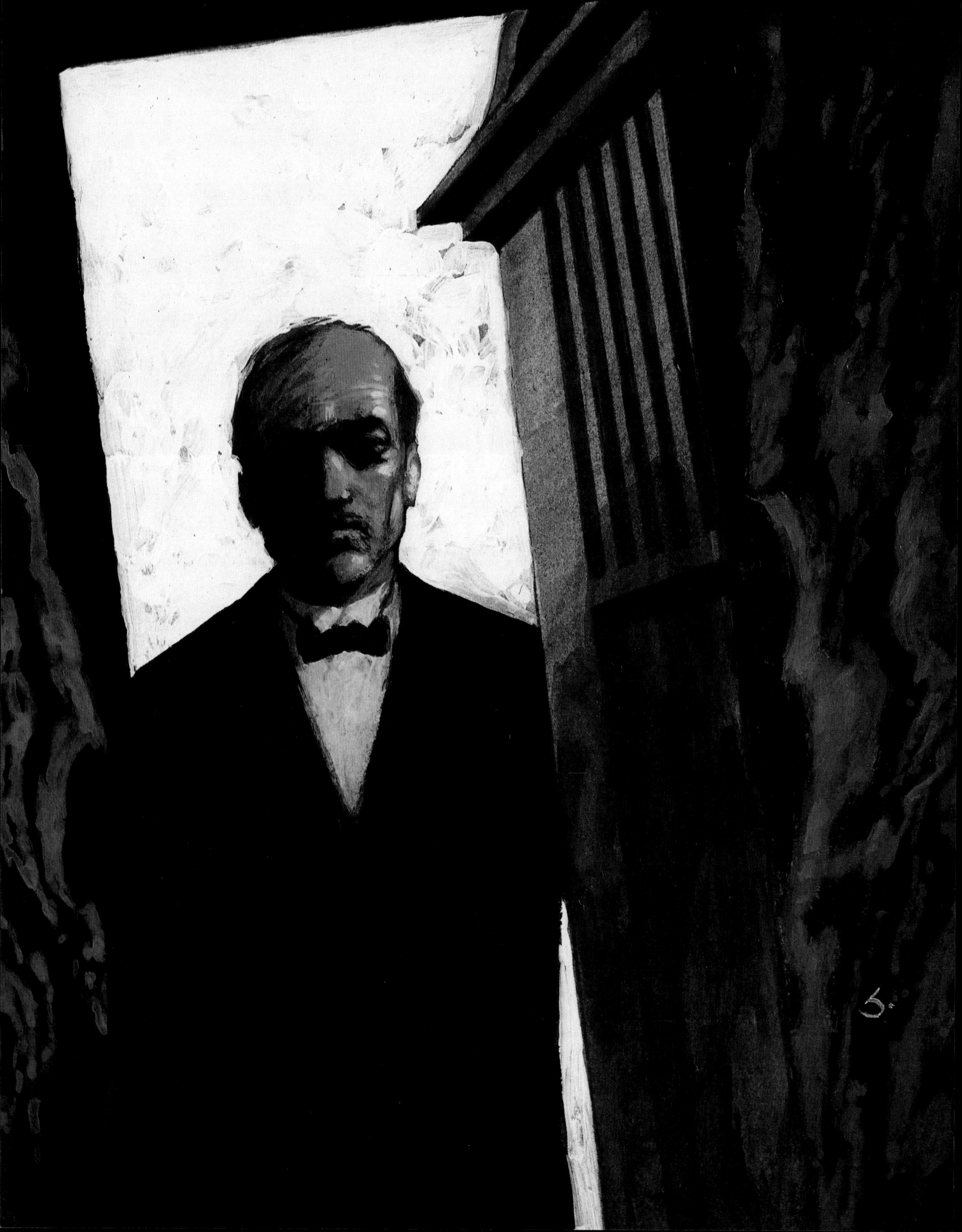

SECRET PASSAGE

The passage is closed. There is nothing more to write. The faithful man sighs, rises, and slowly moves through the hushed halls. He touches the ticking grandfather clock and swings it wide. Below awaits conquered and converted fear, a darkness filled with light.

But no master, not now.

Only emptiness.

ART CONCEPT

Back to the present; solemn Alfred opening the trick grandfather clock revealing secret entrance to cave; we can glimpse the top of the carved rock stairs.

SCOTT HAMPTON'S SOLUTION

"This was the last card that I did for this series. I used the shot that I'd done of Alfred standing outside of Wayne Manor [page 43] as the reference, and I did that same shot again. In a way, it's the exact opposite of the earlier one. There, Alfred is outside Wayne Manor, and very distant from the trappings of Bruce Wayne or Batman. Here, he's on the edge of them, literally standing at the threshold between Wayne Manor and the Batcave.

"Here, Alfred takes over the story. I wanted to show the transition from well-lit and cheerful Wayne Manor to the more creepy and primal Batcave. I used lighting to create a distinction between the two environments.

"I did this card in an hour and a half. I was so late that I couldn't even overnight the painting—it had to be in the office that afternoon. I shipped it through Delta Dash. I was dead tired."

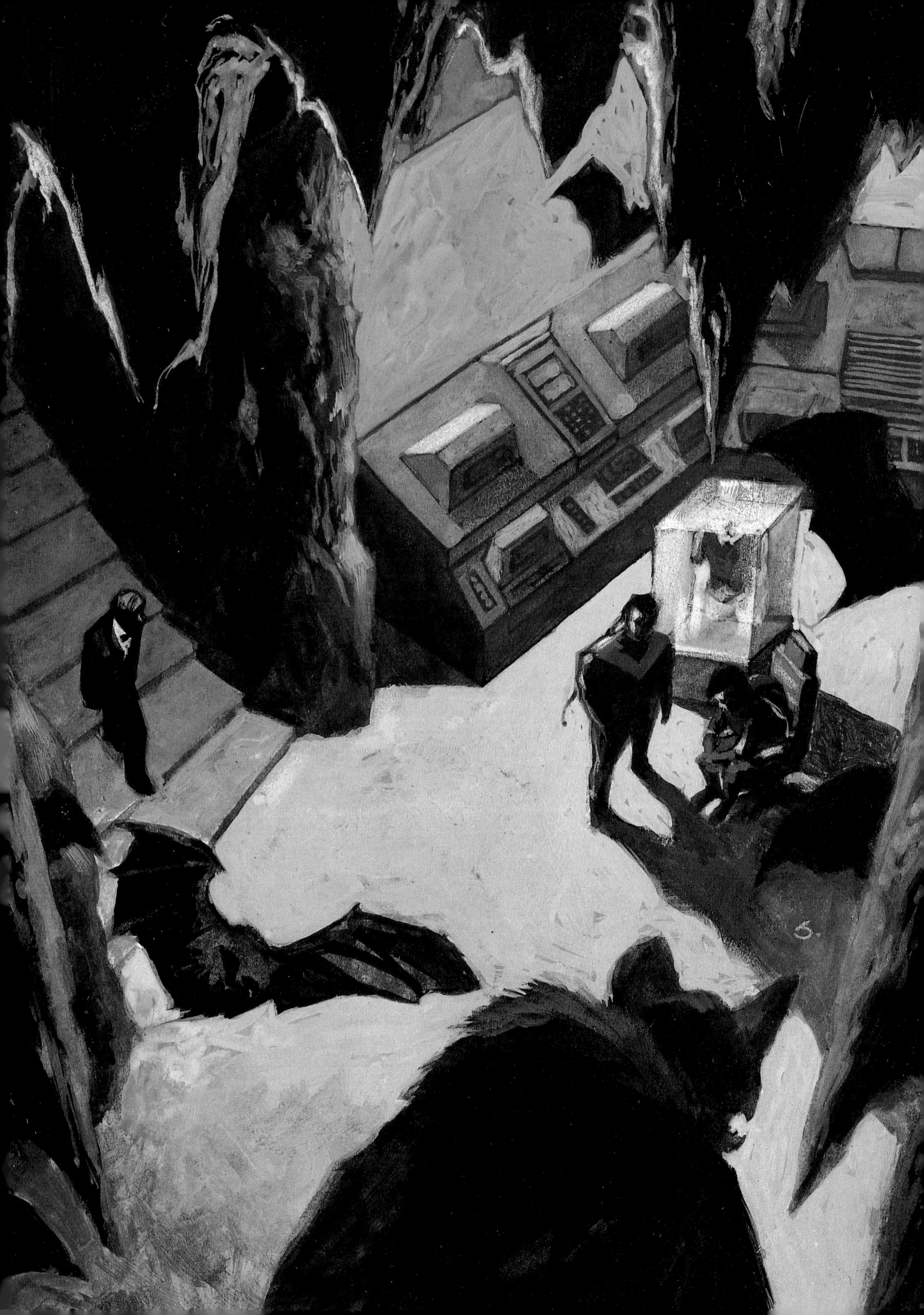

THE CAVE

The echoing descent is marked, as ever, by a wonder at what his Master has wrought. The tools and the vehicles, the stark contrast of it all—*computers* in a *cave*. Primal atmosphere housing modern efficiency. Hell turned haven.

Far off in the forest of stone spikes, night creatures swoop and shriek, as if in mourning. The faithful man hopes he is not alone. . . .

ART CONCEPT

Interior Batcave; in extreme foreground is the bizarrely sleek Batmobile (or at least a cropped portion of it); beyond is the well-lit computer/communications workstation and crime lab; and in the far background, the tiny figure of Alfred is descending the long flight of carved rock stairs toward the workstation; maybe a bat or three fluttering thru scene.

SCOTT HAMPTON'S SOLUTION

"Doing a shot of the Batcave was a trial. I wanted to make this cave more human and alive, but I also had to establish the Batcave portion of the set.

"Further complicating the matter was the fact that I got different versions of how the Batcave worked, and where the steps empty out, and at what angle you could see different things.

"It was almost impossible to get a composition where you get that glass case and Alfred coming down the steps, along with a computer workstation and some actual bats. So I moved some things around, and kept moving them until the composition worked.

"Of course, how often do you get to rearrange the furniture in the Batcave?"

ALFRED DESCENDS STAIRS

STALAGTITES
COMPUTER
ALFRED
NIGHTWING + ROBIN
BATS

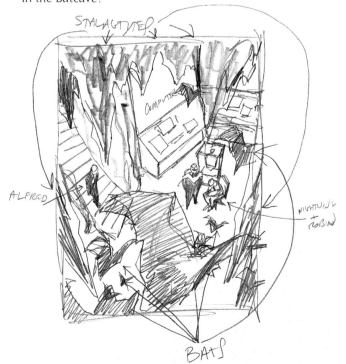

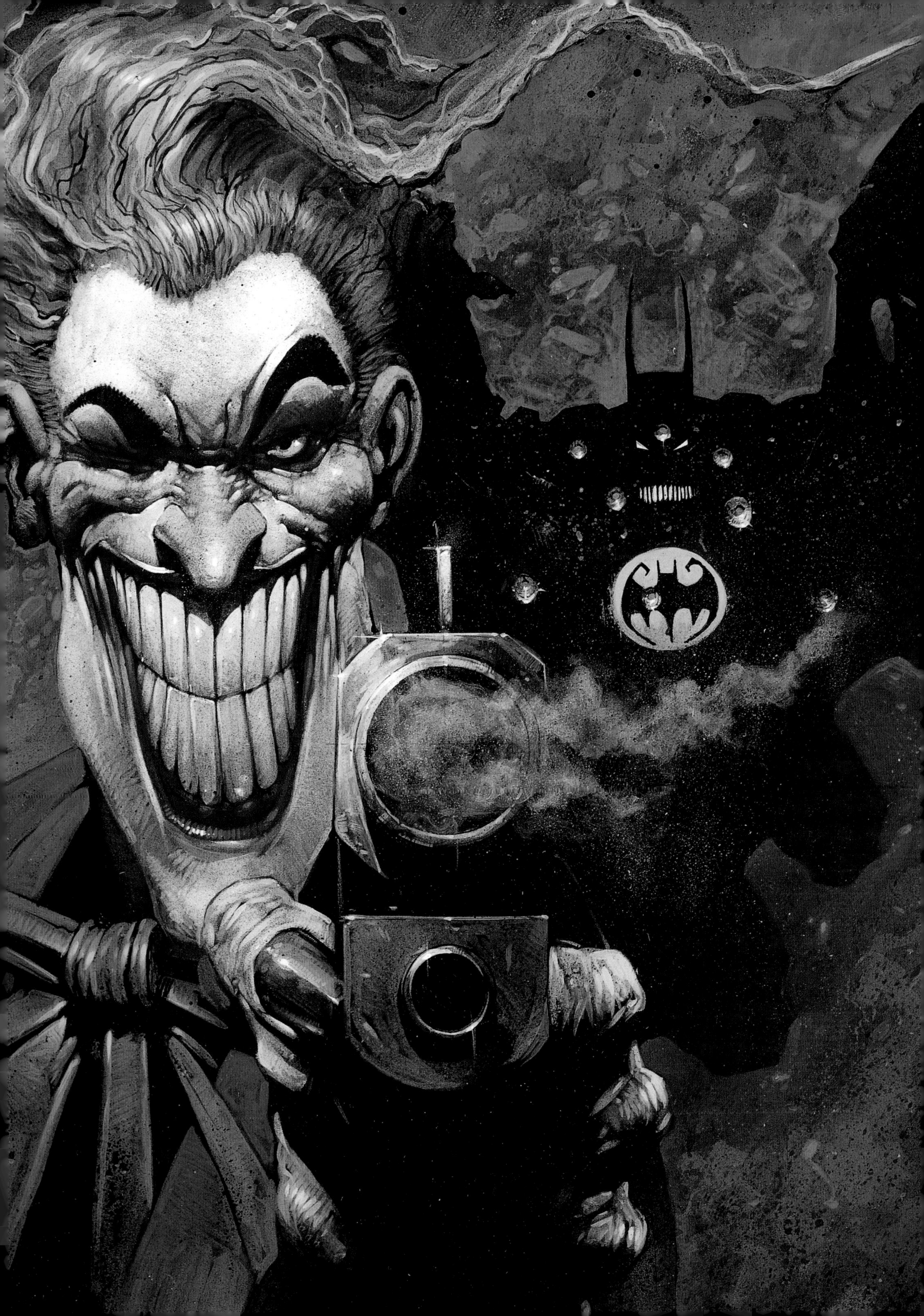

TARGET PRACTICE

"He's *dead* to me . . . " *BAM!*

" . . . he's dead to me *not* . . . " *BAM!*

" . . . he's *dead* to me . . . " *BAM!*

" . . . he's dead to men—What's the *matter* with me? Why can't I let him *fatten the worms?!* Instead of scheming some ghoulishly hilarious *crime,* I'm chasing a big fat *bat* through my *belfry!* Something must be *done* about this *obsession!*"

ART CONCEPT

Joker seen from rear in extreme foreground, blasting his .45 automatic at his (already bullet-pocked) "vision of Batman": A cutout target of a bizarre, twisted (and scary) "Bat-Clown from Hell." This is Batman seen thru the filter of Joker's madness, so Bat-Clown should be truly nightmarish. (Of Joker in foreground, we need see not much more than back of his head & arm/hand holding & blasting the gun.)

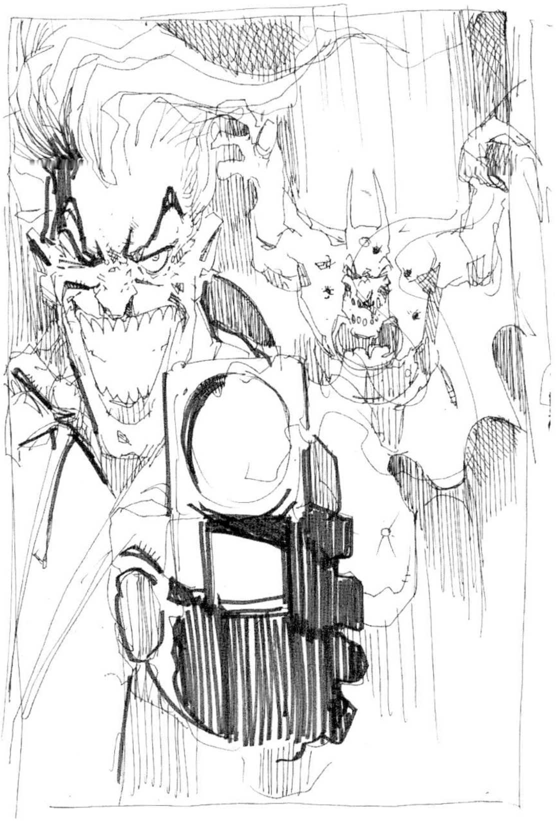

CARL CRITCHLOW'S SOLUTION

"This card required the Joker to be shooting at a 'Batman target,' so I departed here from the 'Big Joker Head' motif, using a double shot with the target behind him.

"The big head was a consistently strong element that helped the card work. If I was more technically minded, I could explain it all in terms of the 'golden section' or 'Fibonacci' or some such. But I just knew it worked.

"It's difficult to have a composition that's very involved if it's only going to be a few inches across when it's printed. As good as reproduction techniques are, you can't get around the size. So you need something that's going to have an impact when it's reduced down to that size, so that you can still see what's going on, I suppose."

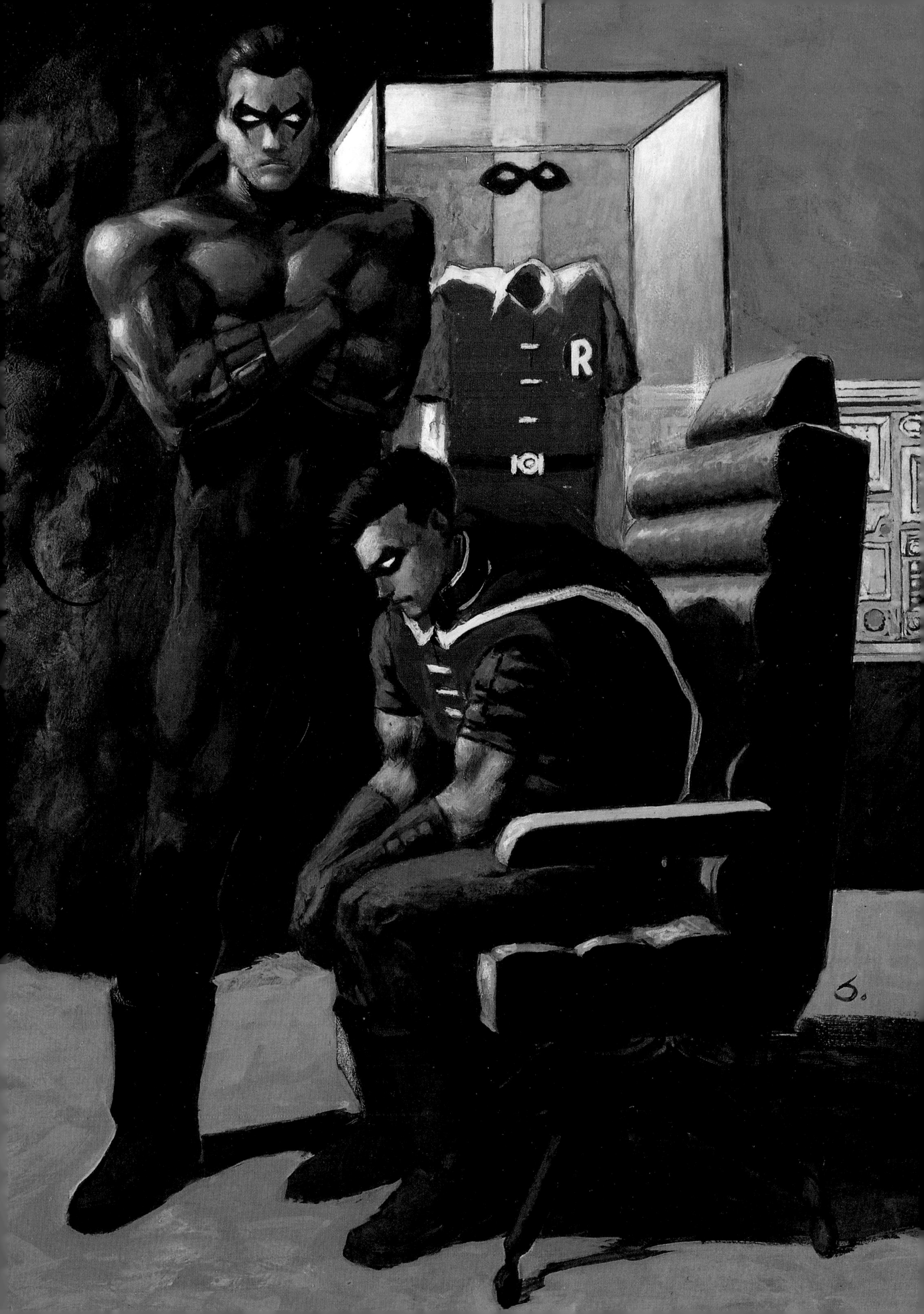

THREE ROBINS

Meeting in the Batcave, Robin and Nightwing mourn their mentor:

"He always did right by his partners, Dick, all three of us . . . even when it ended in tragedy for Jason Todd. He taught us, helped us mature, gave us an example which *seemed* immortal . . . but now. . . ."

"Easy, Tim. If there's anything I can do. . . ."

"Just *talk* to me, Dick. Share your memories. Help me make sense of the senseless. . . ."

ART CONCEPT
In the cave, Nightwing and current/new Robin (both grim, somber, sober) flanking the glass memorial case with the old Robin costume in it. **Overall image:** Showing off the three costumes: Nightwing, old Robin, new Robin.

SCOTT HAMPTON'S SOLUTION
Most people assume there's only one Robin, also known as Dick Grayson. But in comic book continuity, Grayson became a solo crime fighter known as Nightwing. Jason Todd, an orphan Batman encountered while the youngster was trying to steal the Batmobile, became the second Robin. The Joker viciously cut short Jason Todd's super hero career, and Tim Drake currently assumes the role.

"I really wanted to approach this as an establishing shot for the two characters. Nightwing is in a kind of 'great elder' position toward Robin.

"It was also important to establish a relationship between the three Robins, including the 'ghost' of Jason Todd, and the fact that their common link is Batman.

"These cards are very much in continuity. This shot takes place a moment or so after the one before it. While that is common in comic book storytelling, it wasn't so common in this set, and nonexistent in card sets where they are *not* trying to tell a story."

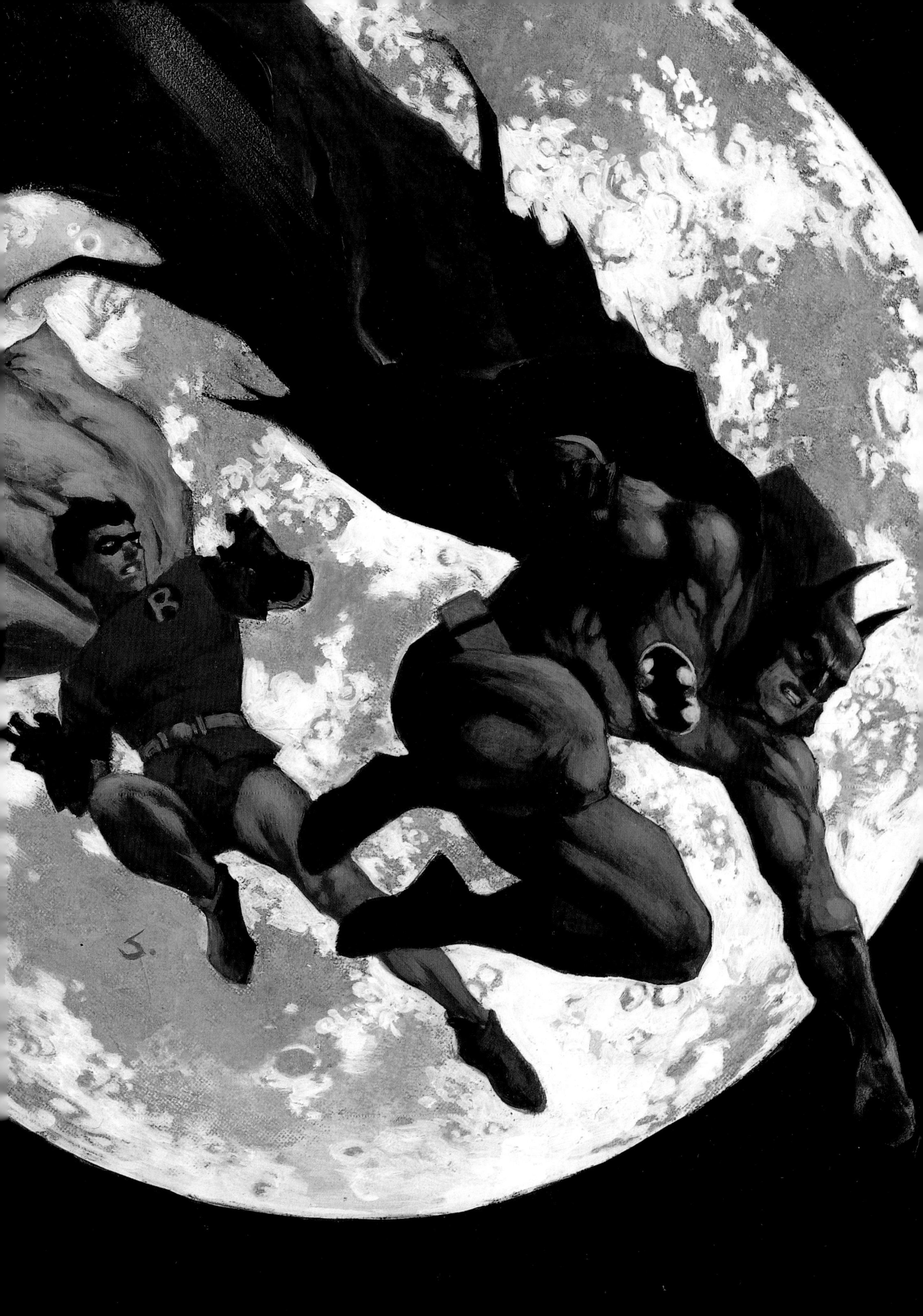

DICK GRAYSON

A Shaken Nightwing Remembers:

"The world was mine when I was a kid—Dick Grayson, high-wire circus star. But the world ended when my parents were murdered. That's when Bruce took me in. He knew exactly how I felt and exactly how to handle me. He became my father, my partner, my role model, my friend. He *remade my world,* Tim, and he *saved my soul.*"

ART CONCEPT

Classic Batman and (original) Robin swinging "side-by-side" into action shot, but with emphasis on the original Dick Grayson "laughing daredevil" Robin.

SCOTT HAMPTON'S SOLUTION

"You can't just do a tracing of the iconic image of Batman and Robin swinging together, but it's fun to take such a classic image and put your own spin on it. That's what I tried to do with this painting.

"The visual that I'm thinking of, I don't think it has a moon, but it's Batman and Robin coming at you, swinging on their ropes. When you've read the comic book, seen the TV show or the movies, you come across this image in different ways. I was very aware of that when I was trying to come up with this card. There's something emblematic about it. I went against that picture, somewhat. I've got their attention shifted off-camera, they're aimed off-camera. It's not as 'in your face.'"

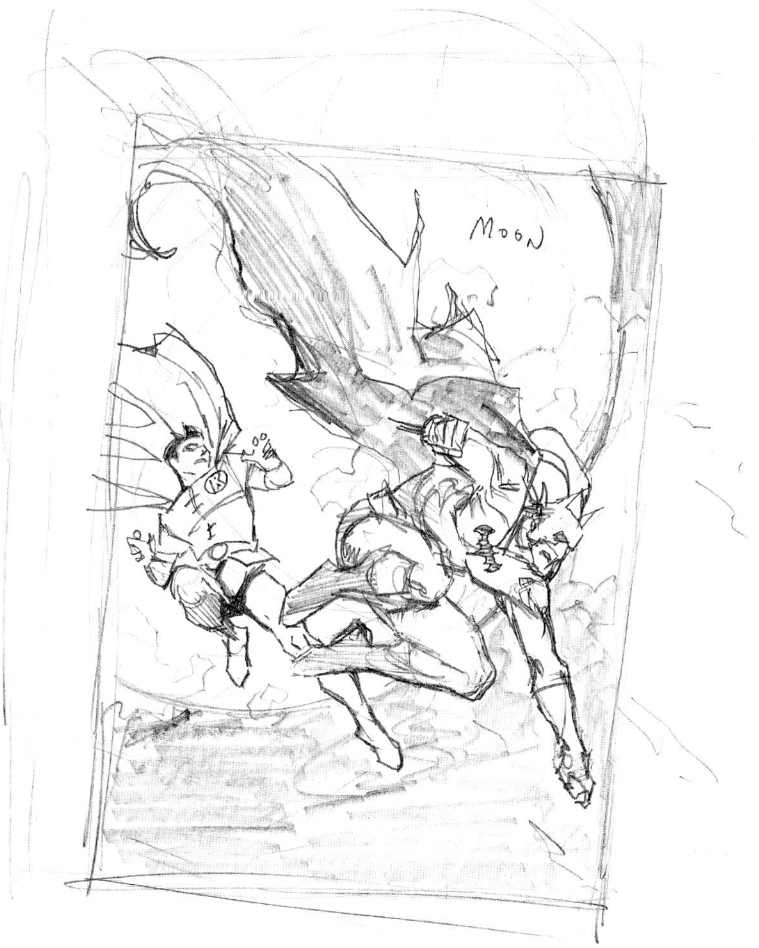
MOON

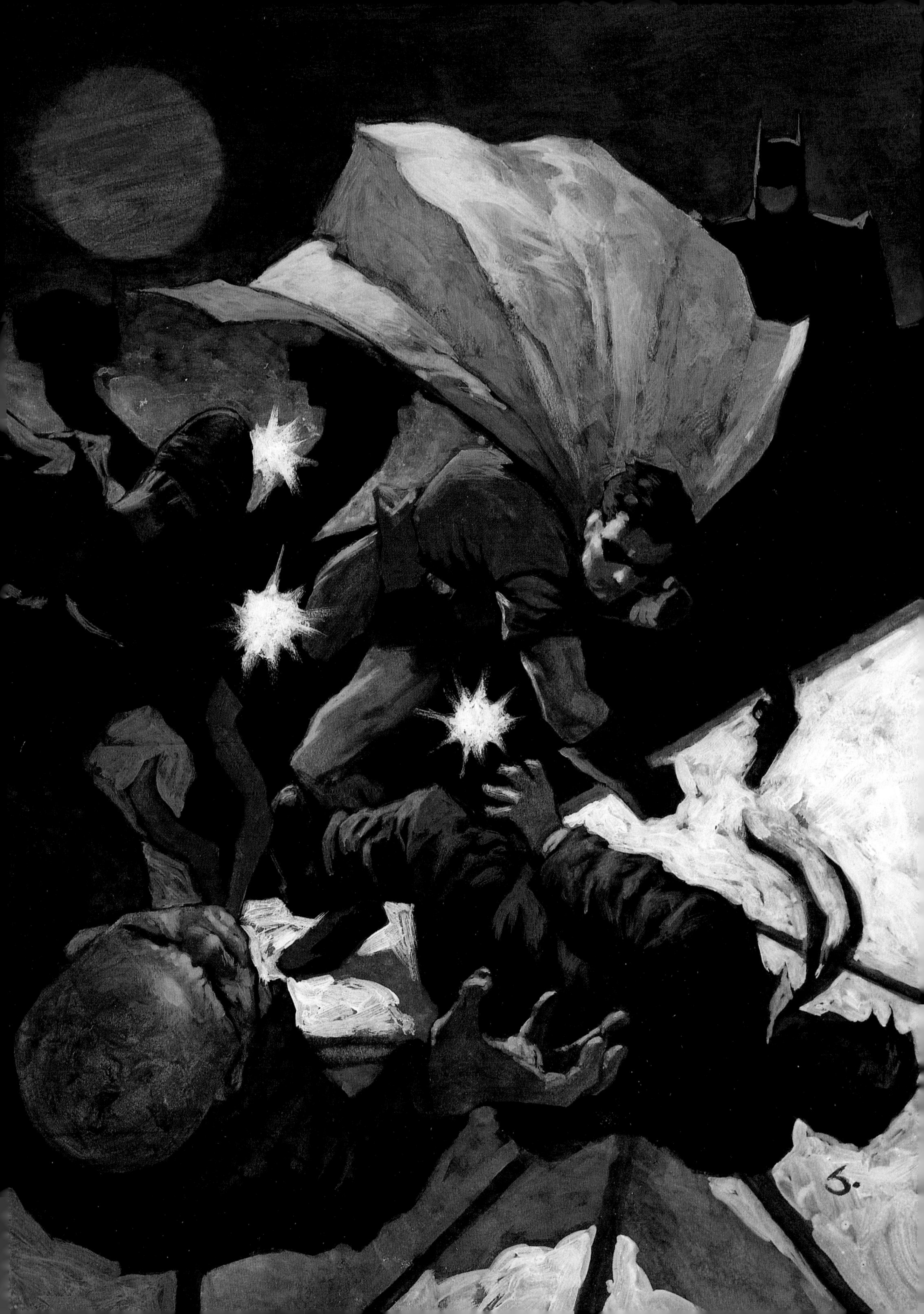

JASON TODD

Nightwing remembers his successor:

"After I moved on to become Nightwing with the Titans, Bruce salvaged another troubled kid. Jason Todd's world could have become one of crime and misery. Instead, through the Batman's guidance and example, Jason learned to respect decency and justice . . . and he used his second chance to become the second Robin."

ART CONCEPT

Street-urchin Jason Todd (in scruffy civilian clothes) caught literally red-handed—stealing hubcap off car & looking up to see Batman looming over him.

SCOTT HAMPTON'S SOLUTION

With this card, Hampton came up with an idea that was quite different from Doug Moench's suggestion. He decided to show Robin handling his opponents by himself, while Batman observes his protégé.

"This one was another of the difficult ones. There are these three thugs, all of whom have to look like they're being hit by Robin in one blow, with the moon and Batman looking on.

"Coming up with a composition that would read, where you could tell what was going on, was tough. But I enjoyed playing with the paint in Robin's cape. There's a lot of shifting from warms to cools and blues and reds. In fact, there's more red and green and gray in that cape than there is yellow. It may be hard to see, but I think the texture is interesting."

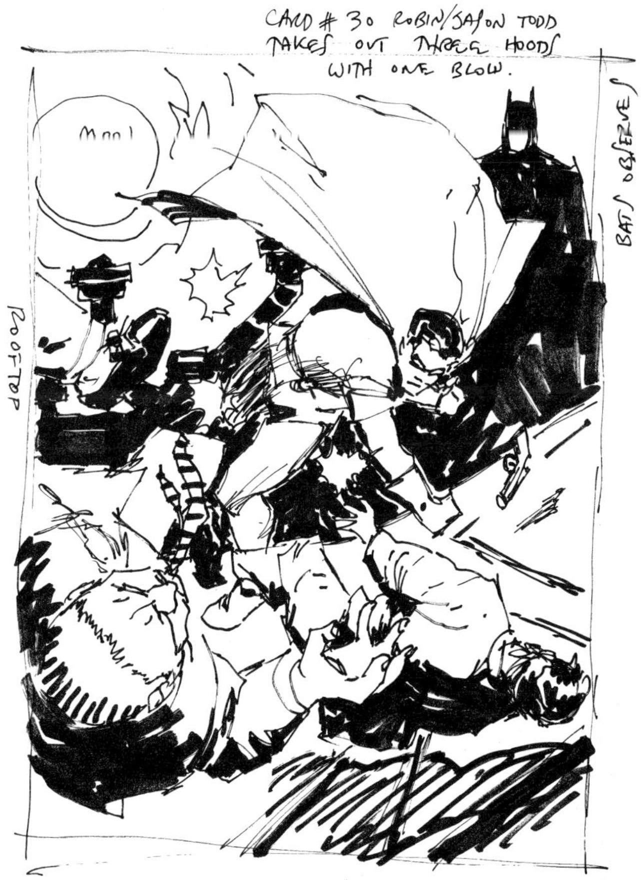
CARD # 30 ROBIN/JASON TODD
TAKES OUT THREE HOODS
WITH ONE BLOW.
Moon
BATS OBSERVES
ROOFTOP

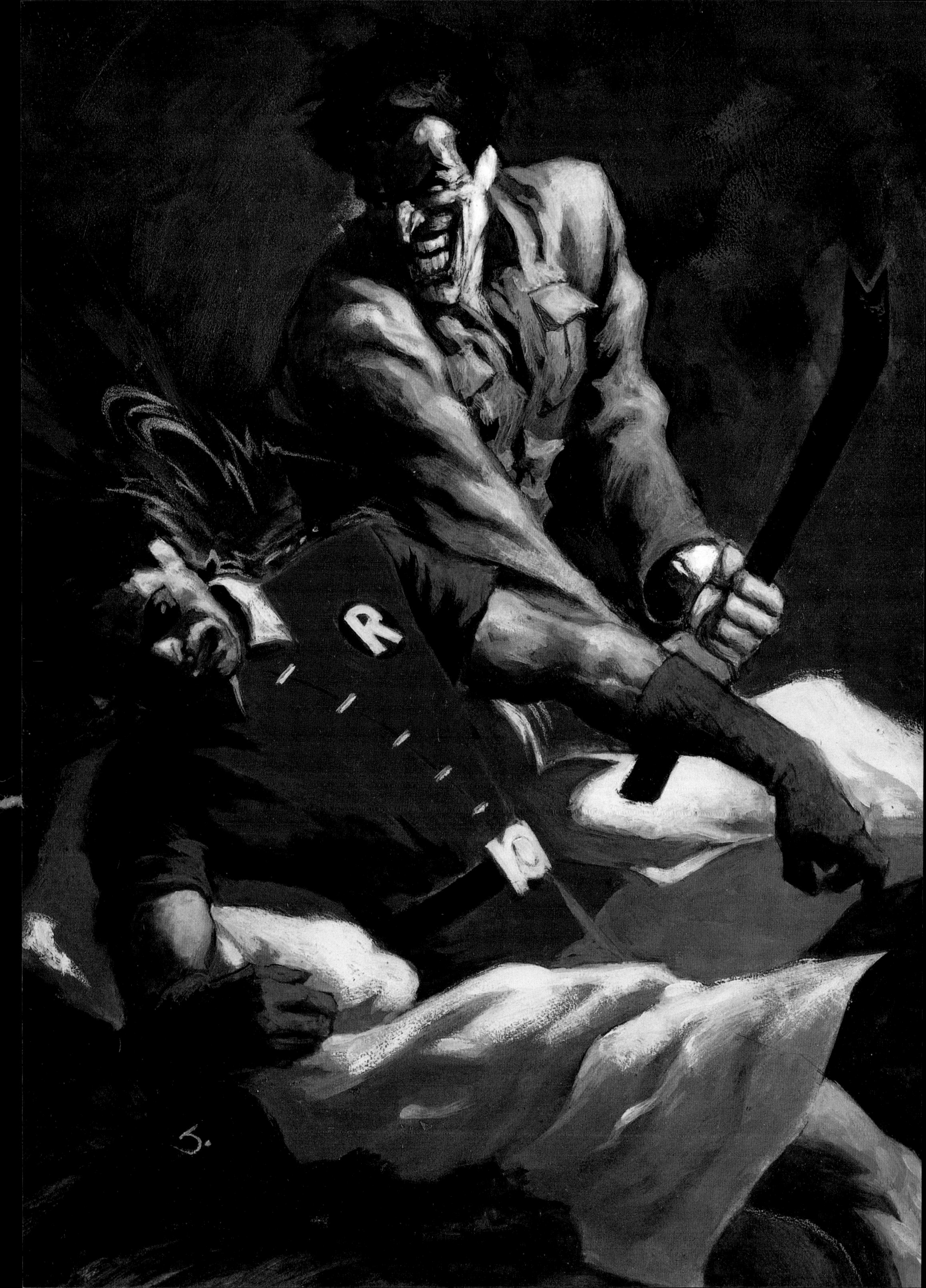

DEATH IN THE FAMILY

Grief-stricken, Robin recalls one of the darkest hours of the Batman's life:

"And Jason Todd did *more* than redeem himself, Dick. He carried on your tradition and he paved the way for me. Bruce said he was a bit too reckless, maybe, but still a good Robin all the way up to his final sacrifice. In the end, a true hero who paid the ultimate price . . . fallen but never forgotten."

ART CONCEPT

Joker savagely and shockingly killing Robin/Jason Todd—that is, Robin wearing same costume seen displayed in glass memorial case.

SCOTT HAMPTON'S SOLUTION

"This was a very disturbing image of the Joker, and again, the tenor of this set is not so dark and grim.

"We went in a lot of different directions with this card. We were trying to figure out what to do with it, how to make it fit a bit more smoothly. Ultimately, the editor sent me a fax based on a sketch that I had done. In my original sketch, the Joker and Robin were full-figure. He asked me to get a little closer to the action.

"The ironic thing was that the fax was very funny, and I used it as the basis for what I did with this image. I used a very cute fax to get to a very uncute and very creepy moment."

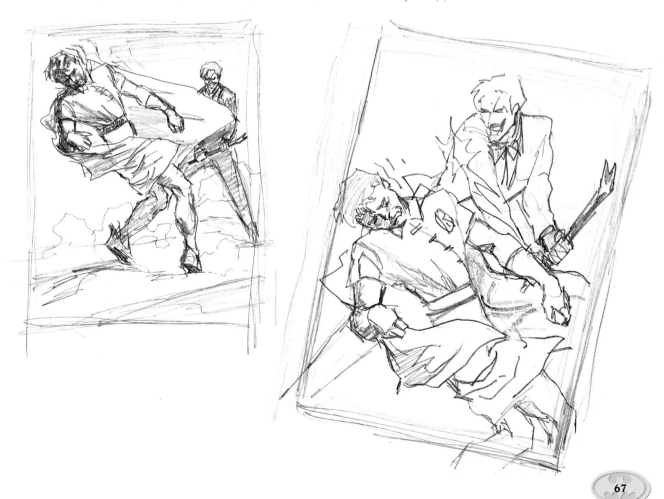

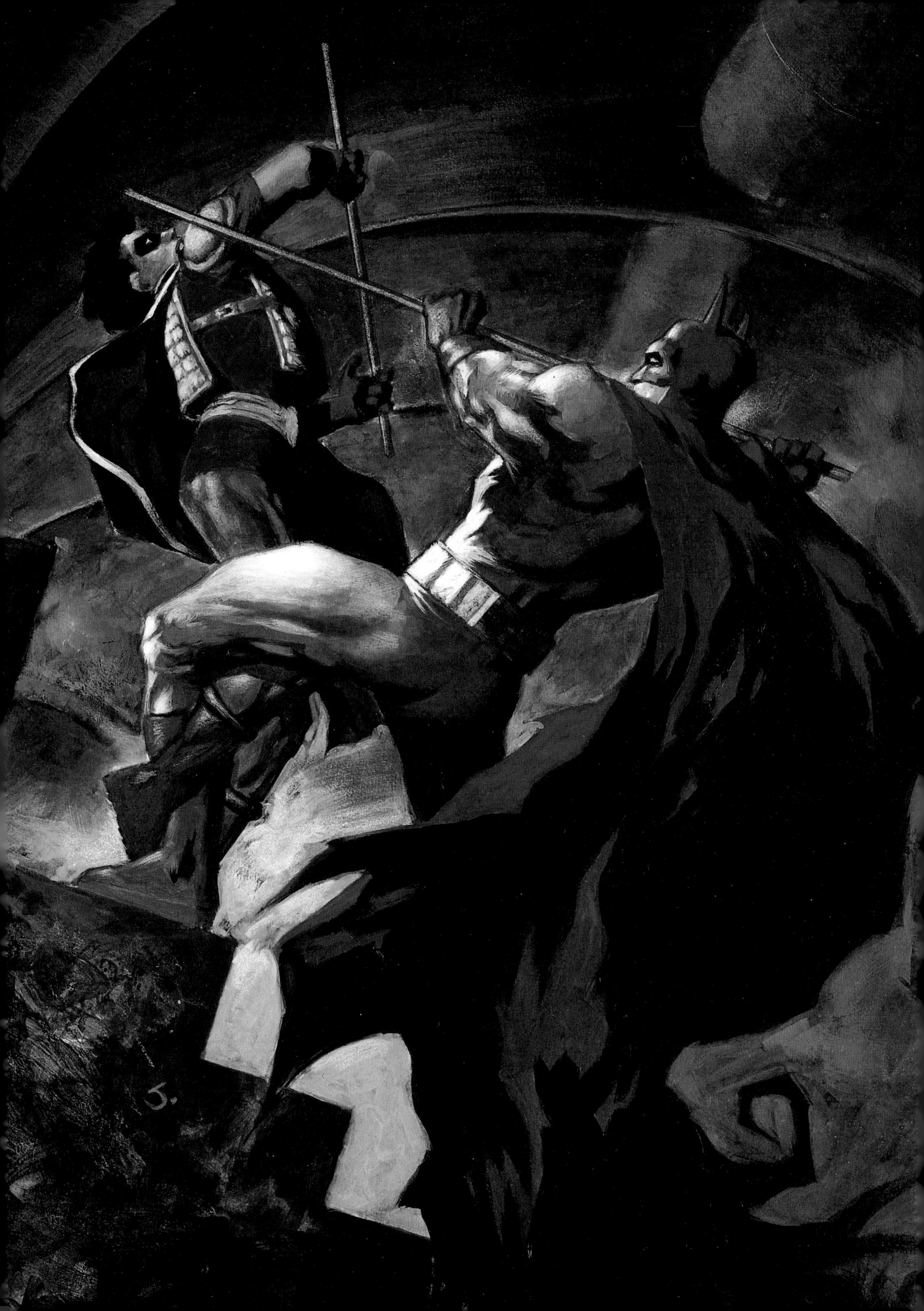

TIM DRAKE

Robin looks back on his life's turning point:

"The loss of Jason Todd was still preying on Bruce when I made a bid to become the *third* Robin. I figured my deduction that he was the Batman would prove me worthy. He disagreed, and put me through more training than a drill sergeant. As much as I resented it at times, I couldn't blame him—and looking back, it was the best thing anyone's ever done for me."

ART CONCEPT

Batman in costume but with cowl/mask off to reveal Bruce Wayne face—startled as he is confronted by Tim Drake in street clothes & "spiky" hairdo. (In Batcave if detailed background is included.)

SCOTT HAMPTON'S SOLUTION

"I wish I could do this one over. When I was doing these cards, one of the things that was hard for me was to be able to look at the whole Batman mythos as not just being dark and colorless and creepy. Now, there's a lot more color in my work, even when I'm going for darks. If I were to approach this now, it would be a lot more colorful. I didn't want this to be a grim card.

"It's such a fun sketch, and I wish I had set it up for greater contrast, and that I had made the figures pop more. But setting it in some sort of underground situation, some sewer under the city. . . . I just wish that I had the background to do over, so I could lighten it and darken the figures, or do something to make it a little more punchy, a little brighter. I was really looking for it to be more fun, but I don't think you get that from this piece."

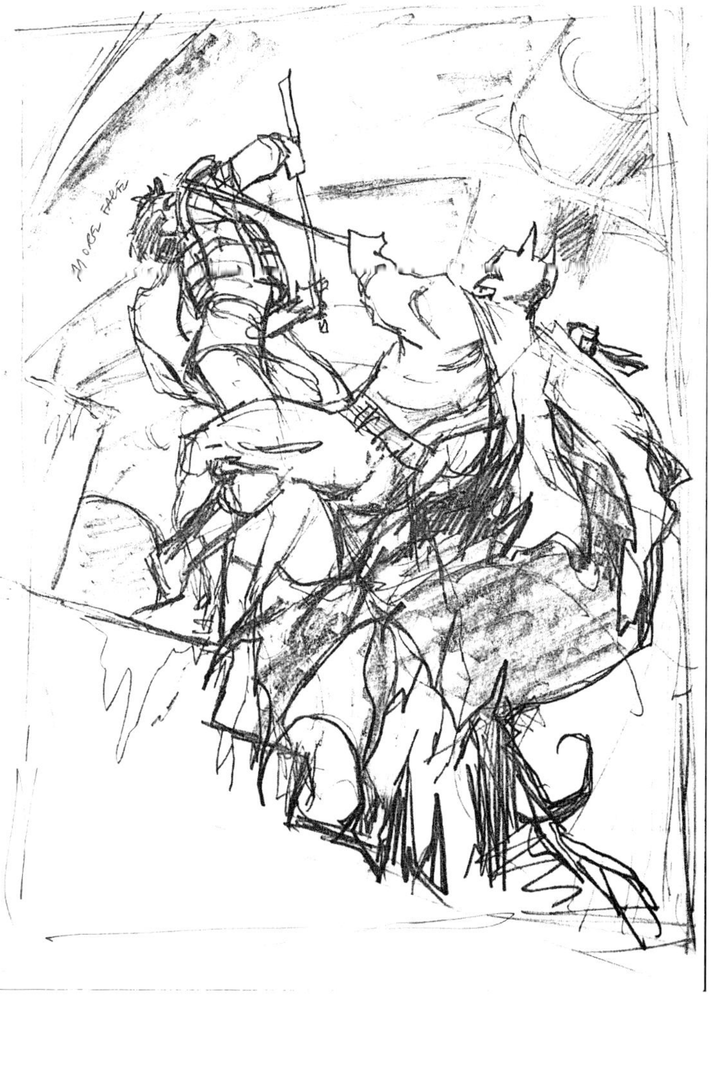

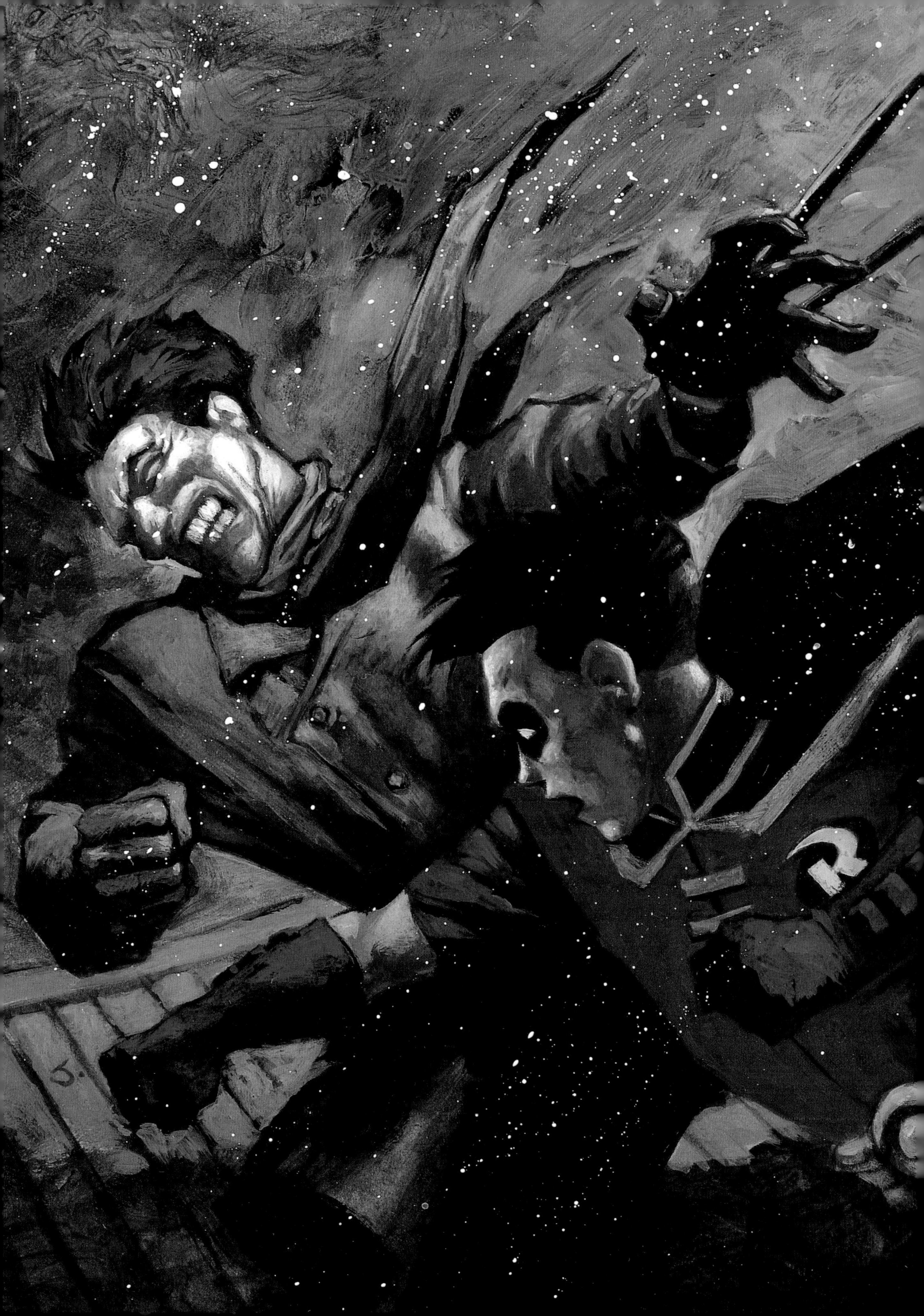

WILD JOKER

Robin struggles with a deepening sense of guilt:

"If only the Batman hadn't *shielded* me so much. I know Jason's death affected him, but the Joker's no laughing matter. He's *bad* crazy, and Bruce never should have faced him alone. If only I'd *been* there, maybe I could have—"

ART CONCEPT

Current Robin (Tim Drake, in new costume) battling the Joker in the snow—from *The Joker's Wild* miniseries.

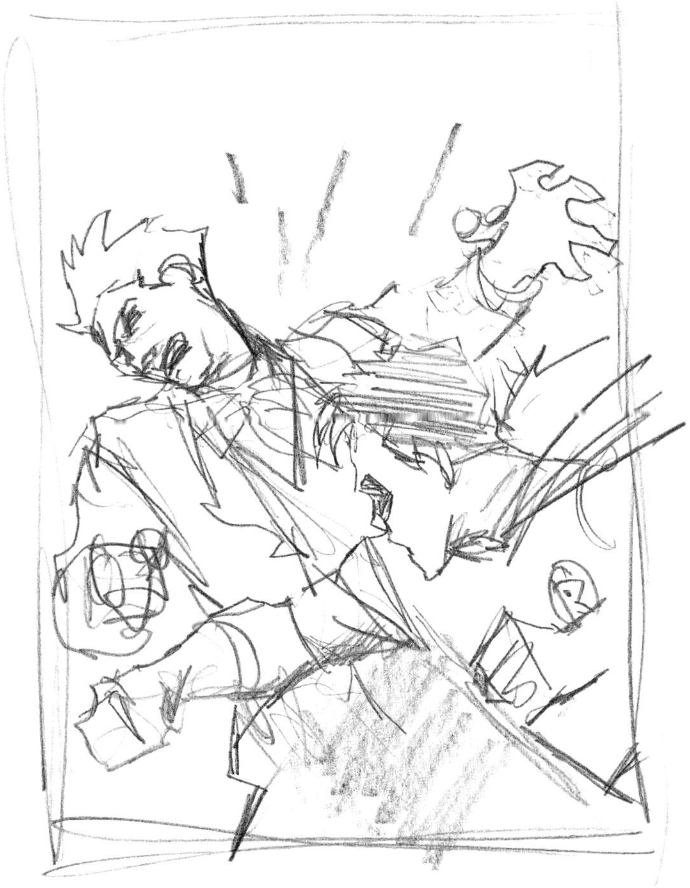

SCOTT HAMPTON'S SOLUTION

"The description for this card said 'Robin fighting Joker in the snow.' I thought that that would be great, and I was looking forward to this one because of that blanket of snow. Most of the other cards take place at night, or are very dark.

"But later, when I did the research on *The Joker's Wild,* the graphic novel this scene comes from, I discovered that Robin was fighting the Joker on a catwalk over a sewer plant, and while there is a snowstorm, Robin's basically just knocking the Joker into a vat of sewage.

"This came as quite a surprise to me. I didn't get to play in the snow!"

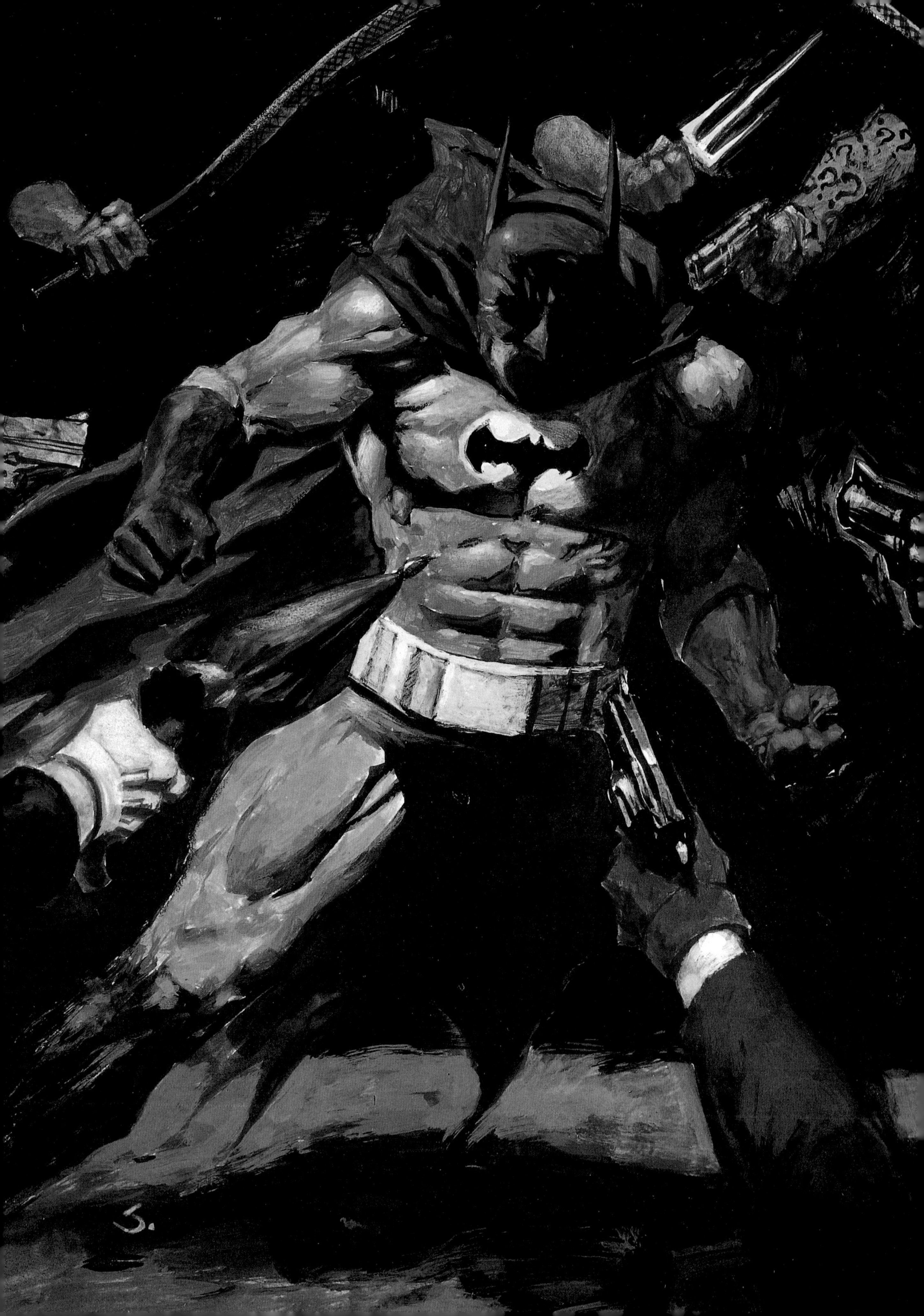

SUSPECTS

"Masters Dick and Tim—I believe grief may have blinded us to the obvious. Is it not likely the Joker had *accomplices* in his dark deed? For Master Bruce to fall, surely he was outnumbered and taken by surprise . . . ?"

"You may be right, Alfred—and it may be time for us to stop mourning and start *moving.*"

ART CONCEPT

Play up the cave formations as Nightwing and Robin turn to face approaching Alfred [attired as seen in the grandfather clock scene (page 55)]. Tiny-but-recognizable figure of Alfred okay.

SCOTT HAMPTON'S SOLUTION

"This one was much more direct. I didn't play with this one very much, in terms of how I painted it. I just kind of laid it in and left it. I felt that it worked okay, just as it is.

"I have a tendency to want to noodle with my painting, and to play with it and polish it somewhat more than I should at times. In this instance, I felt that with the tension of the character and the scene, it was preferable to leave the painting like this, almost half-done."

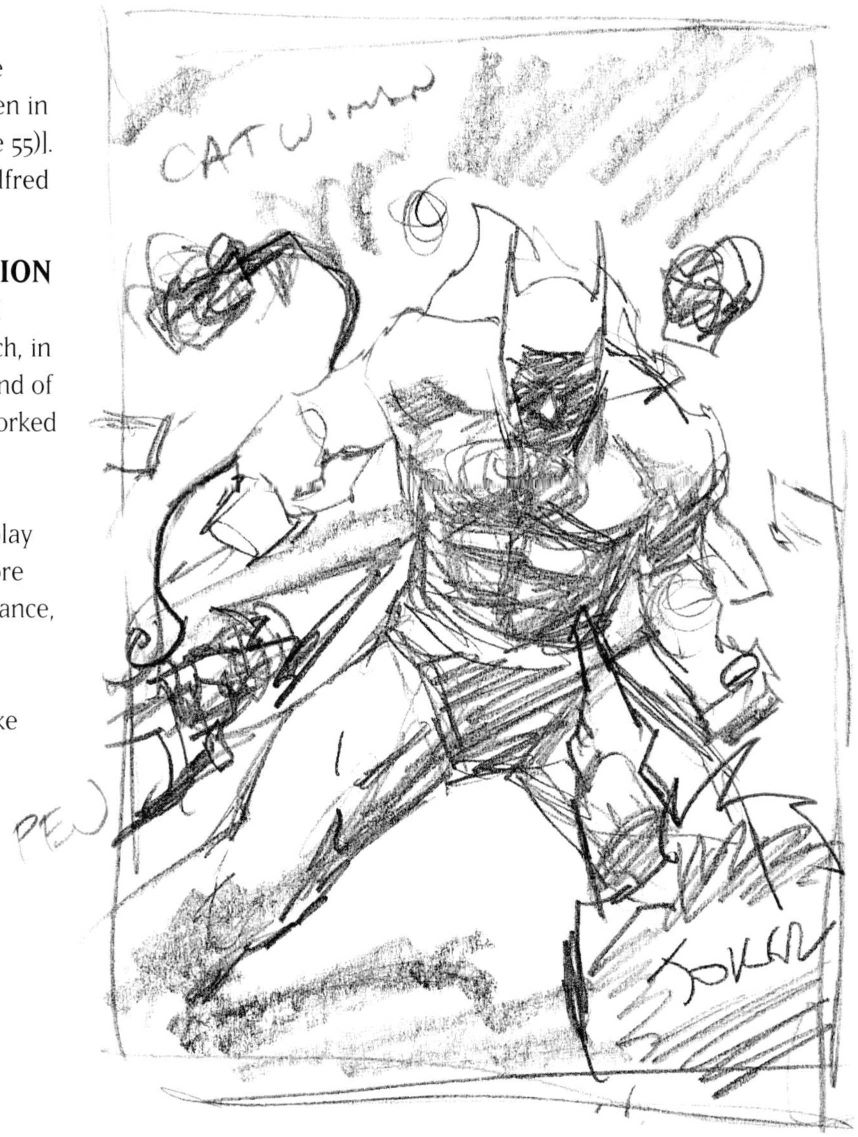
CATWOMAN
PEW
JOKER

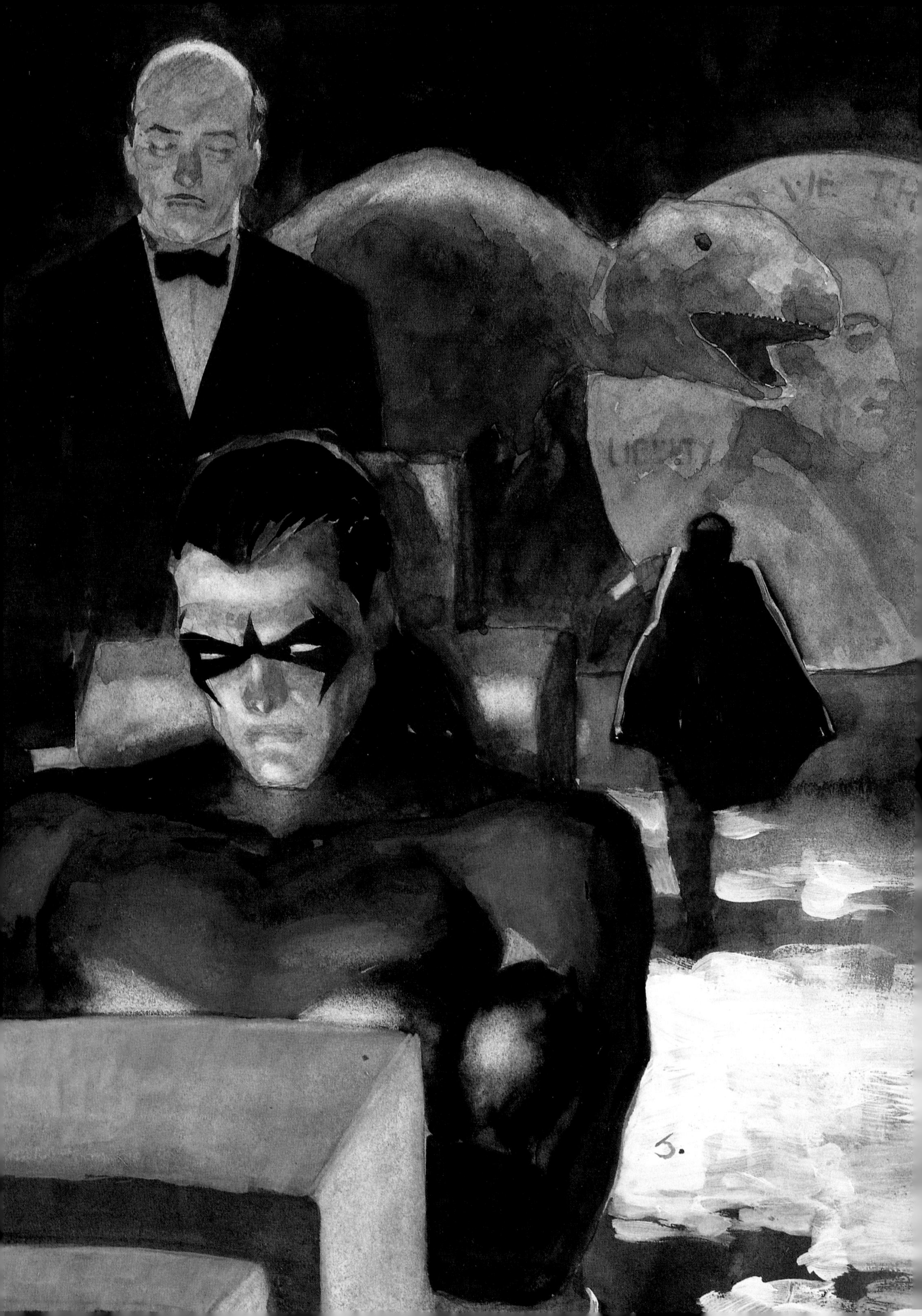

MORE THAN TROPHIES

"This cave holds more information on likely suspects than any other place on Earth. Dick, you and Alfred start accessing my computer files."

"Fair enough—but where are *you* going, Tim?"

"To hunt for even *more* data."

ART CONCEPT

Show off the cave trophies—giant Joker card hanging from cave ceiling, life-size dinosaur, giant Lincoln penny, etc.—as Robin starts to exit, leaving Nightwing & Alfred behind. With focus on the trophies, all three figures can be tiny—blackened silhouettes, provided they're recognizable, would suffice.

SCOTT HAMPTON'S SOLUTION

"This was an image that was troublesome to me. I wanted to show that they were back at the Batcave, back to the present, but also position the characters for the next step of the story. So I had to get all three characters in there—Alfred, Nightwing, and Robin—all three of them doing their own thing. Also, I had to fit in the tyrannosaurus and the big penny. I was thinking, this is a freaking trading card, how am I going to *do* this?

"In the end, I just stacked everything in the scene, and did the thing primarily, although not exclusively, in watercolor."

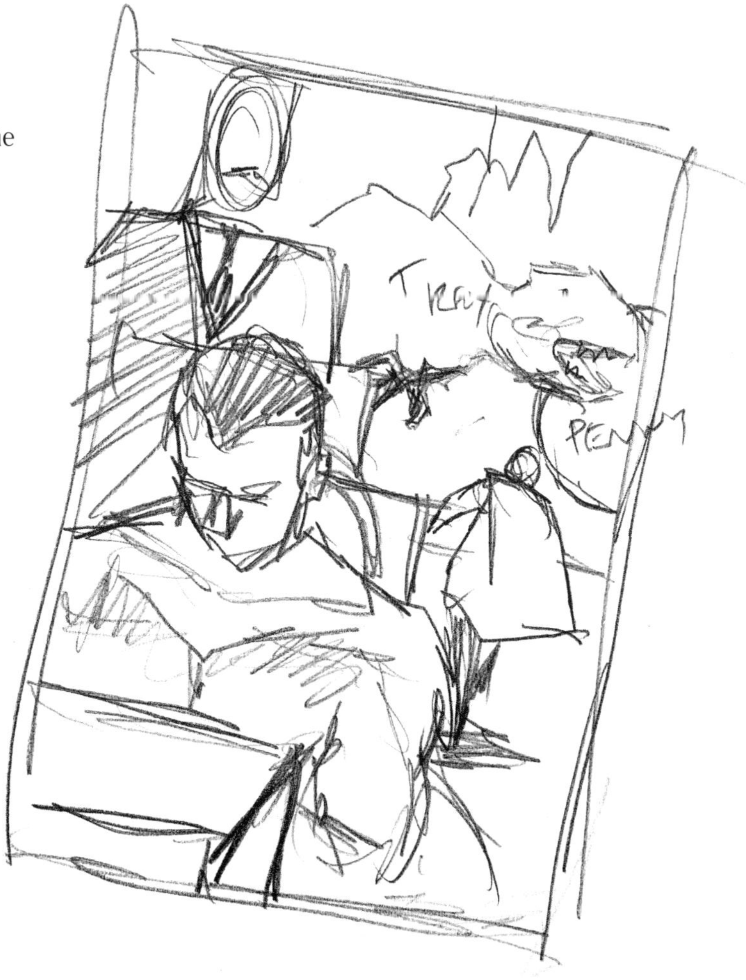

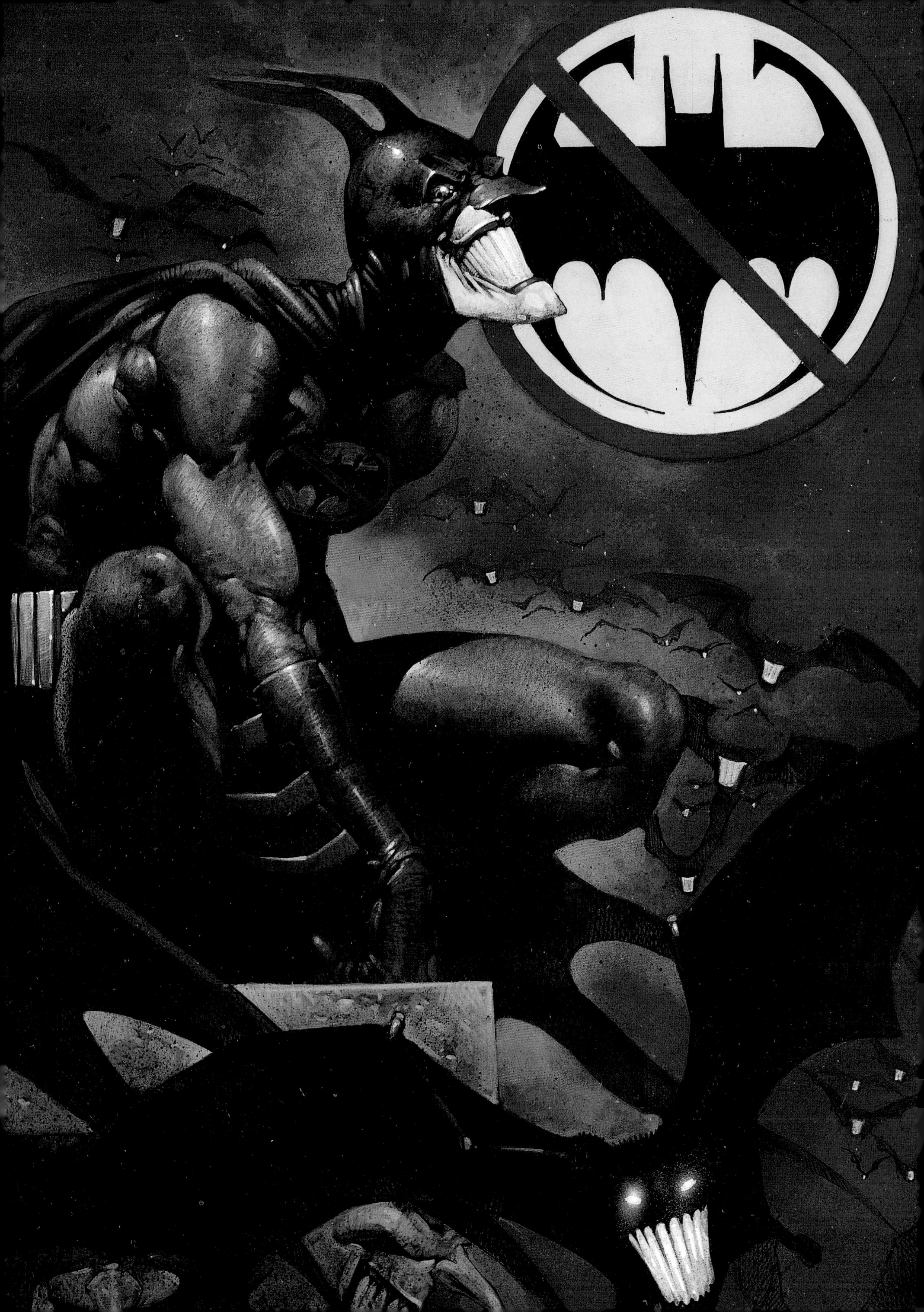

LAUGHING BATTY

"If I were *me*, no doubt I'd *die laughing* but how would I bite the big bullet if I were *Bats?* On the other hand, as Bats I'm *already dead*, so maybe I should *replace* me as Gotham's *new* Caped Crusader—the *Bat-Joker! HYAHAHAHAHAAA! Stop*—I'm *killin'* me!"

ART CONCEPT

Joker hanging upside-down with his legs hooked over a room-dividing curtain rod (or whatever); he is now wearing an ill-fitting and bizarrely wrong Batman costume of his own making (one bat-ear bent and much longer than the other, etc.) with the cape hanging way down past his upside-down head; maybe the chest Bat Emblem has the "universal no" circle & slash symbol superimposed over it; Joker's upside-down leering/laughing mouth should, of course, be clearly visible below/above the bottom edge of the Bat-Mask.

CARL CRITCHLOW'S SOLUTION

"At first glance, you may not see the Joker in this image. But then you notice the teeth.

"I do have a Joker, the Bat-Joker with the big teeth, the white face, the big long nose, and 'no Batman'—that's why there's a bat symbol with a line through it.

"I did the 'no' sign with the help of some tape. With acrylic paint you can get a nice thin line. . . . But acrylics have their limitations. I don't recommend trying to paint anything like a newspaper headline—it just wouldn't work. Especially not at the scale that these trading cards were originally printed in."

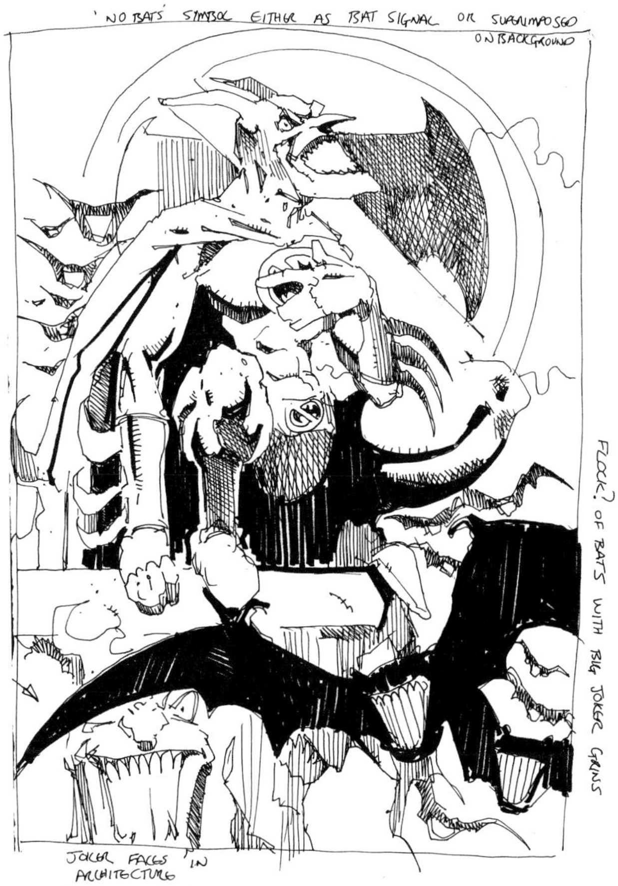
'NO BATS' SYMBOL EITHER AS BAT SIGNAL OR SUPERIMPOSED ON BACKGROUND
FLOCK? OF BATS WITH BIG JOKER GRINS
JOKER FACES 'IN ARCHITECTURE

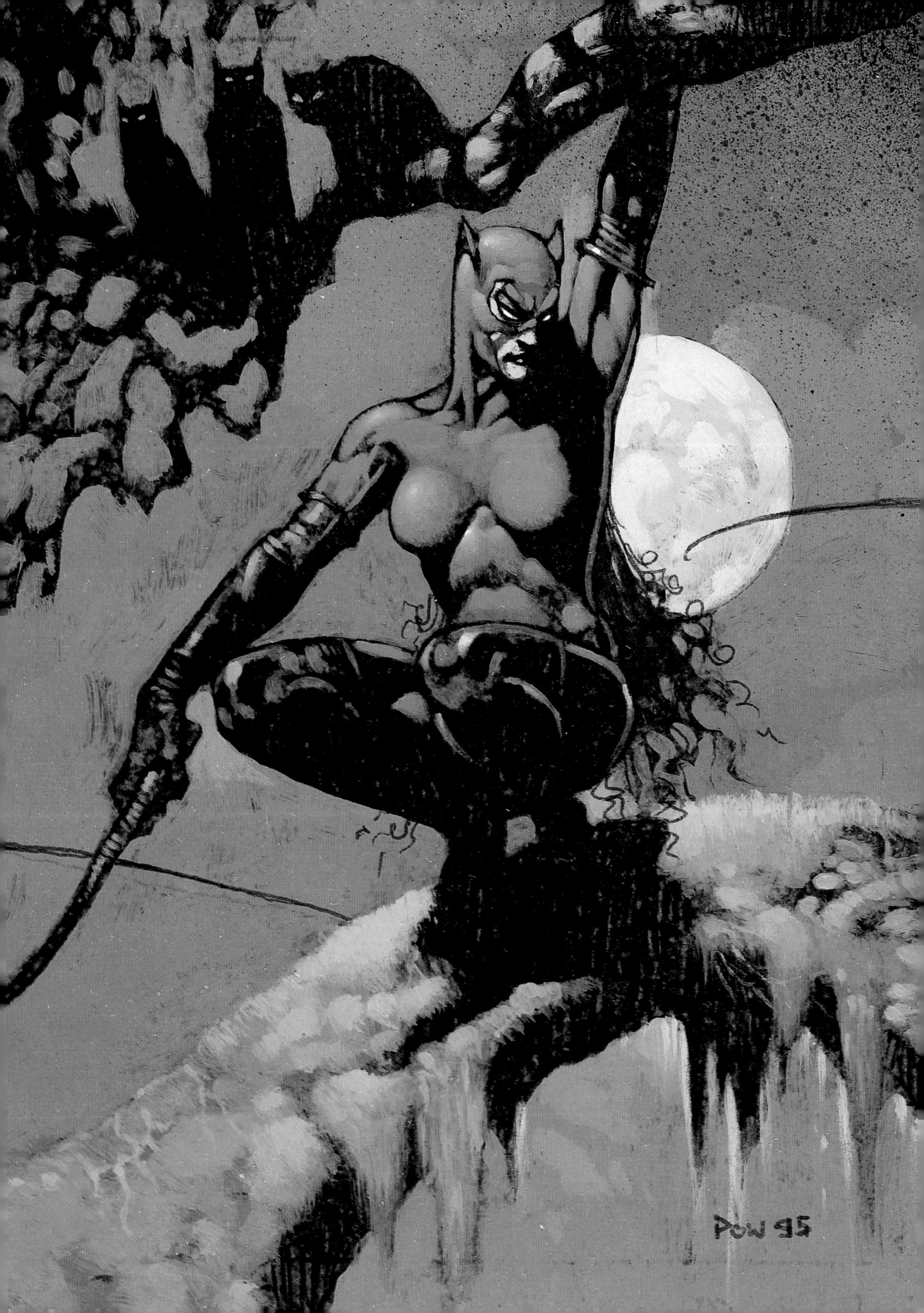
POW 95

CATWOMAN

Alfred and Nightwing go over Robin's files to find out who could possibly be behind Batman's sudden disappearance:

"What about *Selina Kyle*, Master Dick? Perhaps *she* had something to do with—"

"Catwoman's too much of a loner to join up with *anyone*, Alfred, let alone the *Joker*—and she's a *cat burglar*, not a *killer*. Besides, she's always had a *thing* for the Batman."

"You're right, lad. Who's *next* in the computer files?"

ART CONCEPT
Inward-facing profiles (or cropped partial profiles) of Alfred and Nightwing in extreme foreground left & right, with Batcave computer screen framed between them; screen shows full-figure shot of Catwoman with whip in hand.

DERMOT POWER'S SOLUTION
"I tend to go for images that are very brooding, dark and sinister. Catwoman really lends herself to that. I painted Catwoman as I would paint Batman—dark and mysterious. She's kind of like the female Batman really, isn't she? Dark and mysterious and strong. . . .

"I also wanted to use this piece as an excuse to show how I really like Frank Frazetta's work. Thinking about it now, it looks absolutely nothing like Frazetta's work, but I was able to use a little of his style when I painted the moss-green tree Catwoman is perched on."

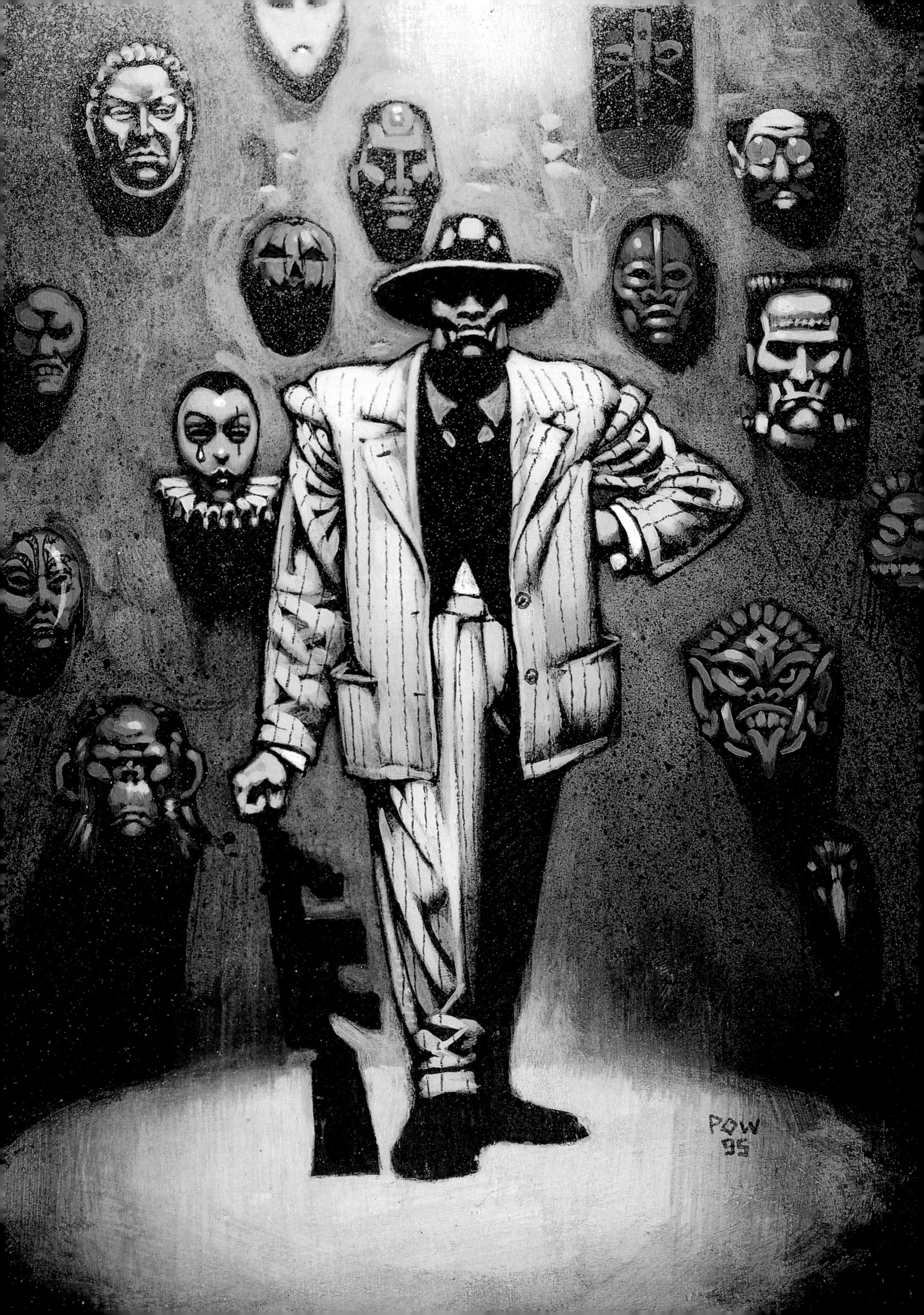
POW
95

BLACK MASK

Alfred and Nightwing spot a likely suspect in Robin's files:

"If the Joker *did* have an accomplice, the leader of Gotham's *False Face Society* is a likely candidate. After all, Roman Sionis *hated* the Master. . . ."

"But only as *Bruce Wayne,* Alfred. In fact, Black Mask is the only member of the Rogues Gallery who attacked Bruce *instead* of Batman—without knowing they were the *same man.*"

"Meaning the Master would have been murdered *out* of costume—so strike Black Mask."

ART CONCEPT
Computer screen showing full-figure shot of Black Mask, surrounded by wall-hanging masks of different types—everything from authentic African tribal masks to dime-store Halloween fright-faces, from a gas mask to the theater symbols of Comedy & Tragedy.

DERMOT POWER'S SOLUTION
"I was disappointed in this one, actually. I wanted to do it where you couldn't see his face, which I thought would've been much better. I would have had his head down and his face would be in shadow, and then with all the masks around him. . . . To me it made a lot more sense. My original seemed to say 'What does he really look like' and 'What mask was he wearing' and all that kind of thing. I wanted to make the Black Mask more mysterious, with

only his masks around to define him. But I guess it wasn't in keeping with the character.

"I used sepia tones to give it a darker feel."

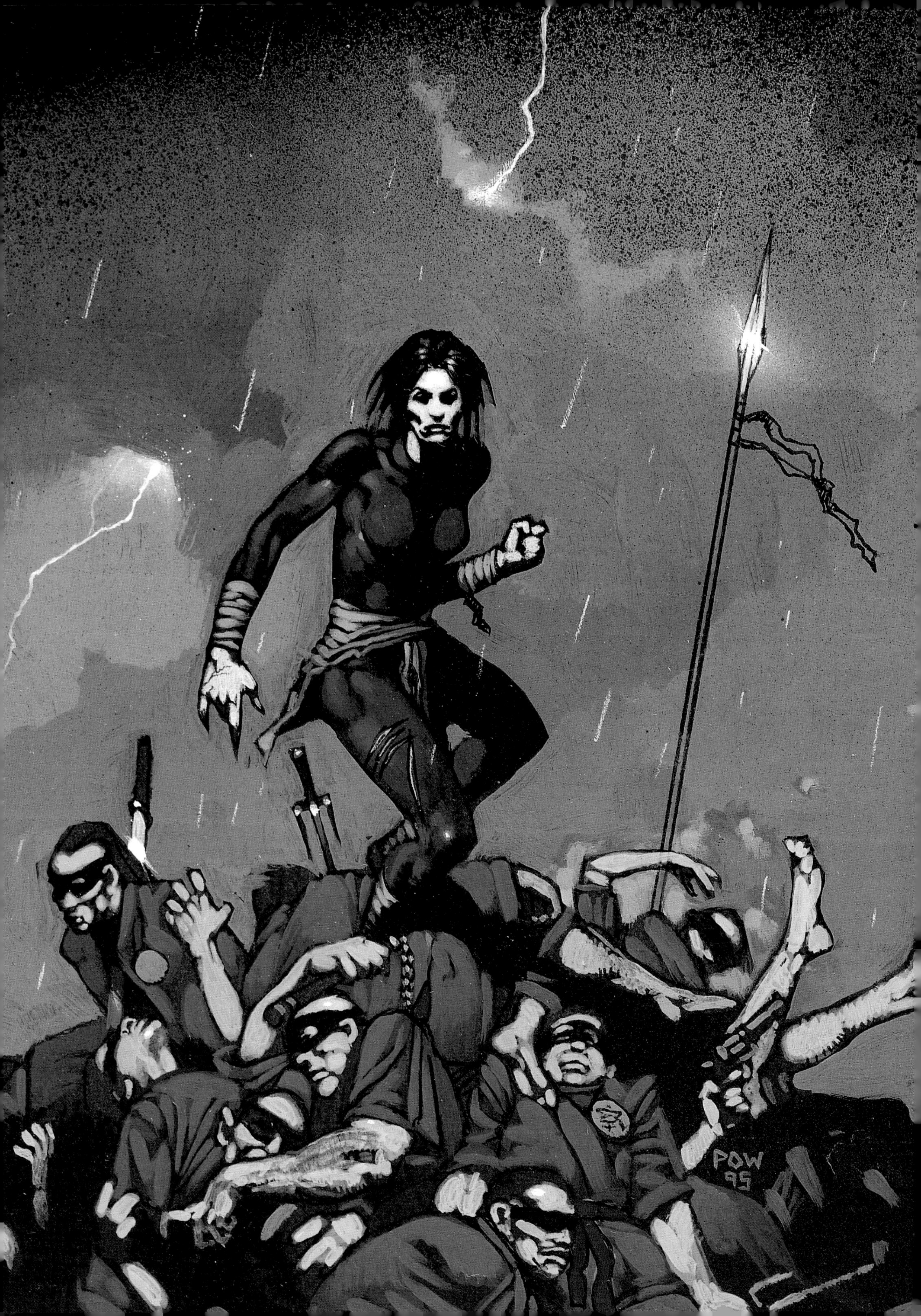
POW
95

LADY SHIVA

A formidable foe—but not a suspect, Alfred and Nightwing decide:

"I think we can scratch *Shiva* as well, Alfred."

"Yes, she always regarded the Batman as little more than a suitable challenge for her fighting prowess. That and a curiosity—a warrior who refused to kill."

"And even though *she* had no qualms about killing, the most accomplished martial artist on Earth would hardly shoot her opponent in the back."

ART CONCEPT
Computer screen showing Lady Shiva in an expert & impressive martial arts pose—executing a high twist-kick or whatever.

DERMOT POWER'S SOLUTION
"I wanted to do a Frank Miller–type thing—Miller sometimes does these shots where one figure gets color, so they stand out—that was my logic. But it didn't work out that way. Not at all.

"Instead, she's all in black, and colored similarly to the rest of the card. Although you could probably say I was influenced by Miller in the way I painted her face.

"If you look at Miller's faces, he tends to get the expression and everything about the face in a couple of quick little lines. I really like that, the simple and open space. . . .

"Now, you can't really leave open spaces in painting, like you can with pencil and ink. Or if you can, I haven't figured out how. One way to get that same effect is to paint the characters' faces in very stark light with very strong shadows. Especially when it's reduced as small as it is with a trading card—you can still read the expression because you've left it very strong. It's as close to line work as a painting can get."

RAIN

HER ENEMIES ALL WEAR GREY SUITS

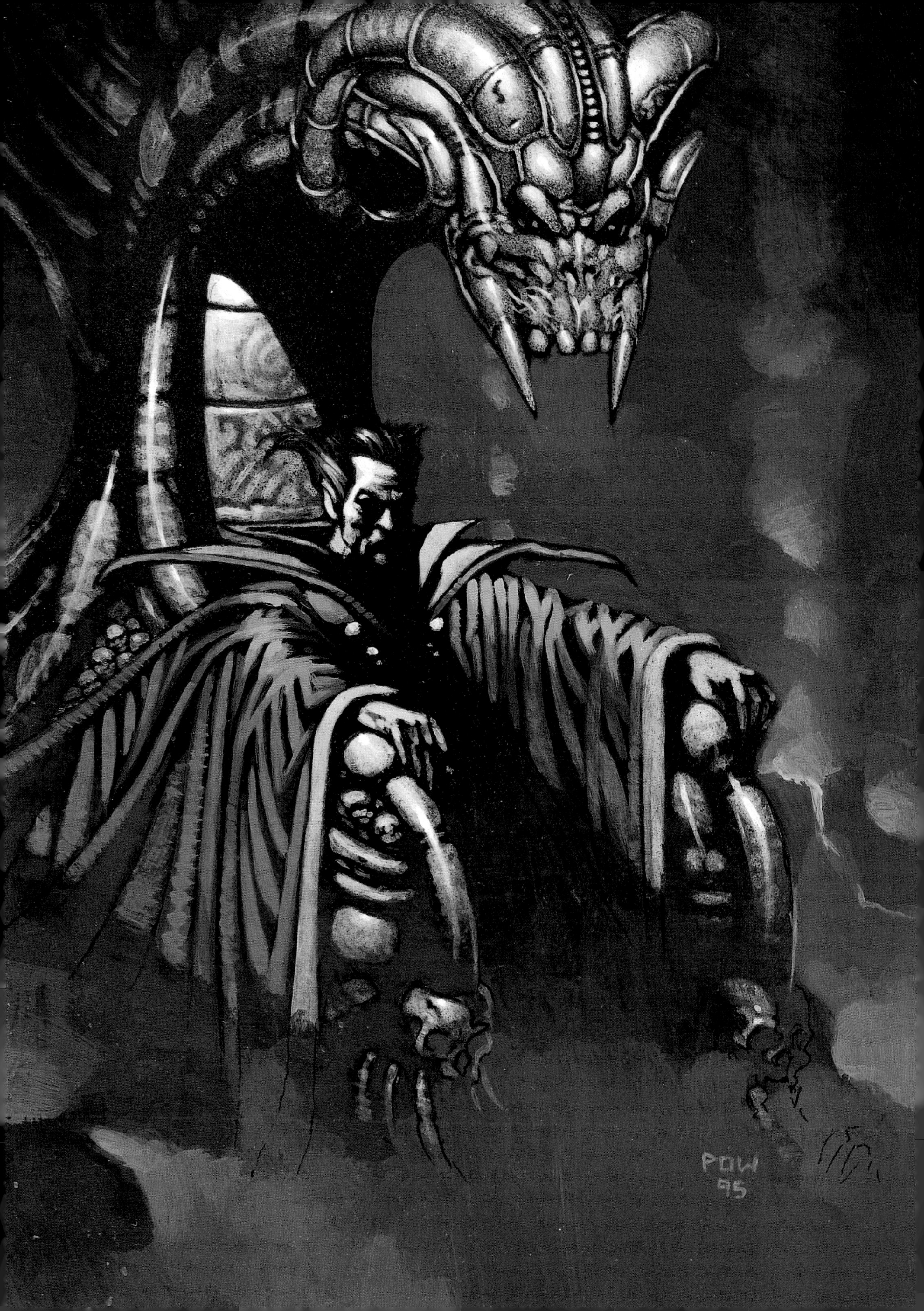
POW
95

RĀ'S AL GHŪL

Alfred and Nightwing take the measure of another murder suspect:

"With the worldwide membership of his Brotherhood of the Demon available, I can't see Rā's al Ghūl needing the Joker for *anything.*"

"Nor, given their mutual respect, would he *want* the Master dead. Indeed, his immortality notwithstanding, Rā's al Ghūl wanted the Batman to father an *heir* with Talia . . . hardly possible for a dead man."

ART CONCEPT
Computer screen showing Rā's al Ghūl—with a giant demon's head looming behind him; see the graphic novel *Birth of the Demon.*

BISU HEAD

BONE-LIKE

DARK B.G. LIKE ORIGINAL CARD,

GREEN MIST

DERMOT POWER'S SOLUTION

"I wanted to make Rā's al Ghūl look really imposing and mysterious, like the dark lord of a far-off castle. I loved painting the Giger-like texture of the throne—H. R. Giger designed the movie *Alien.* I like that kind of twisty, shiny, shell-like stuff; I don't get to paint it nearly enough!"

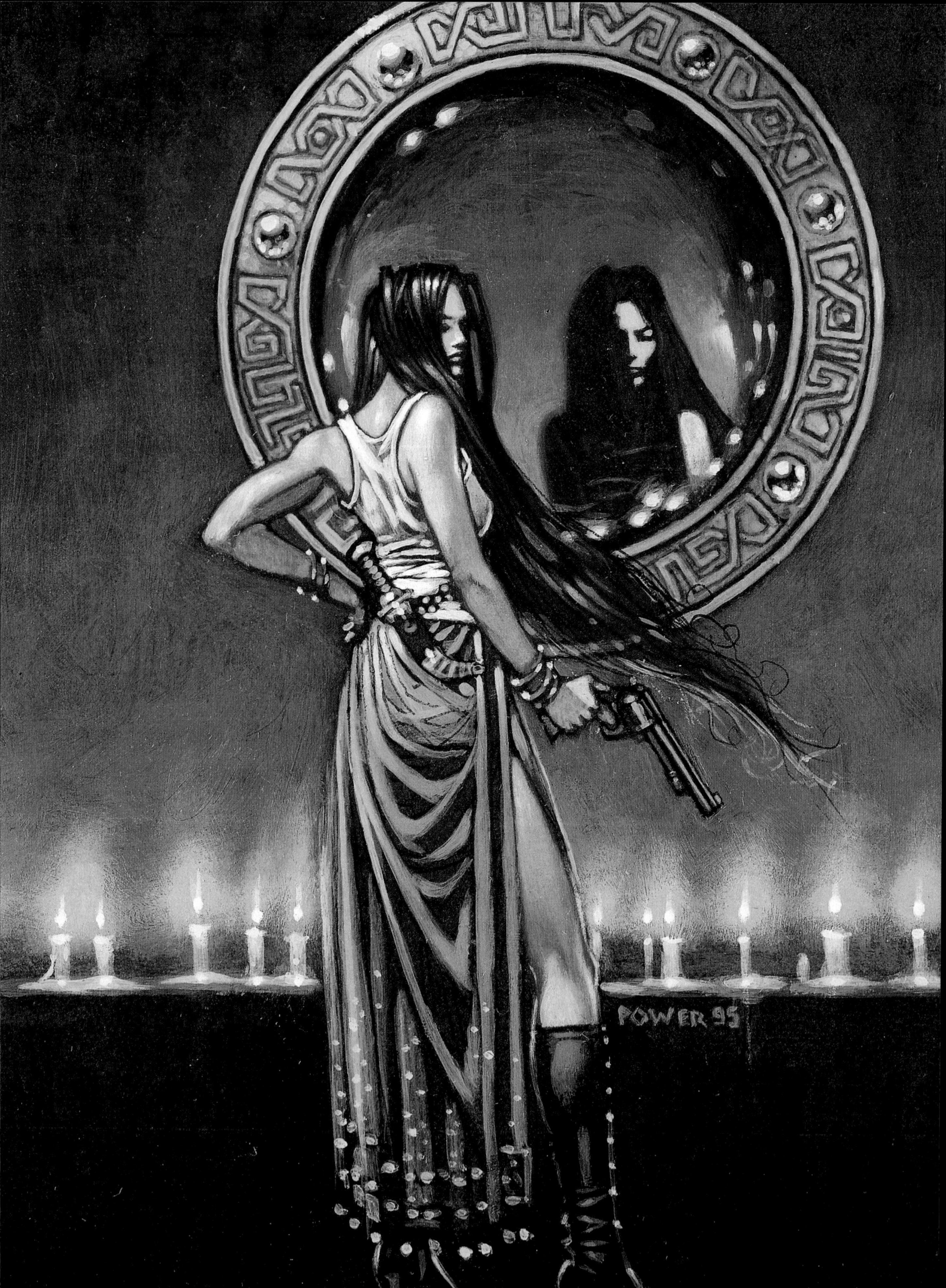
POWER 95

TALIA

Alfred and Nightwing disagree over Talia's files:

"*Talia*—another one who carried a large torch for the Batman, even more so than Catwoman."

"Still, Master Dick, Talia has always been torn between love for the Batman and loyalty to her father."

"True, Alfred, but since we've already *ruled out* Rā's al Ghūl. . . ."

"*Next* candidate."

ART CONCEPT
Computer screen showing gorgeous-but-deadly Talia with an exotic pistol in hand.

DERMOT POWER'S SOLUTION
"This is one of my favorite cards. I'm very proud of the composition—it's nice, and I managed to keep all the colors in one key."

The only complaint that Power has is about the crop. Unlike Hampton, who thought they overcropped his Ghost of a Ghost card [page 17] Power thinks too much of the painting was left in.

"When I designed it, I gave them quite a bit of bleed, and they actually left the whole mirror in. I actually wanted the mirror to be cropped, slightly. . . . It seemed to fit the composition better. I didn't want the mirror to be such a strong element in the composition. I think it distracts away from Talia."

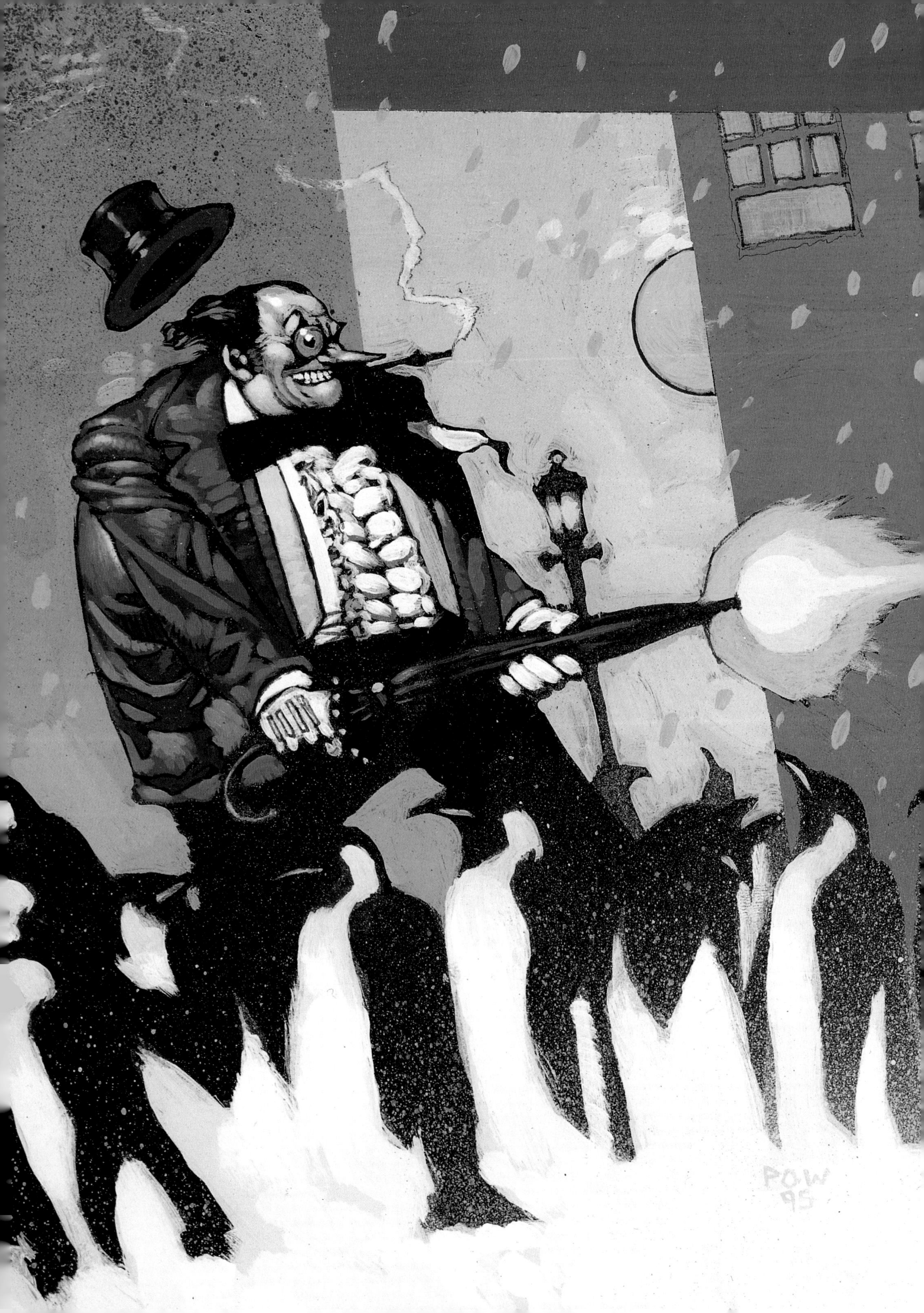
POW
95

THE PENGUIN

This suspect, Alfred and Nightwing decide, is a likely one:

"Oswald Cobblepot makes the most sense so far. He's teamed up with the Joker in the *past*—and he certainly wouldn't mind seeing the Batman dead."

"But if the Joker left *his* calling cards at the crime scene, why was there nothing pertaining to the Penguin's trademark *birds* or *umbrellas?*"

"Good point, Alfred, but let's still file him as a *possible.*"

ART CONCEPT
Computer screen showing the Penguin—either "parachuting" down on an opened umbrella toward real penguins waiting below, or blasting a machine gun concealed inside a closed umbrella, with real penguins arrayed in background.

DERMOT POWER'S SOLUTION
"I was trying to be abstract and a little funny. It's great to draw a character like the Penguin, as you can exaggerate as much as you like—and get away with it. The Penguin is not like Talia, or Batman, or Poison Ivy. You couldn't exaggerate those characters, it wouldn't work.

But with the Penguin, you can completely caricature him.

"I was trying to do a composition that was interesting and abstract, so that the background is all very flat and rigid, full of straight lines. The penguins themselves are just shapes and colors—they don't really come across as real penguins.

"I wanted to make a very simple graphic image—not 'graphic' as in 'graphic violence,' but 'graphic' as in shapes—to create a very blocky feel to the entire piece."

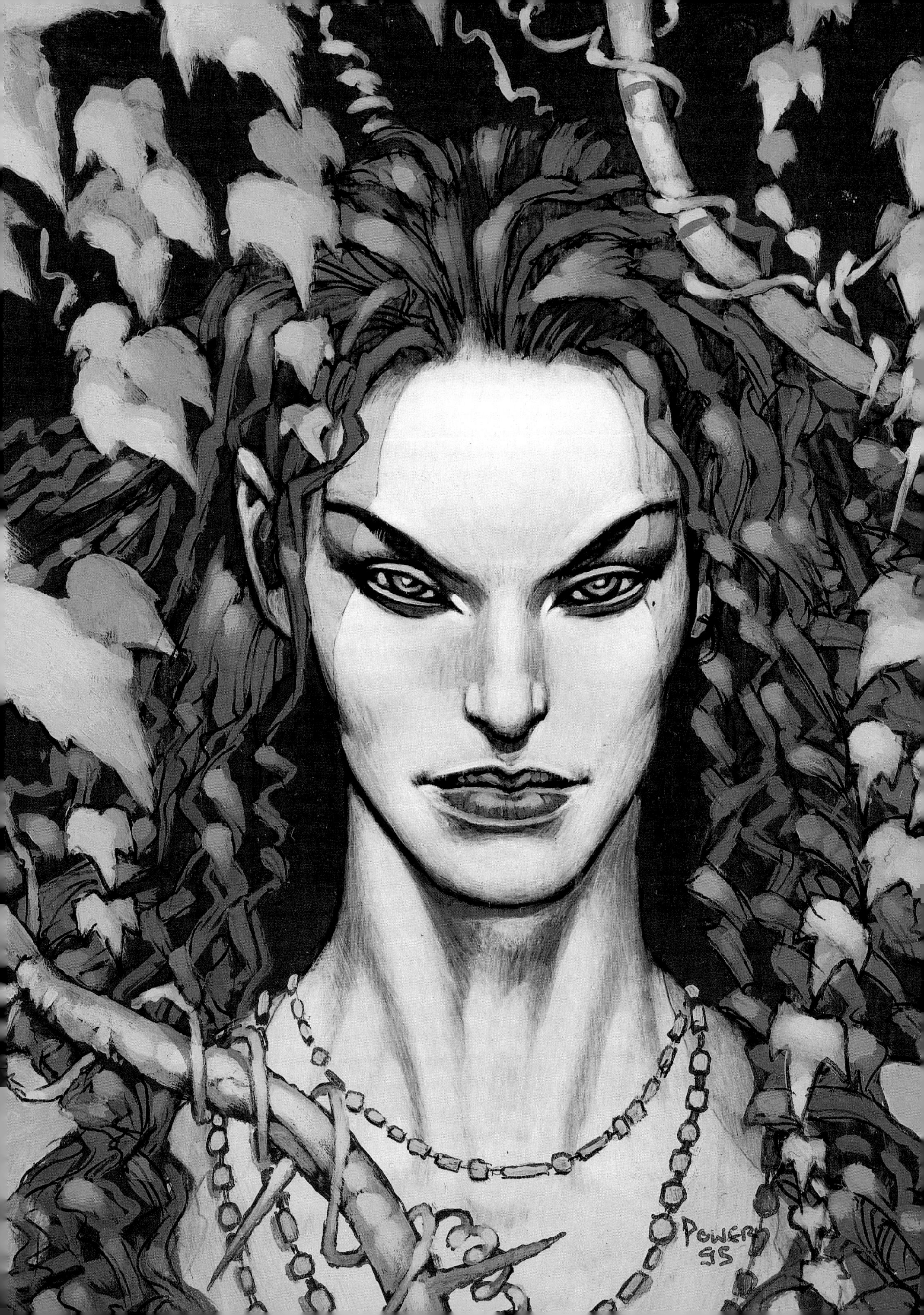
POWERS
95

POISON IVY

Alfred and Nightwing "scratch" another murder suspect:

"Pamela Isley. For a man who used romance as nothing but a crutch for his Bruce Wayne disguise, the Master certainly enjoyed his share of entanglements, so to speak."

"Yes, but Poison Ivy's seductive designs are just a femme fatale's cover for control. She delights in making men *itch* for her, then kills them with her *toxic touch*—and *not* a *gun*."

ART CONCEPT
Computer screen showing seductive-but-evil Poison Ivy in a lush (almost claustrophobic) tangle of vines & leaves.

DERMOT POWER'S SOLUTION
"I loved making her elfin. I wanted her to look more like a child of the seventies, more like a hippie. I didn't like the way Poison Ivy looked in the reference that I was sent, so I changed her. I made her softer, and made her look more magical. I love things that have to do with the magical quality of woodlands. I love greens and kind of woody colors. When I can, I like to bring a mythological fairy-tale quality into my work, and this seemed like a good opportunity to do it."

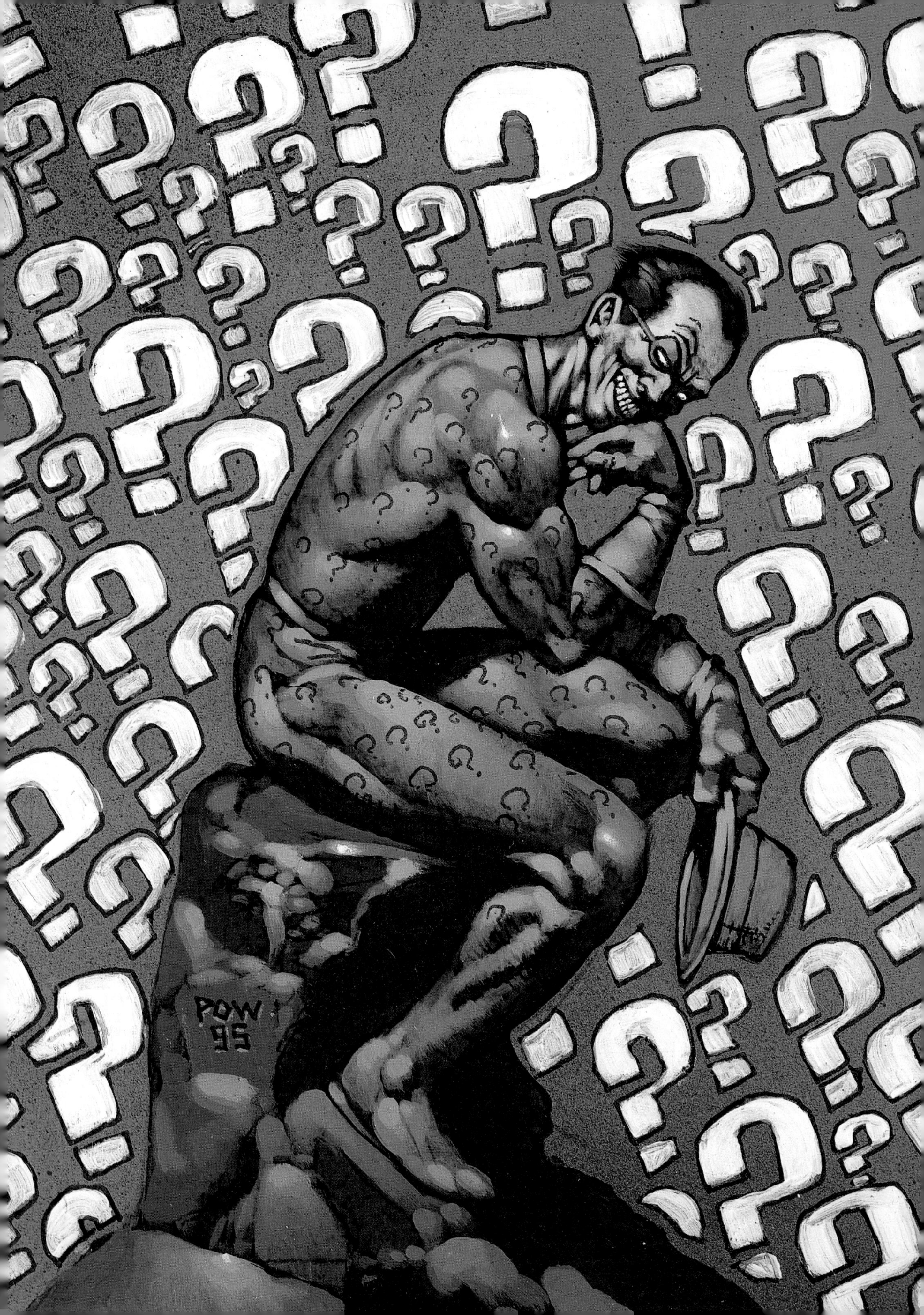
POW
95

THE RIDDLER

Alfred and Nightwing puzzle away: Did the Riddler do it?

"Edward Nigma *is* an enigma, Alfred. I've never been able to figure out if he *hated* or *needed* the Batman."

"I suspect *both,* Master Dick. He *needed* the Batman in the same way a chess master needs a worthy opponent—but he *hated* the Batman for always matching his wit, solving his riddles, and foiling his crimes."

"Which makes him another *possible.*"

ART CONCEPT
Computer screen showing the laughing Riddler surrounded by giant question marks, much larger than the question marks on his costume.

DERMOT POWER'S SOLUTION
"I based this on Rodin's *The Thinker,* which I think is fairly obvious. It's not exactly groundbreaking to have the Riddler surrounded by a lot of question marks. But it is different for me—normally, I would have done something more realistic. Truth be told, I was being a bit lazy when I thought of this. It's just a very simple, somewhat traditional portrait. But I know that it works."

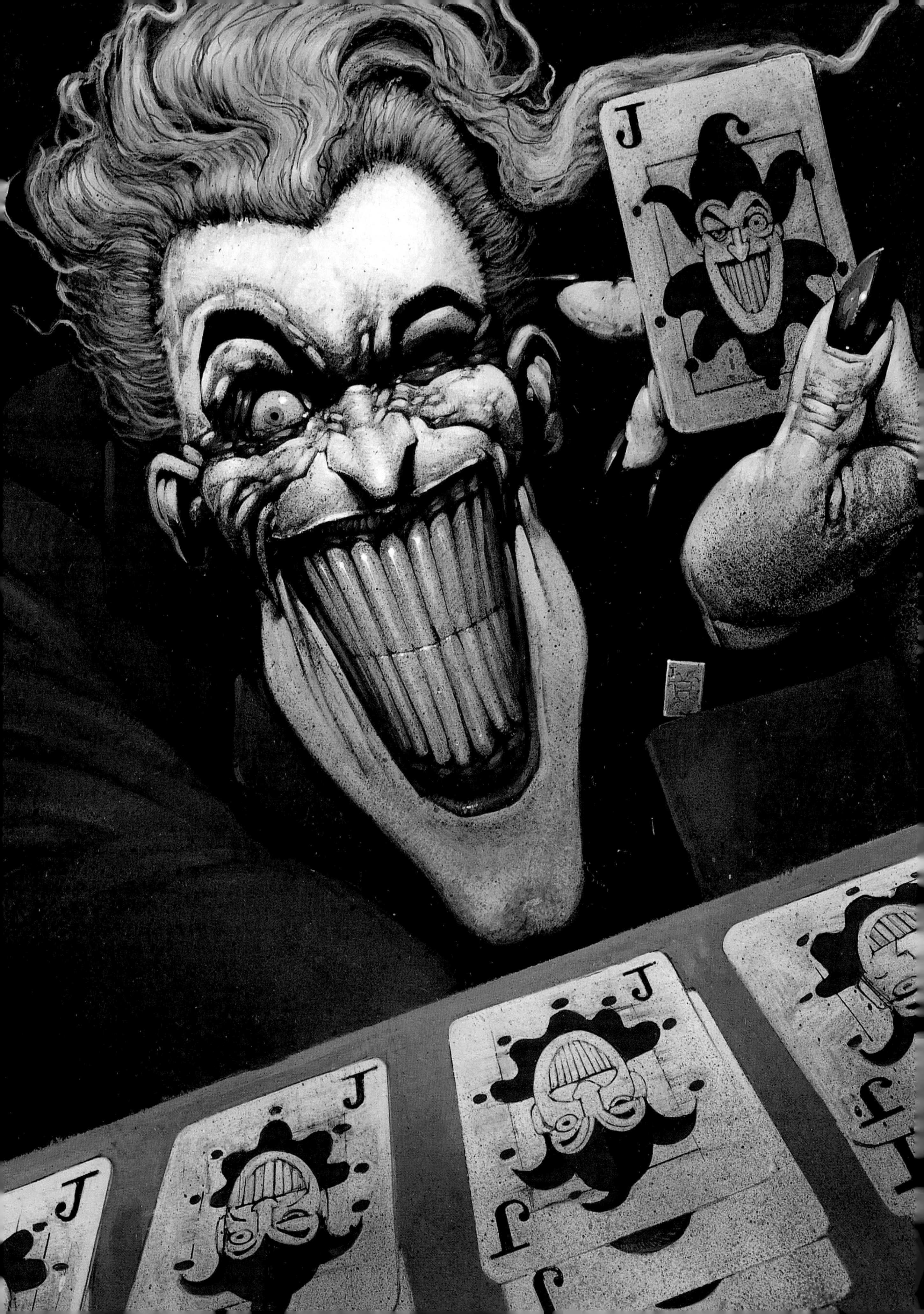

SOLITARY MADNESS

"With Bats gone, I'm forced to compete against myself—and either the deck is *stacked* or I'm not playing with a *full* one! Probably *both,* but no fun at all—so maybe I should *investigate* this murder which has somehow slipped my mind. Such as it *is.* Indeed, I do believe the time has come for . . . *Sherlock Jokes!* *HYAHAHAHAAA!"*

ART CONCEPT
Loony Joker seated at a table facing us, part of a deck of cards in hand; other cards dealt in a solitaire pattern on table in front of him—and we can see that every face-up card is a Joker.

CARL CRITCHLOW'S SOLUTION
"The further I got into the set, the more I started pushing it. Pushing all the elements of the Joker's face.

"Having done the previous ones, I wanted to see how far I could take the elements of the Joker's face, how much I could exaggerate them, and still leave him with a workable-looking face.

"It looks like it works, doesn't it? I mean, he wouldn't really be able to shut his mouth, but you don't really notice that unless you start to think about it."

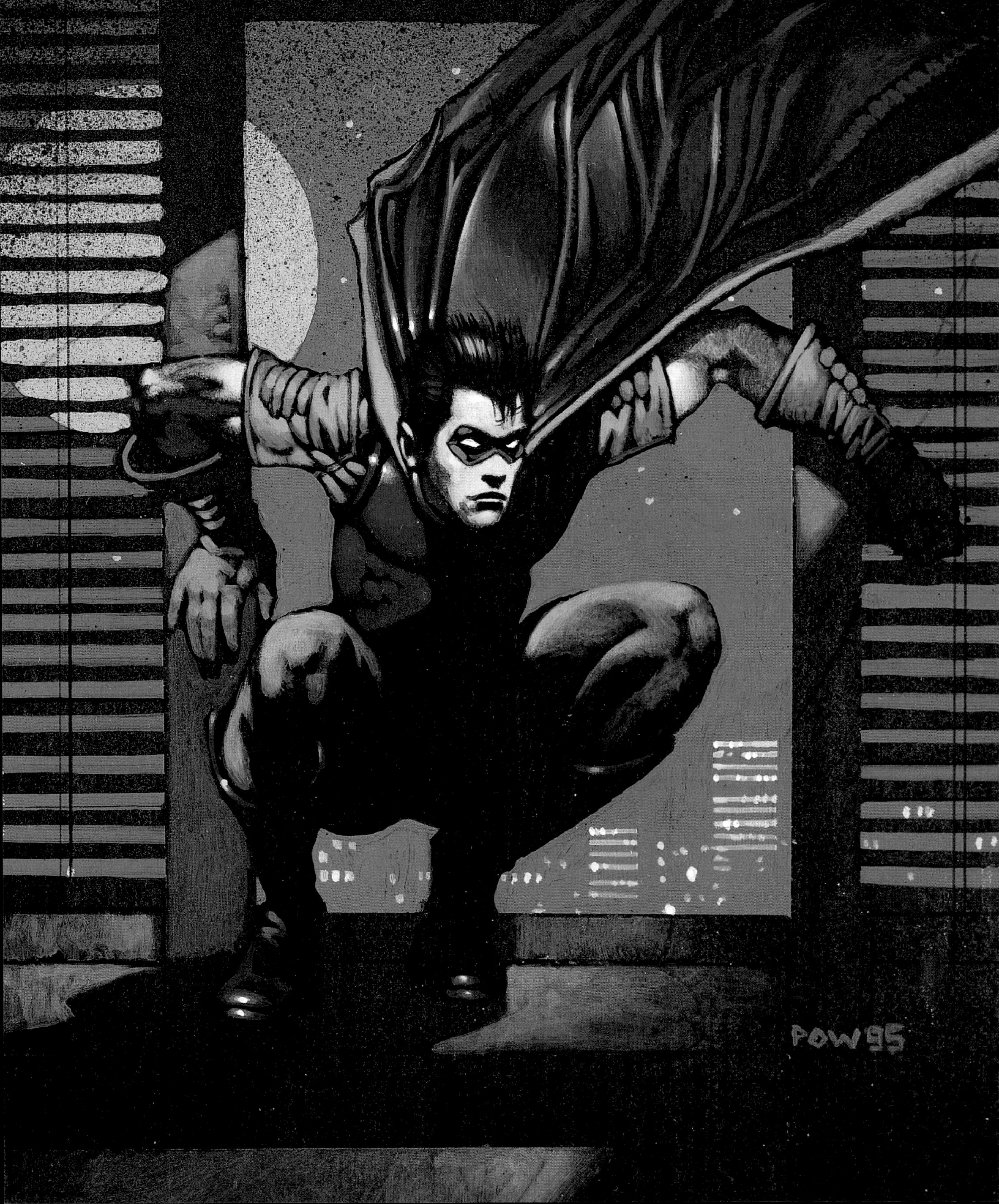
POW95

HARD COPY

Robin slips through the Police Commissioner's high window:

"Good, Gordon is gone for the night. He's old-fashioned enough to prefer paper, so I couldn't tap his files from the cave—but I can read them by his desk lamp. The lock on that old file cabinet shouldn't be too hard to pick."

ART CONCEPT

Interior Gordon's gloomy office; looking between Gordon's desk and an old-fashioned wood filing cabinet, we see Robin (current Tim Drake version) stealthily slipping in thru the window, his eyes on the filing cabinet.

DERMOT POWER'S SOLUTION

"Robin is difficult to do because he's only fourteen but he has muscles. I found it really difficult to put such a young face on such a well-developed body, but I took a break from it, and then I was able to make it work."

Power's version of "taking a break" is very much his own.

"I'd pick four cards, and sit down at my drawing board. I would do some sketches for one until I couldn't think of anything else that might possibly work.

"Then, I'd move on to the next one, and do the same. Then on to the next one, move on to the next one, and then go back to the start of the first one. I'd look at all the sketches and rough notes that I'd put down. When you let it go cold like that, over a day or so, you can then pick out what's good in your original sketches, what's worth pursuing."

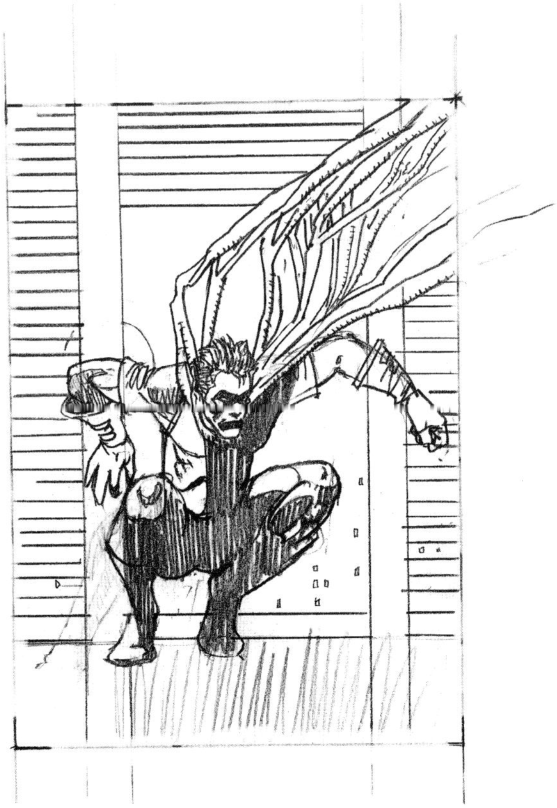

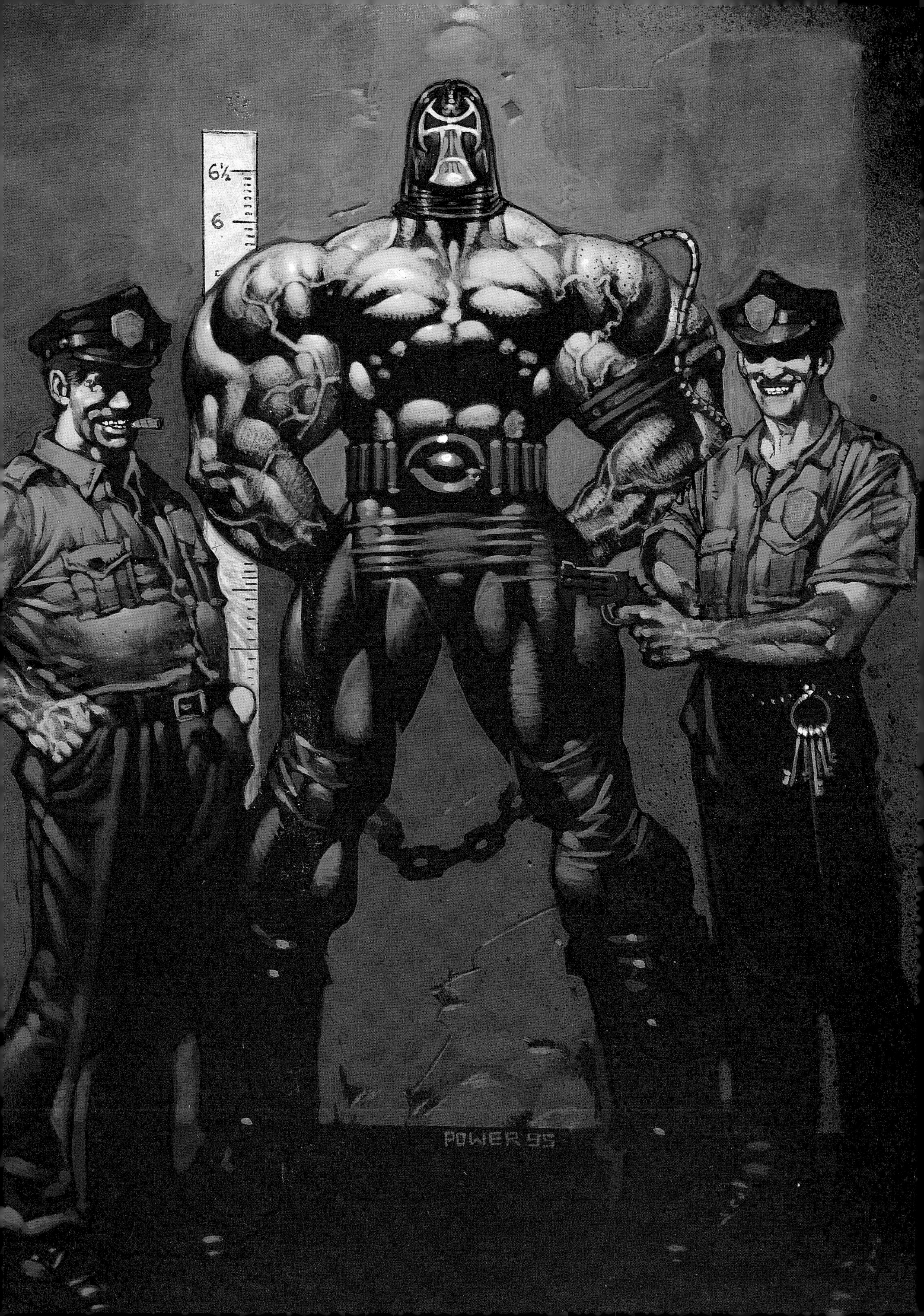
6½
6
POWER 95

BANE

Robin reads Gordon's files:

"It says here Bane came to Gotham after escaping from prison on island of Santa Prisca. Severely injured and forced temporary retirement of Batman. Briefly ruled virtually all criminal enterprise in city. Apprehended by replacement Batman, and still safe and sound in Blackgate Prison."

ART CONCEPT
Full-figure shot of Bane (in full costume & mask) standing against police lineup wall with height marks calibrated on it; Bane is about 6'6".

DERMOT POWER'S SOLUTION
"I like this one, actually. This is the way I like to paint: murky colors and very high-contrast skin tones. I think it worked out fairly well.

"It also has a humorous element to it. The look I wanted here was of two guys who had just caught a really big shark. I wanted them to show their pride, but I also wanted to show that Bane is still extremely dangerous and it's kind of foolhardy of them to be acting the way that they are acting. They look proud of themselves, but the implication is that they are not going to be long for this world."

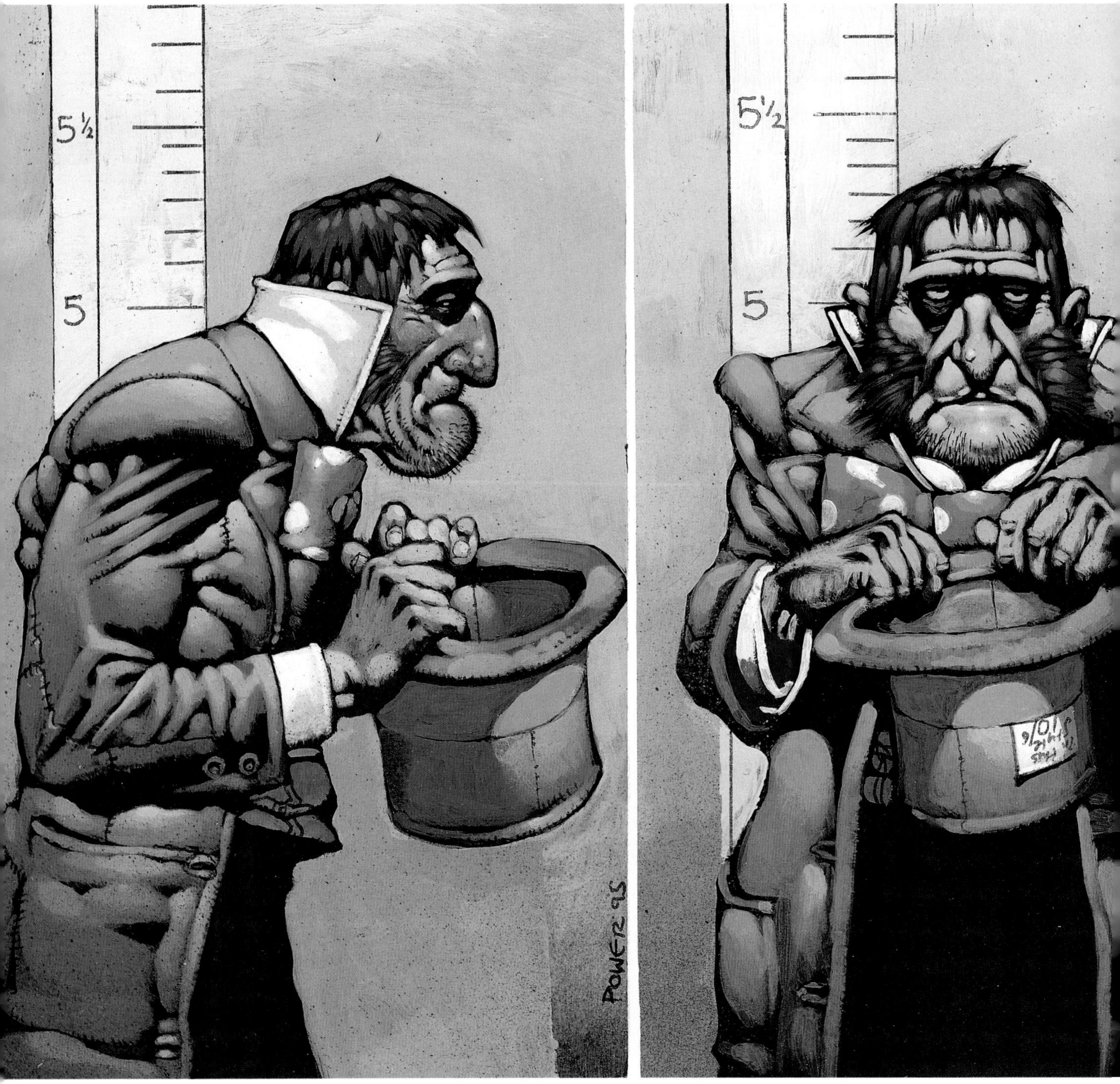
5½
5
POWER 95
5½
5

MAD HATTER

Robin reads Gordon's files:

"Criminally insane, obsessed with hats, lethal 'tea parties,' and Lewis Carroll's *Alice in Wonderland*. Uses headgear-concealed electronic devices to alter and control brainwave patterns of zombie-puppet wearers. Pet chimp bites. Apprehended numerous times by Batman.

"Nothing here that isn't in my computer files, and I've already eliminated the Hatter."

ART CONCEPT

Medium (from waist up) profile & full-front mug shots of Mad Hatter, complete with goofy hat, bow tie, & waistcoat.

DERMOT POWER'S SOLUTION

"It's like two cards for the price of one!" Power laughs.

"I'd done the Mad Hatter before—he was one of the villains in the *Batman/Judge Dredd* comic that I had worked on, and in an illustration that I had done once for a computer game. All of those illustrations were based on the traditional Mad Hatter, and I was bored with that image.

"My thinking was to make him more Dickensian. I wanted to portray him as miserable-looking, dirty and depressed, as if he was from the 19th century."

Mad Hatter is the only horizontal painting in the set. "I wanted to portray him in profile—I think in profile he works quite well—but because I was doing a completely different Mad Hatter, I also gave the front view. It was as if this was a style guide to how he's supposed to look."

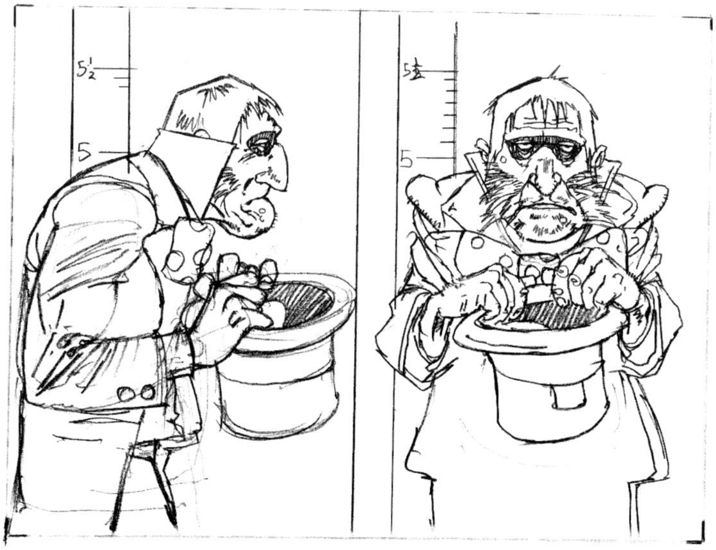

5½
5
5½
5

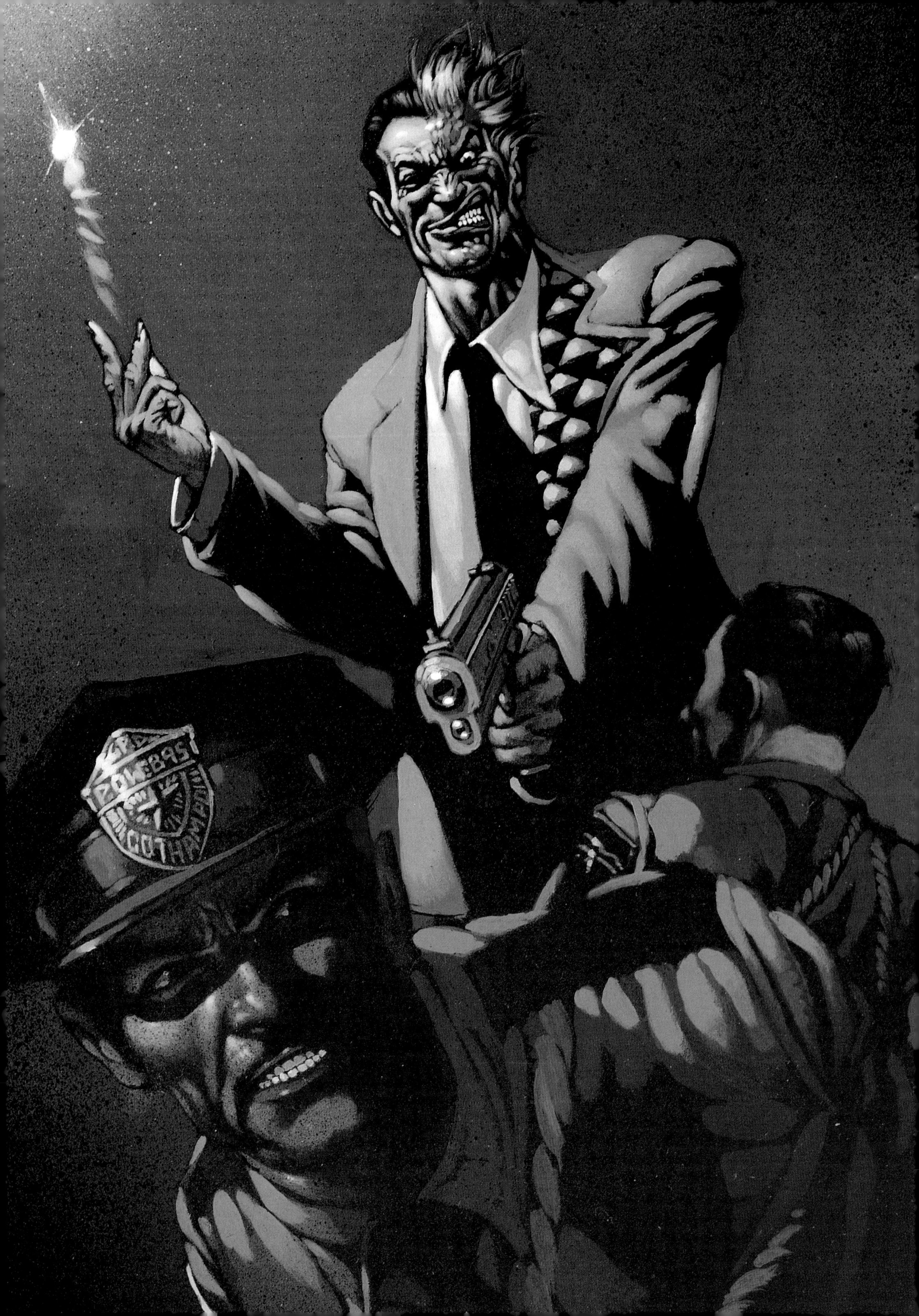
GOTHAM

TWO-FACE

Robin reads Gordon's files:

"Former Gotham District Attorney gone bad and driven to crimes of twisted 'justice.' Embittered by Batman's perceived 'betrayal.' Doused by vial of acid during prosecution of Vincent 'Boss' Maroni. Incident disfigured face and tipped mind into madness. Now has fetish for the number two. Actions dictated by flip of double-headed coin, one side scarred.

"He would be a perfect suspect, except for the fact that he's locked down in Arkham."

ART CONCEPT

Three close-up mug shots of Two-Face (two profile shots framing full-face shot in center); from left to right: Profile showing nothing but the normal Harvey Dent side of face; full-front showing the vertically split face, one side normal, other side disfigured; and opposite profile showing nothing but disfigured side of face. The two profiles should be facing inward—at the full-face in center.

DERMOT POWER'S SOLUTION

"I had to do this sketch three, no   four times. The first time, it was kind of a composite of a photograph of Two-Face, a file, a couple of coins, things like that. I still think that was the best one, but the editors didn't feel it was interesting enough. . . .

"Then I designed a card where Two-Face was holding a gun on two policemen; one of the policemen was dead, and the other looked completely petrified, but that was too gruesome. Then I did a card which was more or less the same, except that both policemen were alive, but they still looked too scared. Finally, I hit upon this one, where the policemen seem to have a bit of a chance. . . .

"If you look closely at the policeman's cap, you can see that I snuck my name into the art."

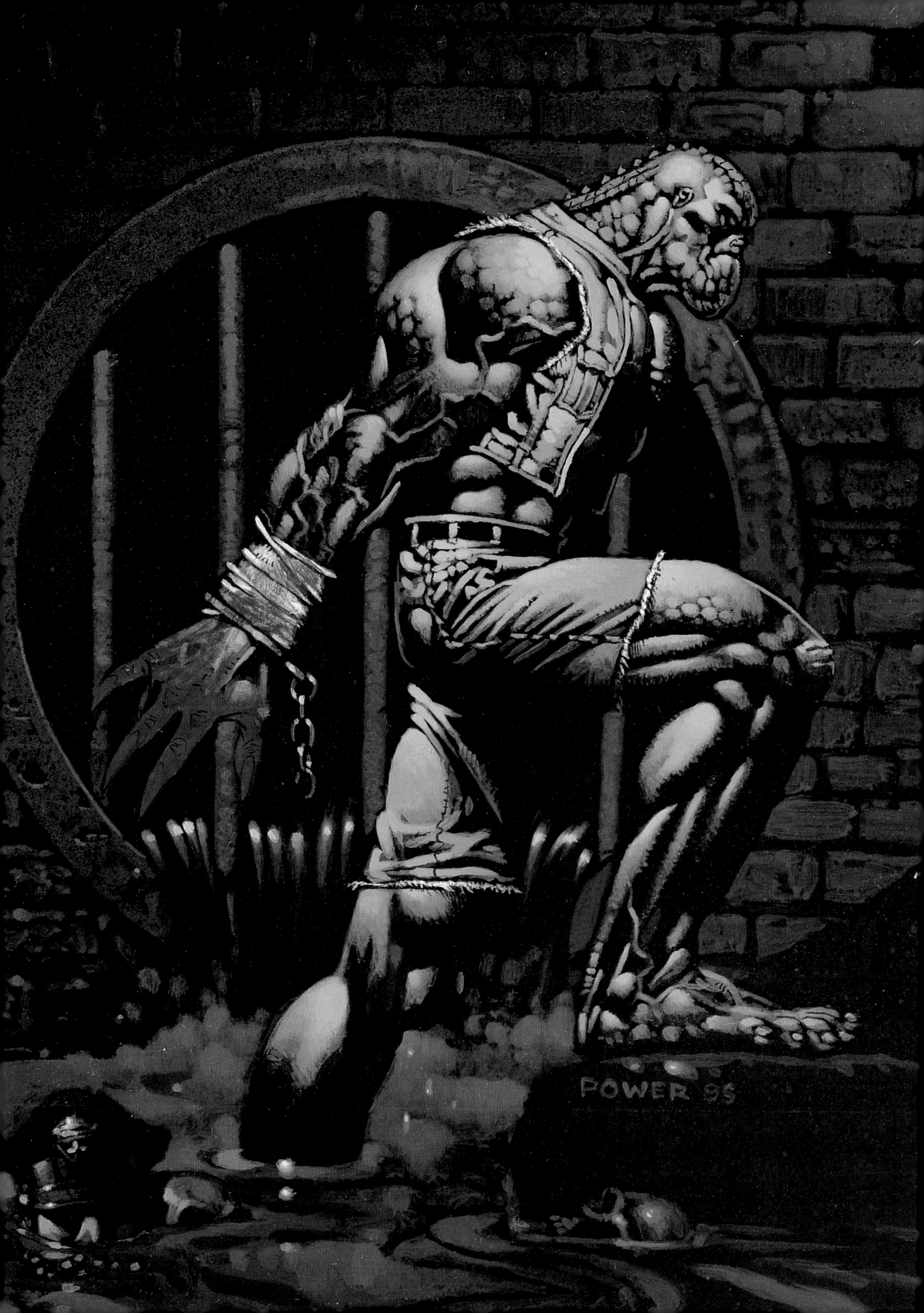
POWER 95

KILLER CROC

Robin reads Gordon's files:

"Rare hereditary condition results in appearance of humanoid reptile. Once a Gotham crime lord, but mentality and behavior progressively disintegrating to bestial levels. Now acts almost purely on instinct. Incredible strength & ferocity.

"And unlikely to use a gun at this point. Besides, he was last seen in a Louisiana swamp."

ART CONCEPT
"Photograph" of enraged Killer Croc taken thru cell bars—which he is fiercely gripping & shaking as he snarls/bellows out at us.

DERMOT POWER'S SOLUTION
"It's just the usual thing that I kind of go for: all the background is muted and very, very dark, while Killer Croc is very bright and stands out.

"I was able to sneak in the dead policeman in the water because the background is so dark. Even though the piece is on the darker side, I feel that I got the colors just right, especially the blood red on Croc's hands and the dim outline of the sewer.

"Except that I think that I colored Croc a bit wrong—I think his green is a bit too acidic."

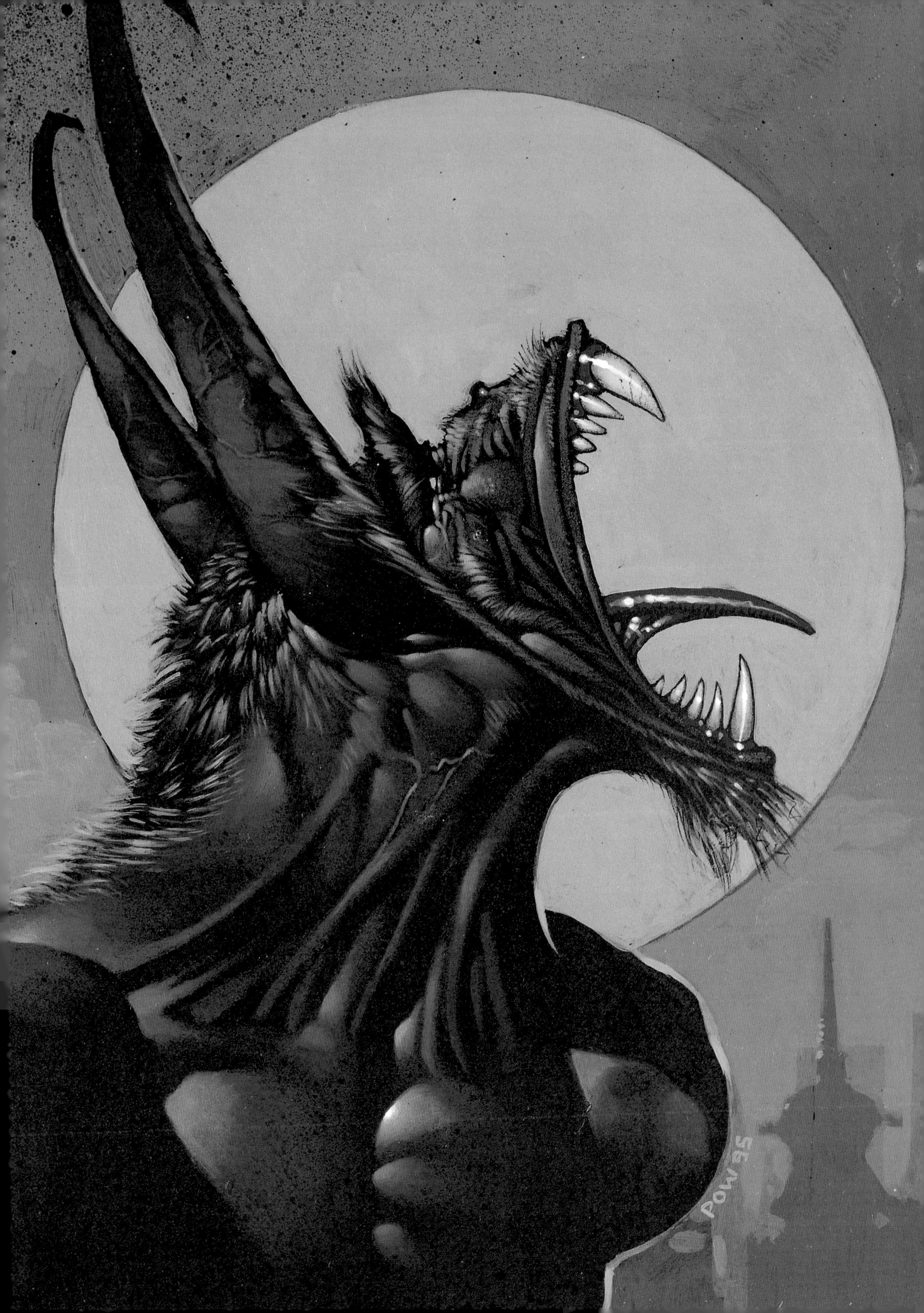
POW 95

Robin reads Gordon's files:

"Tragic case. Scientist (expert on bats) who tried to help the blind but doomed himself to horror. Unpredictable transformation to bizarre batlike creature. Loss of humanity and conscience, no awareness of his other self. ․

"Tragic is right—and like Killer Croc, Man-Bat is hardly a gun nut. Besides, I checked—and Kirk Langstrom's been normal for months."

ART CONCEPT

"Photograph" of Man-Bat in bizarre flight against Gotham's gothic skyline.

DERMOT POWER'S SOLUTION

"It's a very strong composition, another of my favorite pieces. It's quite simple, which is not a bad thing. I think my best work comes when I get the piece right in the first try. When a painting works without too much repainting or changing things around, it makes for a better piece and this one was like that for me."

One of the most common mistakes that Power sees is people putting too much detail in their work. "Too many LPI," he says.

LPI?

"Lines per inch. It shows indecisiveness. Some people seem to think that if they have hundreds of lines per square inch, there's so much work there that it's a good piece of work. Of course, it's never the case.

"Lots of time spent on something often doesn't relate at all to how good it is."

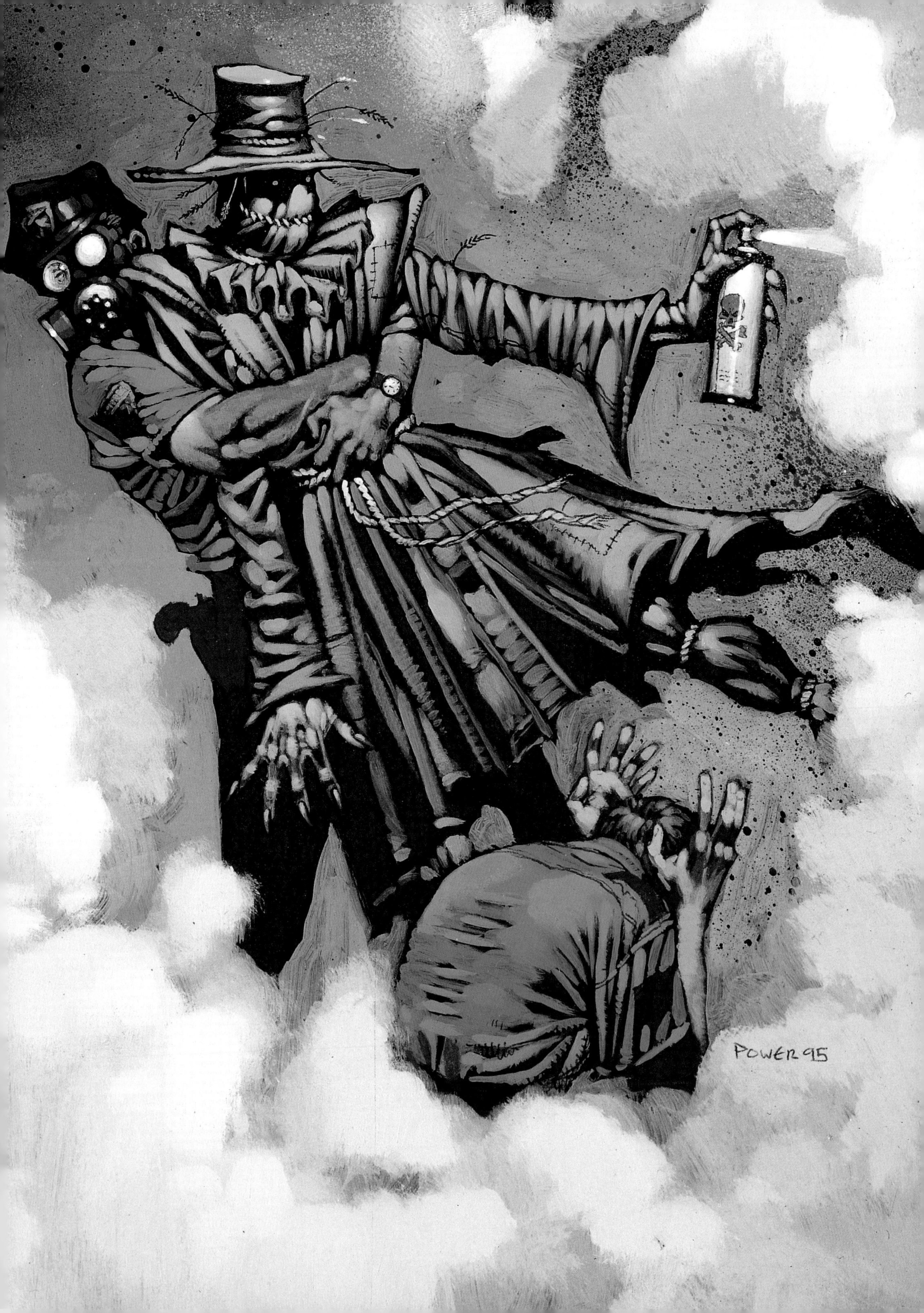
POWER 95

SCARECROW

Robin reads Gordon's files:

"Extremely deranged and dangerous. Former psychology professor, now fancies himself the 'Master of Fear.' Pronounced hatred of Batman. Uses panic-inducing psychoactive agent called 'fear-gas.' Revenge most frequent motive. Pet crow named 'Craw.'

"Jonathan Crane prefers scaring—rather than shooting—his victims to death. But still . . . a definite possibility."

ART CONCEPT

Full-figure Scarecrow (in costume) standing against police lineup wall with calibrated height marks; he's about six feet tall (without his hat). **Optional:** Inset or superimposed mug shot close-up of Jonathan Crane, who looks very much like Sleepy Hollow's Ichabod Crane.

DERMOT POWER'S SOLUTION

"In the comics, Scarecrow has this little hand-spray canister. But that's useless, it doesn't really give you the feeling that he's emptying out a whole can of poison. So I gave him a longer spray can, and put a skull on it.

"Scarecrow looks like a heavy bag of bones—there just doesn't seem to be a lot to him."

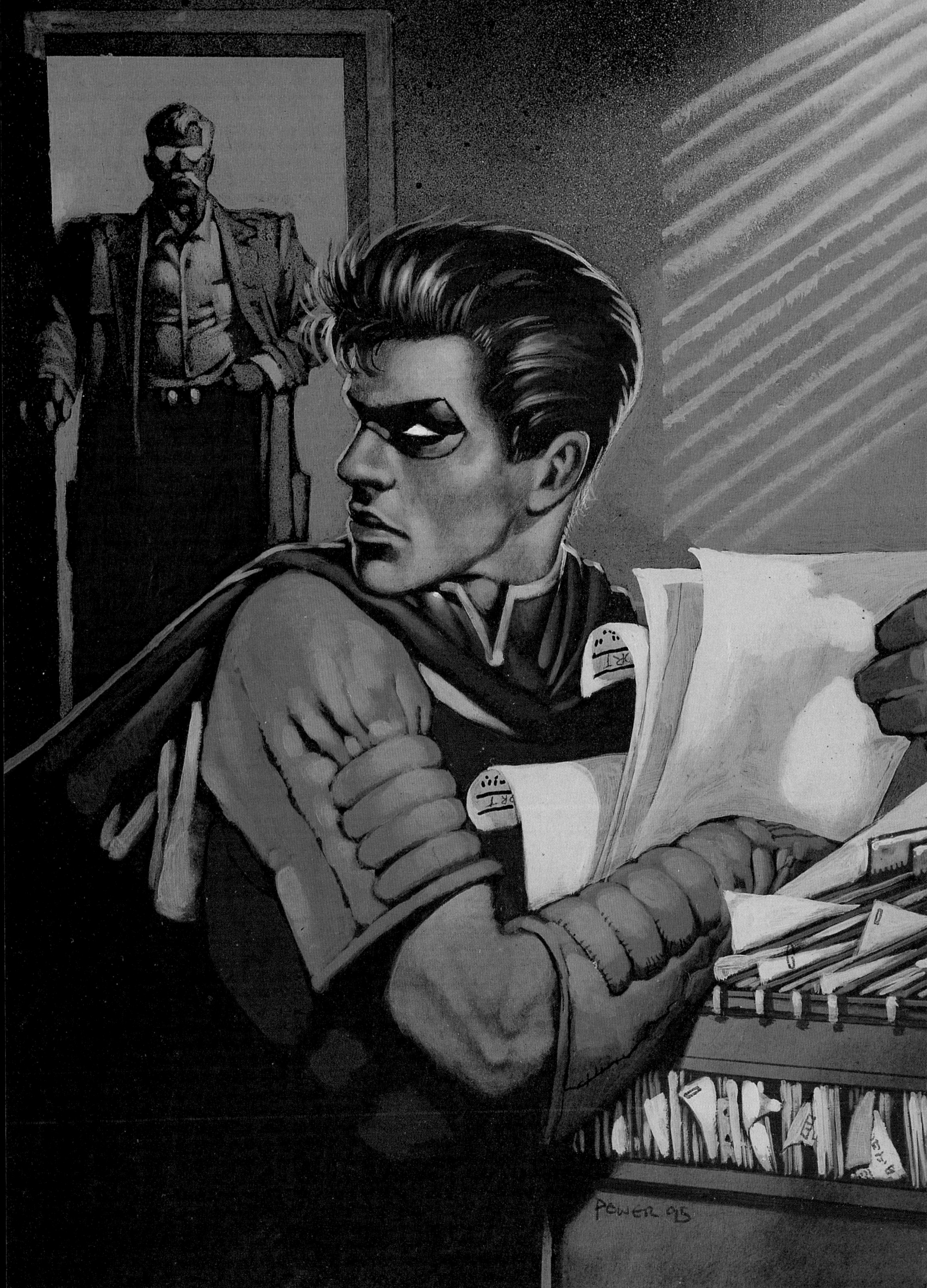
POWER 95

"The *files* won't help you."

"Commissioner Gordon! I . . . I was just—"

"I know what you were doing, Robin—the same thing I've already done a *dozen times,* and believe me, *it won't help.*"

"But how do you know—"

"Surrender the chair, lad. We need to *talk.*"

ART CONCEPT

Master shot noirish interior Gordon's office; Robin seated at desk with file folders under desk lamp (sole light source)—startled & jerking his head up as grim Gordon unexpectedly enters thru doorway.

DERMOT POWER'S SOLUTION

"When I think of Robin, he's very intense, and he's very earnest, but unlike Batman, he tries to be cool. Robin's a bit of a dork.

"This was one of those pictures where you feel like having a coffee break the entire time you're doing it. I knew that it was important to the storytelling, but I couldn't think of an interesting angle, a clever spin.

"But a filing cabinet . . . how can you make office furniture interesting? I couldn't think of a way to get Robin at the filing cabinet and Gordon at the door, and working all that into a dynamic shot."

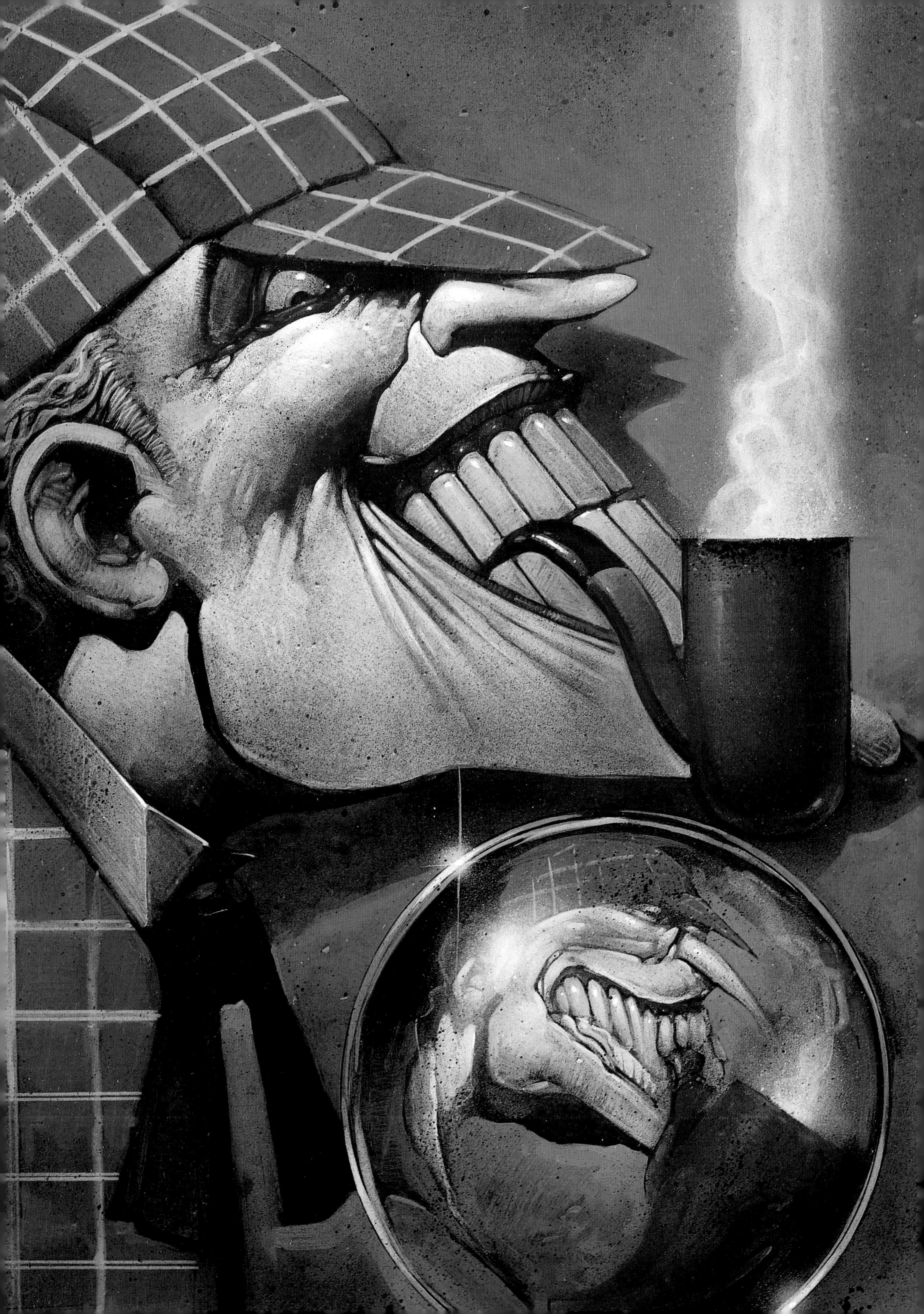

CLOWN PRINCE OF CRIME DETECTION

"*Sherlock Jokes* on the *case*—and for my *first* suspect, I shall grill . . . *me!* Did I have the *motive?* Yes! Bats drives me *batty!* The *means?* Of *course*—since I *always* pack at least *one* .45! *Opportunity?* I *guess* so, if I *escaped Arkham,* which I *apparently* have, haven't I? *Verdict?* Guilty! *Off with my head*—except I'm *already* off with my head, *way* off, and *I know I didn't do it . . . don't I?* Smash the mirror and bring on the *next* suspect!"

ART CONCEPT

The Joker as Sherlock Holmes, complete with deerstalker cap & pipe, in front of a mirror, gleefully/insanely speaking to his absurd reflection.

CARL CRITCHLOW'S SOLUTION

"On this one I did exactly what was asked of me. I just put the extra image in there to make it look like a magnifying glass, just to try and show that it was working, and then make it a bit more interesting. Get a bit of something going on."

For the most part, Critchlow prefers minimal art instruction

"If they have too specific of an idea of what they want, you can sort of get stuck. There are certain things that you may not be able to do, just on a technical level.

"I prefer when they trust me to know what I can do best and what's going to work best, and what isn't."

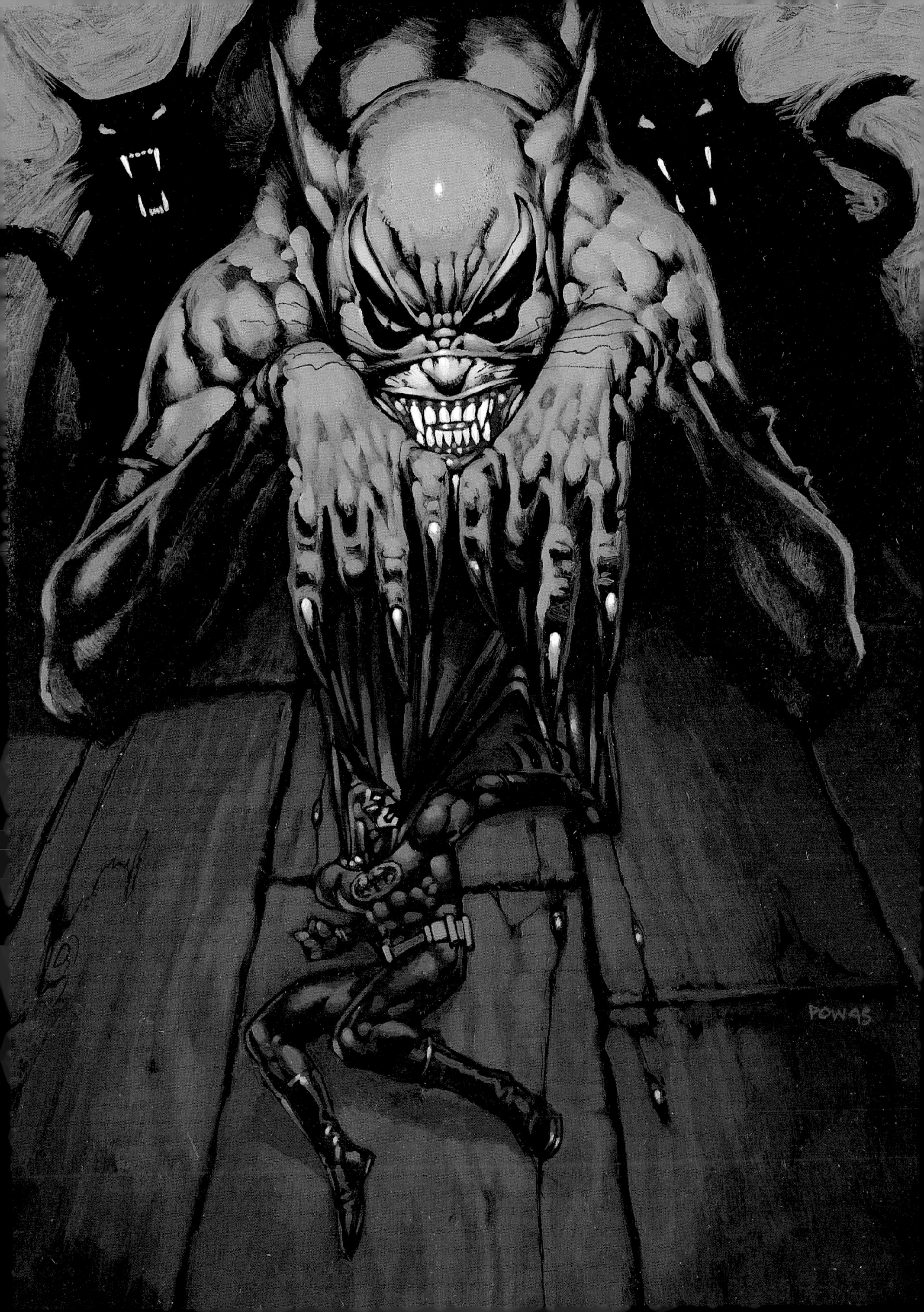
POW 95

KITTY KILLER

The Joker ponders:

"My next suspect has always treated Bats as her *personal plaything*—and cats *do* play with their prey before the *kill,* don't they? On the *other* paw, Catwoman is no killer. She might like to *steal* Bats' heart, but she would hardly rip the bloody thing from his *chest.* Drats! Scratch the cat's claws and summon the *next* miscreant before the great Sherlock Jokes!"

ART CONCEPT

Giant Catwoman on elbows & knees in feline pose—with tiny mouse-sized Batman trapped between her two "clawed" hands—a cat with her "plaything." Catwoman with a smirk which is both lubricious and predatory. If it looks cool (and since this is Joker's warped vision), Catwoman can even have cat's whiskers.

DERMOT POWER'S SOLUTION

"It was very easy to work with the art suggestion on this piece. Batman is this extremely serious, mysterious, and dark figure; to shove him to where he looks ridiculous gives a nice contrast to the character."

Power used this card to work on a style that he had been developing.

"I built up the paint in layers of contrasting color. Purple up to blue up to green. But acrylic paint the whole way . . . and maybe a bit of glazing or dry-brushing after that.

"I work in acrylics, because they can take a lot of punishment, and still hold up. You put your paws on it and it won't smear; you can put masking tape on the paint surface and when you peel it off, it won't peel away the paint."

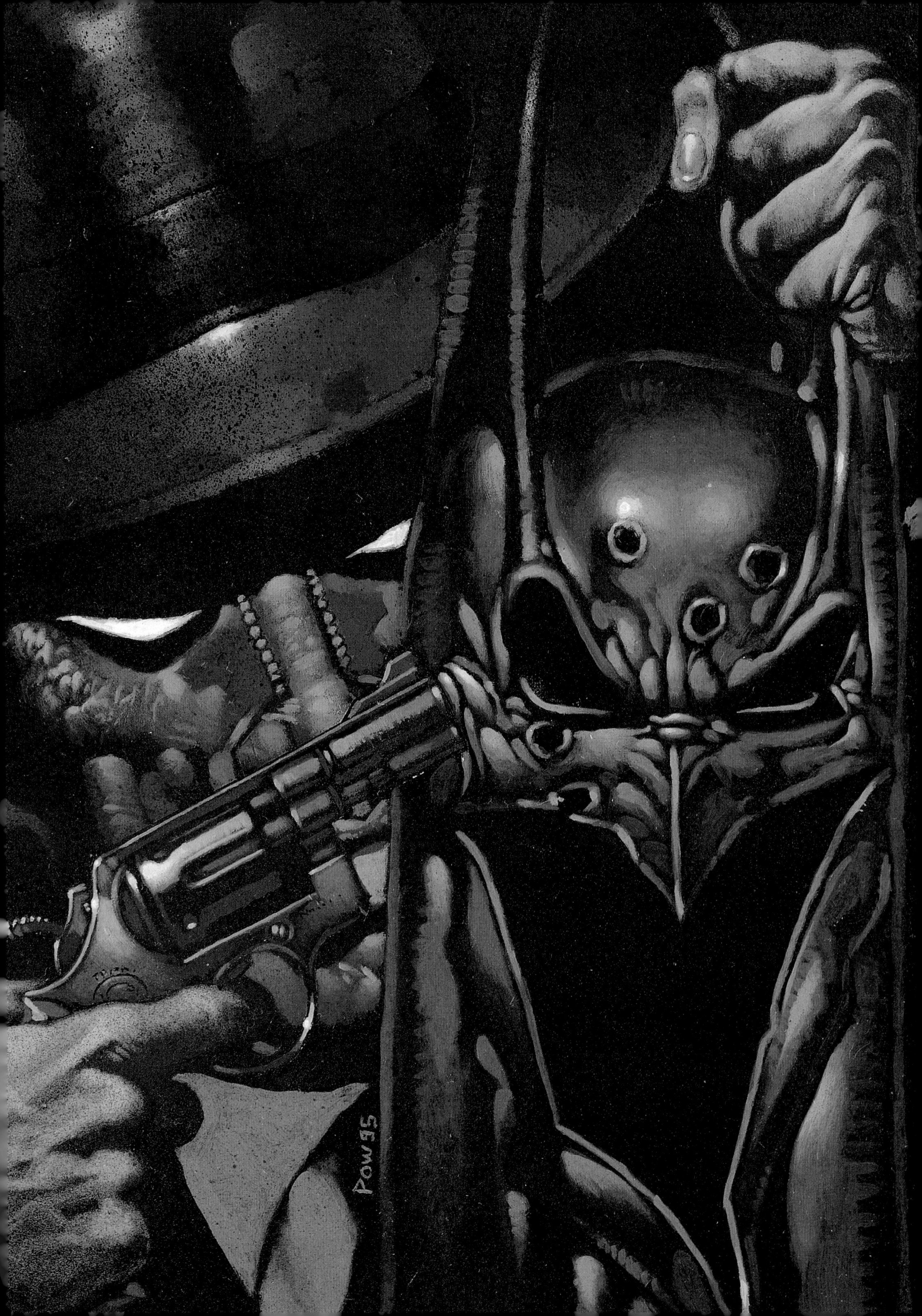
POW 95

MASKS OF BLACK

The Joker's singular mind tries a new tack:

"Maybe the motive was *jealousy,* and maybe the target was the *mask* rather than the *man*—in which case, employing elementary but impeccable logic, my dear Yoks-son, maybe Black Mask was trying to murder the only mask darker than his *own* . . . and Bats got in the way by stupidly *wearing* it!

"Wait a minute. That doesn't make sense even to *me. . . .*"

ART CONCEPT

Two masks side by side, minus the faces/heads: Black Mask's black mask (carved from ebony wood) and Batman's empty mask/cowl riddled with bullet holes—many more holes than were seen on the Pier 13 card [page 13]—and many of them are thru the head portion of mask, not just thru the cape as seen previously.

DERMOT POWER'S SOLUTION

"I liked the gun in this piece best—it looks so real you could almost pick it up. This was a switch for me because when I work I'm not interested in getting objects to look realistic, but with a piece like this it was important because the gun is the focus.

"There's a nice storytelling quality to this piece. You see the bullet holes in the mask and you wonder if Batman was in the mask when Black Mask shot it. It ties in with the piece that Scott Hampton did, where they are pulling Batman's bullet-ridden cowl from the river."

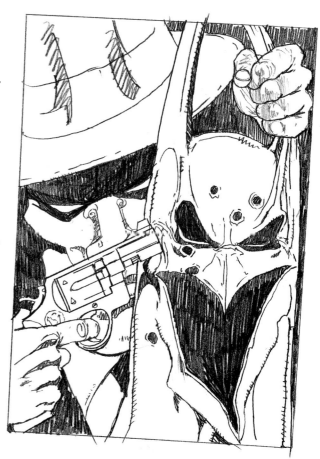

POW 95

DOUBLE-MUG

From the deerstalker thinking cap of the Joker:

"*Harvey Dent* could've put a few .45-caliber dents through Bats' back, depending on how his coin flipped. He always hated Bats for *betraying* him, and a revenge motive makes him the *perfect suspect!* Why, even as I escaped Arkham Asylum, I recall Dent raving from his cell across from mine, saying how *two-faced* Bats was and. . . .

"Oops. That meant Dent was *behind bars* on the night of the murder. Never mind."

ART CONCEPT

Close-up Batman as Two-Face—vertically bisected bat-masked face with one side normal & other side hideously disfigured; on the hideous side, even the mask is wrinkled & tattered, the bat-ear bent & broken, etc.

DERMOT POWER'S SOLUTION

"This one was just quirky. I knew I was never going to get another excuse to do Batman as Two-Face, so it was great to do it this way when I had the chance.

"That's the thing I really liked about a lot of the cards—it was an excuse to show Batman and his supporting cast in unusual settings. I think Batman as Two-Face could be an interesting story, but you know that's never going to happen.

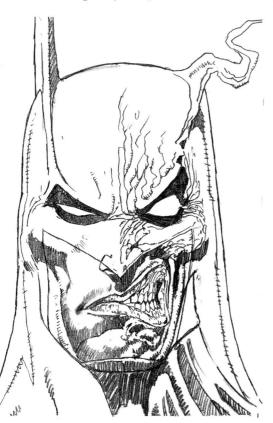

"I love this piece because people are going to look at it and think, what the hell is going on? This is totally not Batman. There's a lot of detail, especially in the teeth, and I think that just enough detail is what makes a piece work."

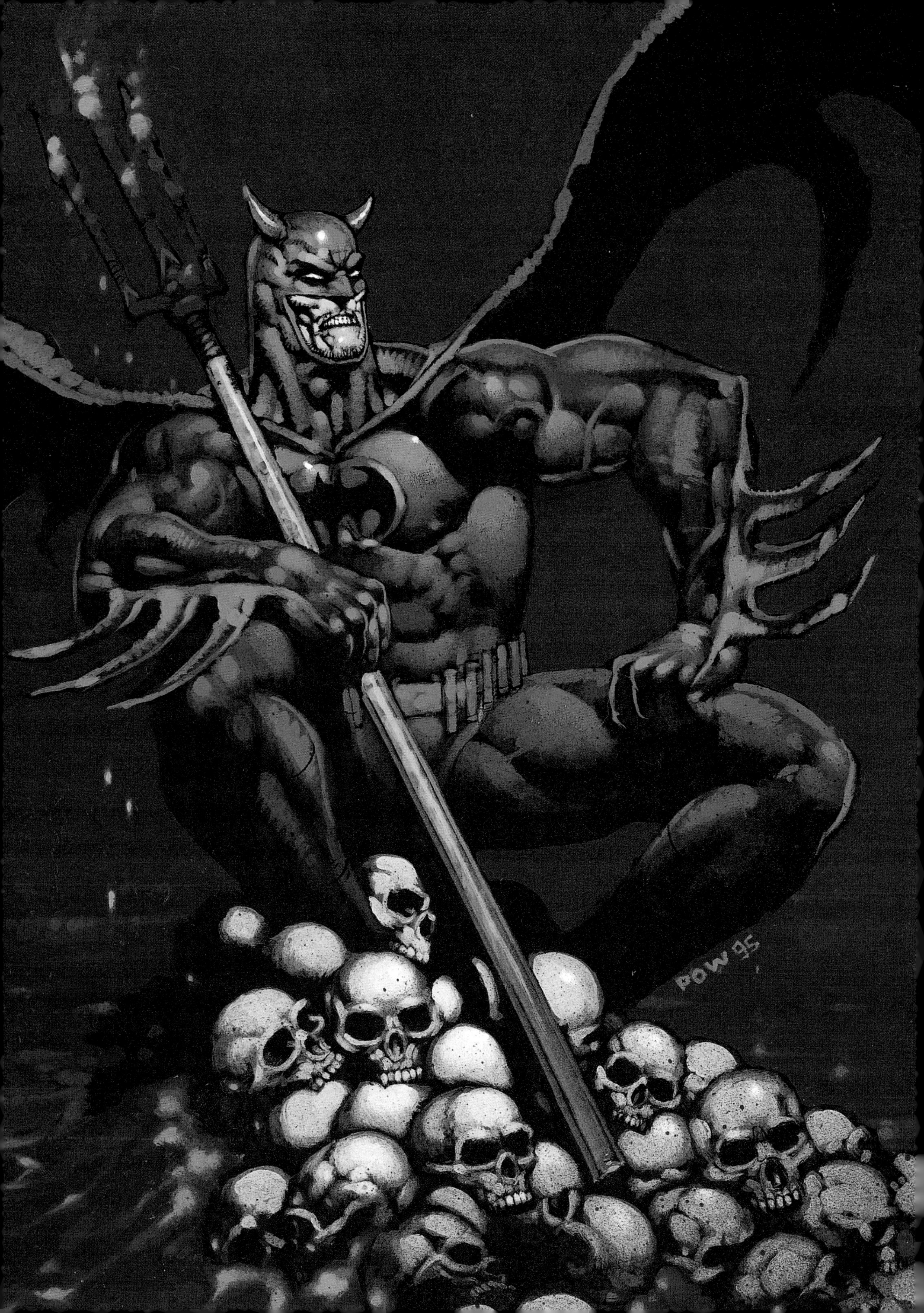
POW 95

DID THE DEMON DO IT?

Sherlock Jokes sleuths on:

"Don't know much about this *Rā's al Ghūl* character, but they call him *'the Demon'* and he's had some hellacious run-ins with Bats. *Why,* I wonder? Maybe in *his* eyes, *Bats* is the demon—in which case, what we're looking at here is a *bat-demon blowout.*

"Doom for the *Devil Bat.*

"A smoking *hole in Hades.*

"A *.45 automatic exorcism.*

"A diabolical snuffing of . . .

"*Nah.*"

ART CONCEPT

Batman as a demon, his bat-ears like devil's horns, eyes evil, bared teeth bestially pointed with the incisors elongated fangs, spread wings extremely batlike, maybe even a devil's spade-tail and a pitchfork/trident in hand. Background of lurid hell flames.

DERMOT POWER'S SOLUTION

"If I had this piece to do over again, I would do something about that orangeish background. It seemed like a good idea at the time, but I'm not so sure now! I wanted to convey a sense of flames and fire.

"I put Batman in hell, and then I lit him from above with a strong white light. I tend to light everything that way, but I don't think that I would do that now. I think I would light him from below, and make him look a bit darker."

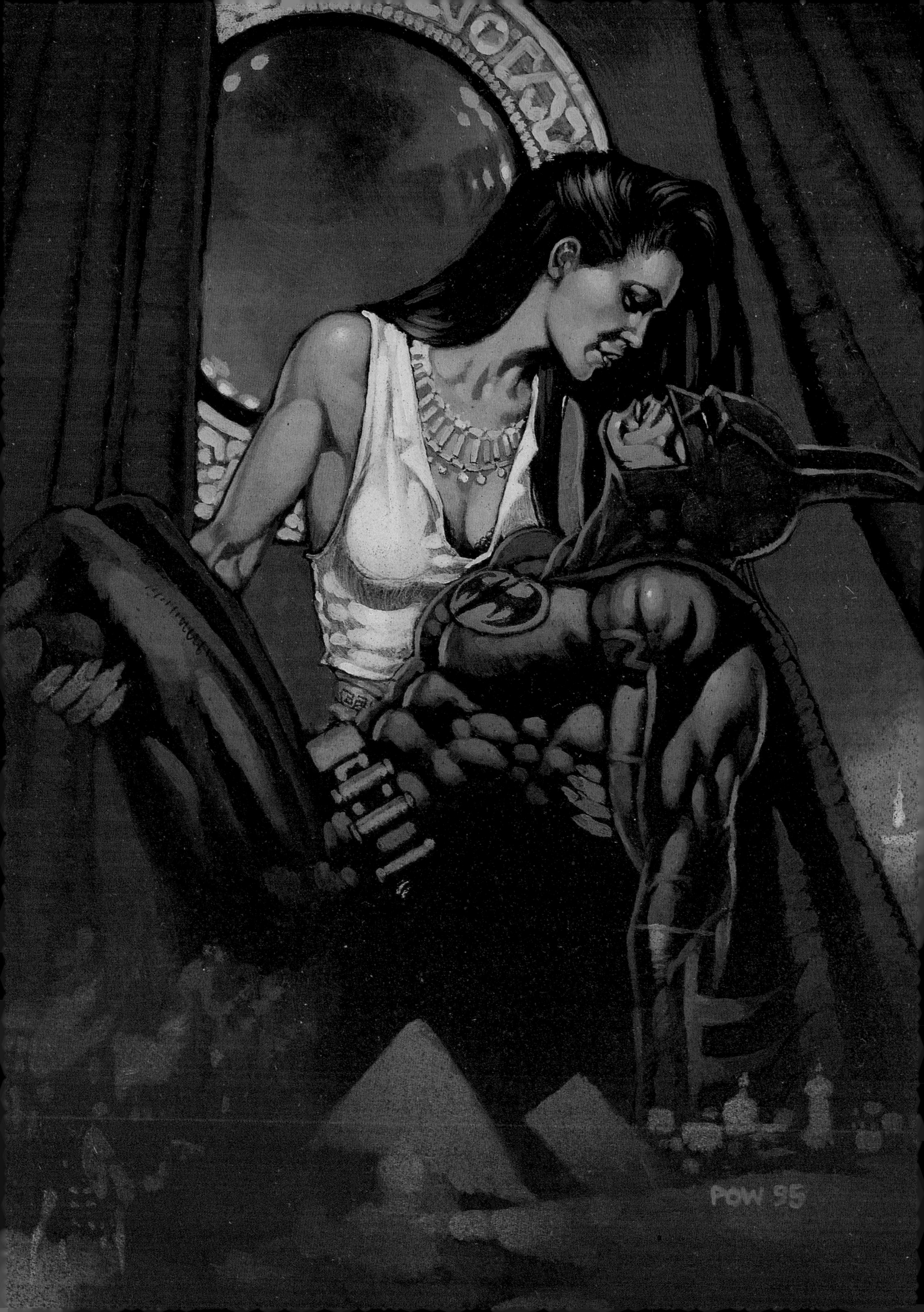
POW 95

GONE WITH THE DEMON'S DAUGHTER

For once, the Joker stops laughing:

"Word is, the Demon has a daughter and the daughter's name is *Talia,* who supposedly has some sort of warped fixation on Bats, so maybe the motive was *unrequited romance.* But *yuck,* how could any woman love a *human bat?* We're talking *Fledermaus* here—nothing less than a *flying rodent.* What would she *do?* Kiss him in a *cave* hanging upside-down over puddles of *guano?*

"*Stop*—before I *puke!*"

ART CONCEPT

Full figures; exotic Talia embracing & kissing Batman, maybe framed by an Arabian arch; do this one in exaggerated "gothic romance novel" style—Batman as a tall dark handsome hunk who happens to be wearing a bat outfit.

DERMOT POWER'S SOLUTION

"I did the opposite of what the editors wanted. They wanted a 'romantic and brave' embrace with Batman and Talia, so I did the poster image from *Gone with the Wind,* except with Talia holding Batman. I thought it was funny, and I liked showing Talia as such a strong character.

"It's just purely tacky, which I liked. I threw in red curtains, everything that I could think of to make it more tacky.

"I put the same mirror in, just to refer back to the previous card that Talia was in [Talia, page 87]. Also, I just love circles in compositions. I know that's not very sophisticated, circles in compositions, but that's me.

"I have to admit that a lot of my art style is not the most sophisticated. I'm going for very strong lines, very much of the Renaissance school, lots of circles."

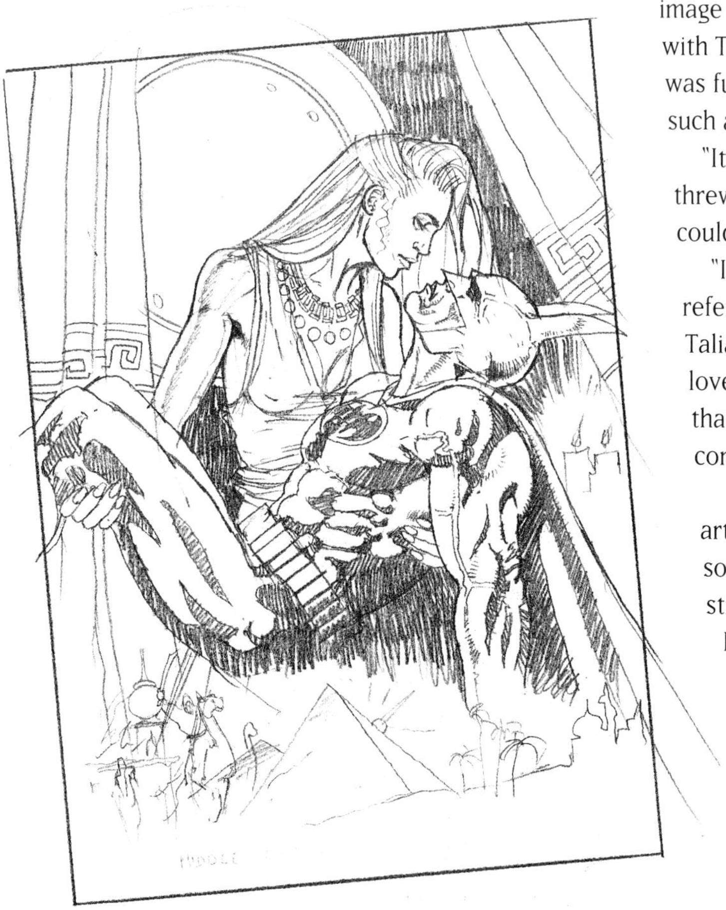

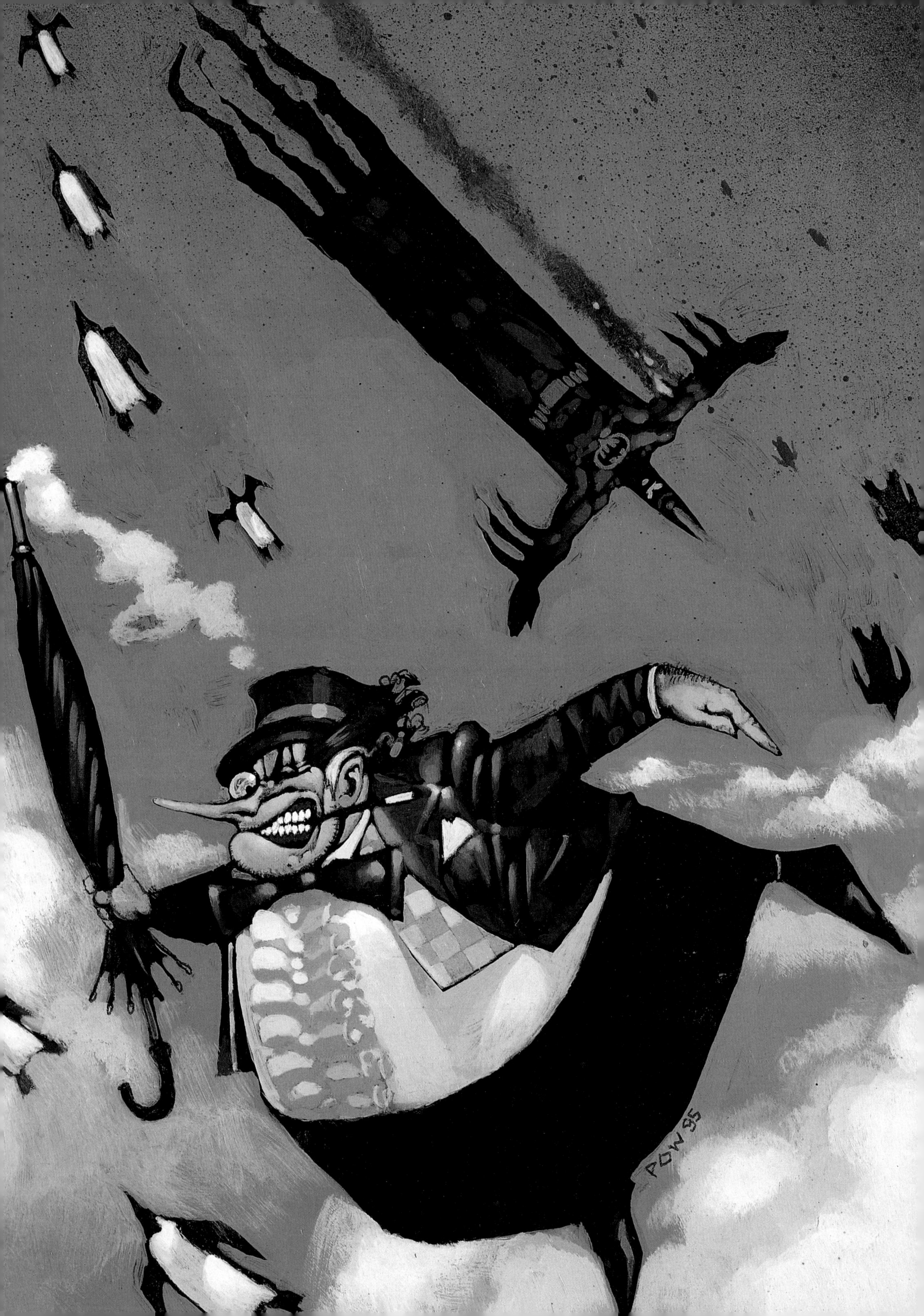
POW 95

BIRDBRAINED BUMBERSHOOTER

The Joker eliminates another possibility:

"That pipsqueak *Penguin* always makes a likely suspect, but I wonder if a .45 automatic could be concealed in one of those trick *umbrellas* of his. Probably irrelevant. Knowing Cobblepot's proclivity for birdbrained schemes, even the *best* bumbershoot would result in nothing more than a *bumble*-shoot."

ART CONCEPT

Batman on an ice floe, starting to crumple (having just been shot in the back)—surrounded by a half-dozen mildly curious real penguins—and the Penguin, holding a smoking umbrella (concealed gun inside it); maybe snow falling.

DERMOT POWER'S SOLUTION

Power wants to make one thing clear about this shot: the Penguin is not just falling out of the airplane: "He's flying!"

"When I first submitted this piece, there was a bit of concern about the birds, since normally penguins don't fly. Finally, we decided that the scene was just a product of the Joker's twisted mind, and if Batman could fly . . . so could the penguins.

"I don't know if people got that card. It was supposed to look as though the Penguin has just shot the Batman down. Like a World War II dogfight."

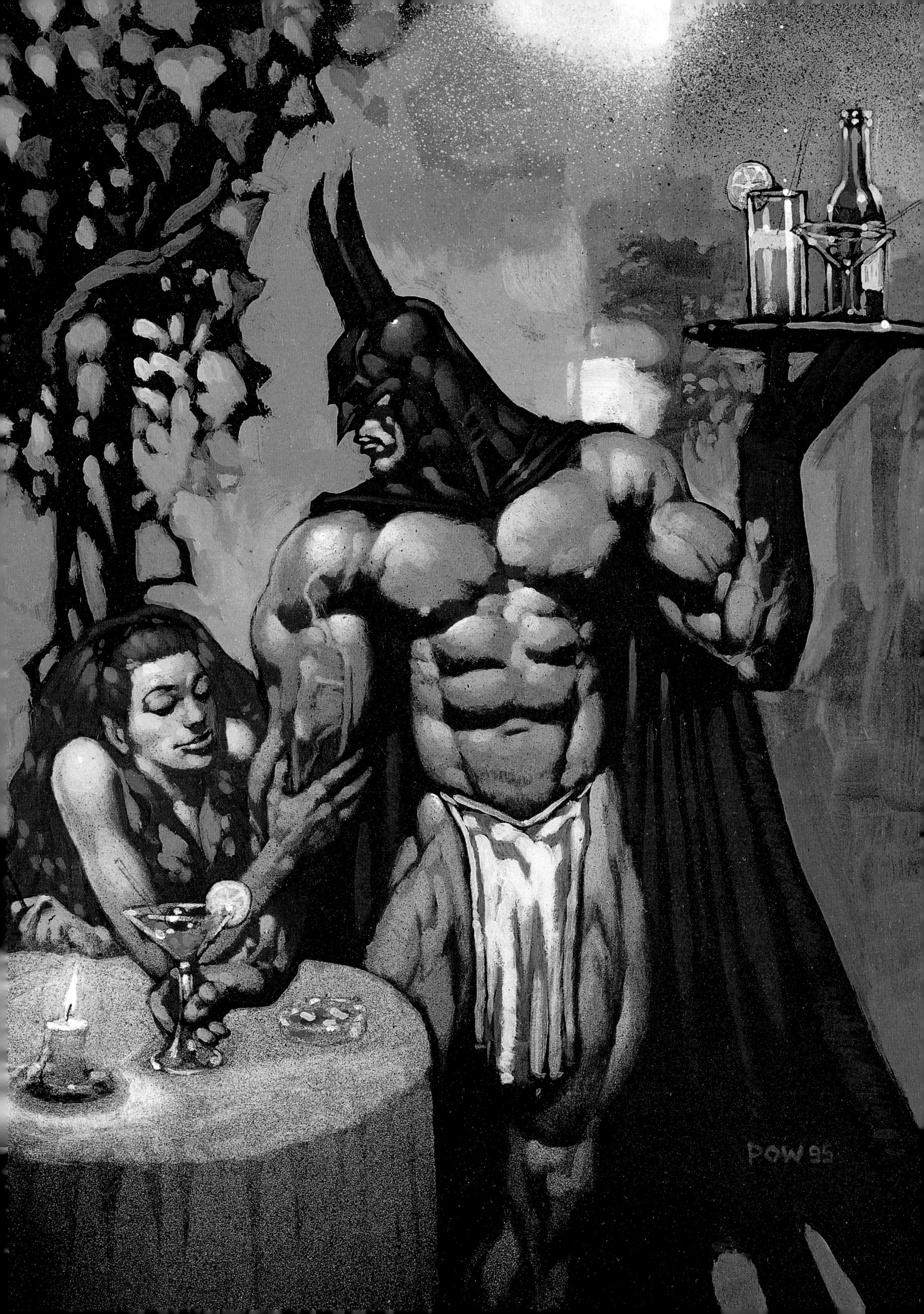
POW 95

AN ITCH TOO FAR

The Joker turns the color of his hair with envy:

"Poison Ivy always bragged that Bats was nothing but dreamboat putty in her toxic hands. Of course, he never *did* itch for Ivy, but that hardly shattered her illusions. And what *is* it with these voluptuous villains? Why do they all fall for a geek who styles himself after a *furry nocturnal bug-feeder?*

"And anyway, if *Ivy* did it, Bats would have died of *terminal rash,* not gunshot."

ART CONCEPT

In a lush jungle-of-vines setting, Poison Ivy is languorously lounging at a cocktail table, sizing up a "Chippendale-zombie" Batman standing submissively for her inspection; Batman wearing nothing but mask/cowl/cape and trunks, muscled torso & legs bare. (This is Joker's perception of how Poison Ivy would like to see Batman.)

DERMOT POWER'S SOLUTION

"The loincloth was my idea," chuckles Power. "When I submitted the sketch for approval, I had Poison Ivy's eyes up. But when I painted it, I had her eyes down.

"I think this is a very cool card. It completely takes away the pompous nature of Batman. It's kind of humiliating for Batman, but it portrays Poison Ivy as very powerful."

Was Power laughing the whole time he worked on this image?

"No . . . but my girlfriend was."

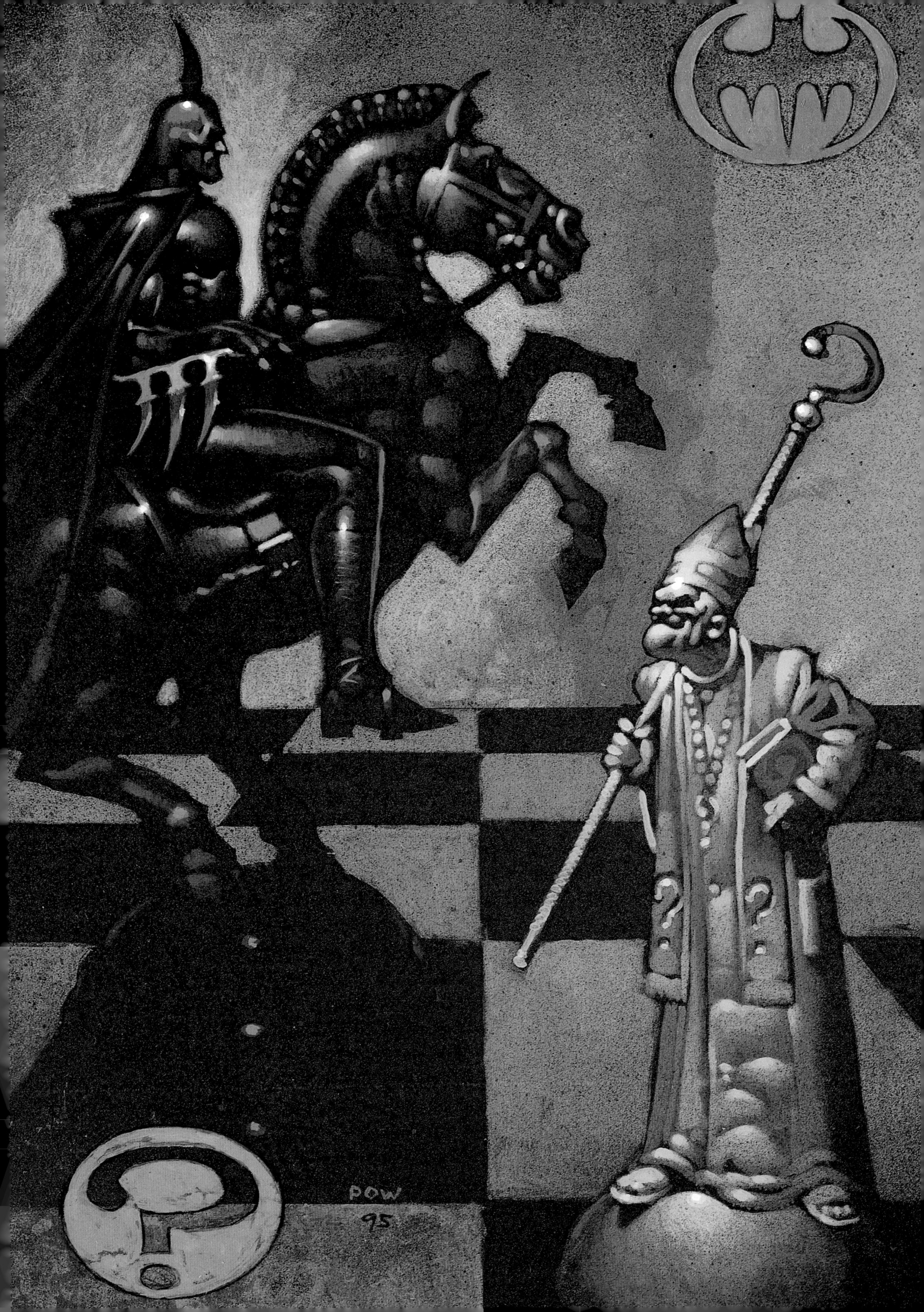
POW
95

The Joker considers one last suspect:

"Would the Riddler kill his own *punchline?* Possibly—if Bats punched him out once too often. But then, who would the witless E. Nigma match wits with? And furthermore, riddle me *this*: what's *green* and *masked* with *question marks* all over?

"Another *rejected suspect,* that's what!"

ART CONCEPT

Riddler & Batman opposing each other as stylized chess pieces on a giant checkerboard surface of question marks (light question marks on dark squares & dark question marks on light squares); Riddler as a stylized bishop; Batman as a (what else?) dark knight astride a horse.

DERMOT POWER'S SOLUTION

"I really liked putting Batman in such a formal setting. The play of light off his costume came out well. And then there's the Riddler, who makes a perfect bishop, in my opinion.

"Someone pointed out to me that I made the Riddler look like the Pope. It wasn't my intent, but since they pointed it out, I can't look at this image without thinking that. That kind of ruins it for me, really.

"Compositionally, I had a hard time with this card. I put a little symbol of Batman and the Riddler in the corners because I wanted to balance out the image a little more. I was trying to make it less awkward."

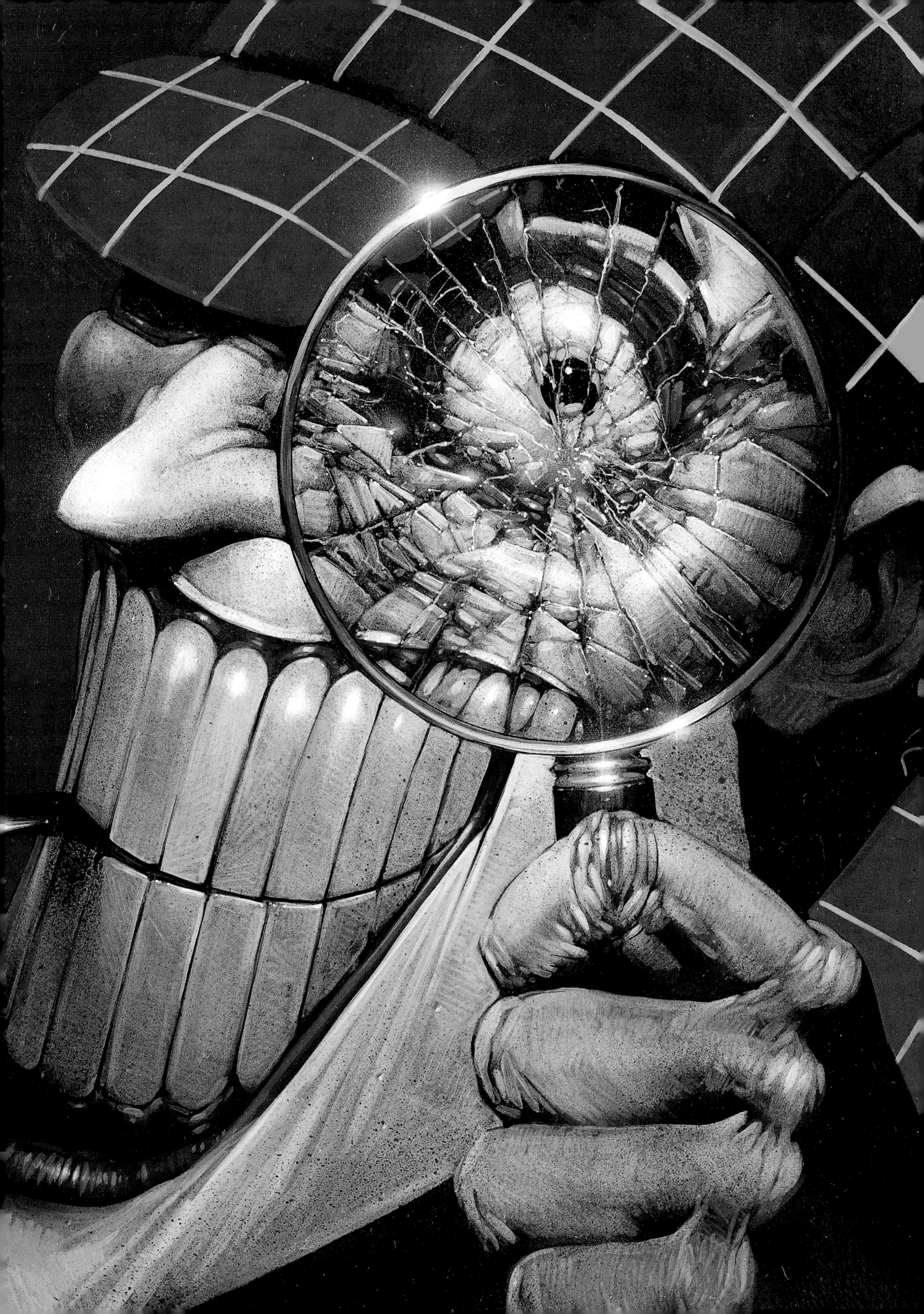

SHERLOCK JOKES STRIKES OUT

"*None* of the others did it?! I'm the *only one* with motive, means, and opportunity? This intensive investigation is giving me *brain strain!* Or maybe I'm just not *cut out* to be a *detective*. Maybe I'm a better *criminal* and maybe I really *did* murder Bats. Maybe I'm even getting *homesick* for the dark and madly soothing asylum of *Arkham . . . HYEEEHAHAHAHAAAA!*"

ART CONCEPT

Insane Joker as "Sherlock Jokes"—bizarre Sherlock Holmes; see Clown Prince of Crime Detection card [page 113]—holding his now-jaggedly-cracked magnifying glass up to one eye and dementedly peering thru it at us; eye & portion of surrounding face seen thru the cracked lens are both magnified and fragmented/distorted.

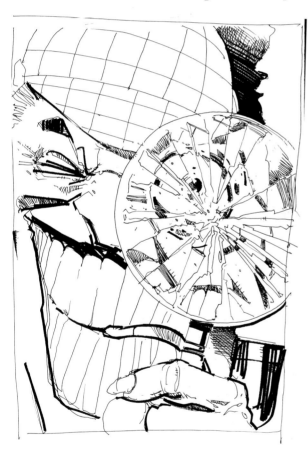

CARL CRITCHLOW'S SOLUTION

Critchlow did not smash a magnifying glass for this image.

"If you smashed it, it might not look like you'd expect it to. So I drew it like you'd expect it to look, without really looking at a smashed magnifying glass.

"The first thing is always getting the drawing right. But it's when the drawing is a bit boring, or it's not a very interesting composition and you try covering it up with flashy paint techniques, that's when you get into trouble. The main thing is getting the drawing right. If it works well as a drawing, then it'll probably look good as a painting. If you think it looks just okay as a drawing, but you can get away with it when it's painted, because it will have all fancy sort of shines and effects and nice colors on it. . . . Then it's probably still going to look like rubbish when it's a finished painting."

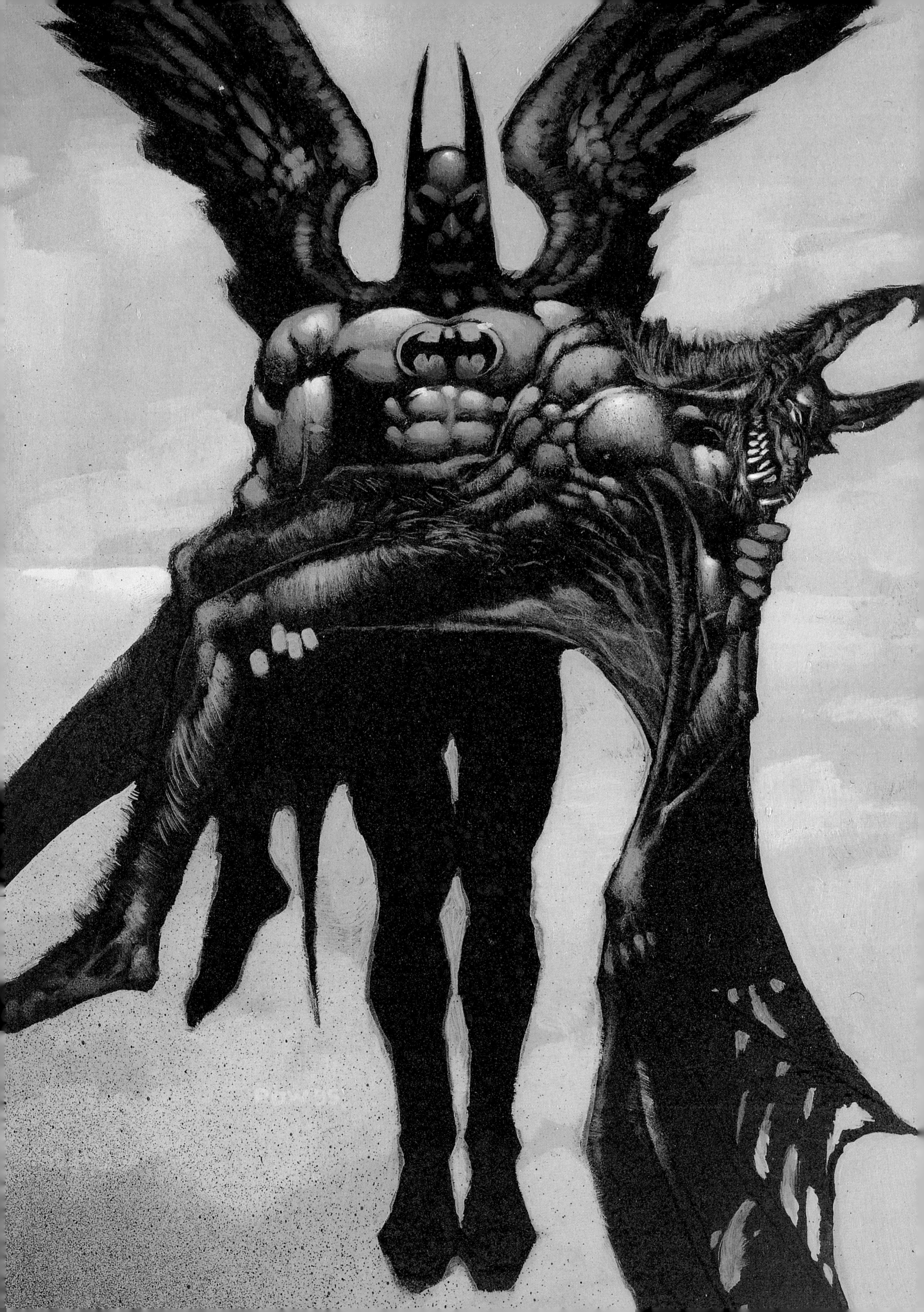

DARK ANGEL

Dr. Kirk Langstrom pauses in his lab to gaze out at the night:

"I have been to hell, time and again, a man shaped into a beast of my own making. And each time I have been rescued by the same entity . . . a dark savior who has delivered me from the curse of the bat. Now that entity is gone. Now . . . I am alone."

ART CONCEPT

Aerial shot; bestial & horrific Man-Bat "poised" in flight and beholding Batman as an "angel" descending toward him. Hands & arms beatifically outspread, as if to help/save Man-Bat & not to battle. Batman's mask & cowl are as usual, but his cape is gone & replaced by dark angel wings.

DERMOT POWER'S SOLUTION

"This is my kind of card! It's dark and brooding. . . . Mixing the dark, indistinguishable colors with a quasi-religious feel makes this card really creepy and beautiful at the same time.

"It has an altarpiece quality to it, kind of like the Pietà or something like that, but it's not blatantly obvious. I painted it to look like something that might go in a church."

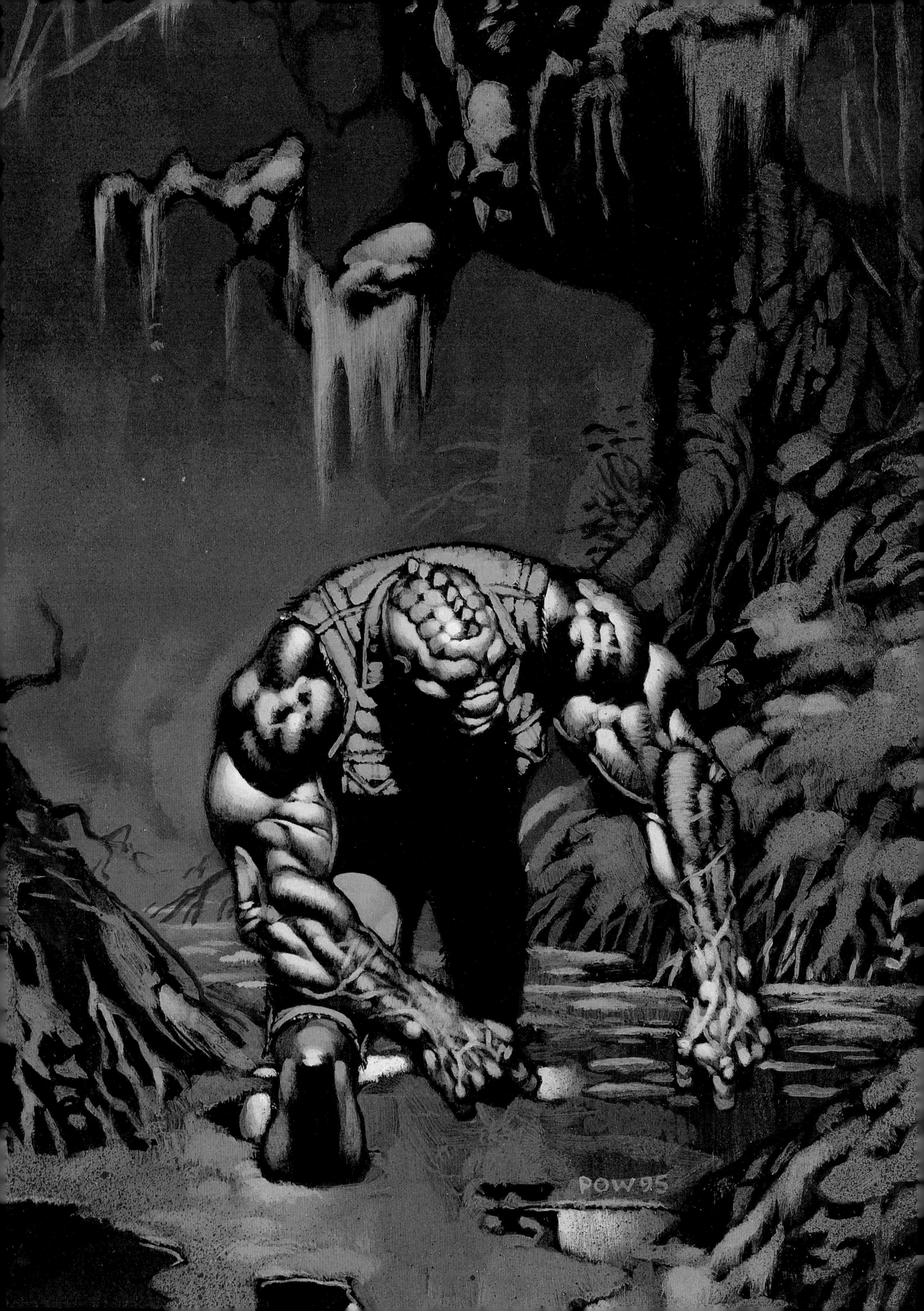

CROCODILE TEARS

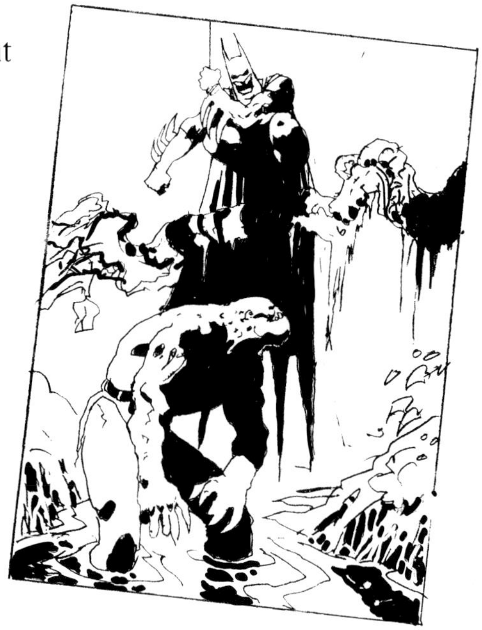

Slithering silently through the swamp, a strange killer suddenly finds his dull reptilian mind filled with a vision. For no apparent reason, he sees the dark but perfect being who has repeatedly bested him in primal struggle, turning predator to prey, and who forever haunts his nightmares. Were he aware of this perfect being's passing, he might exult in savage joy. But the vision fades, and his dim thoughts return to nothing but food.

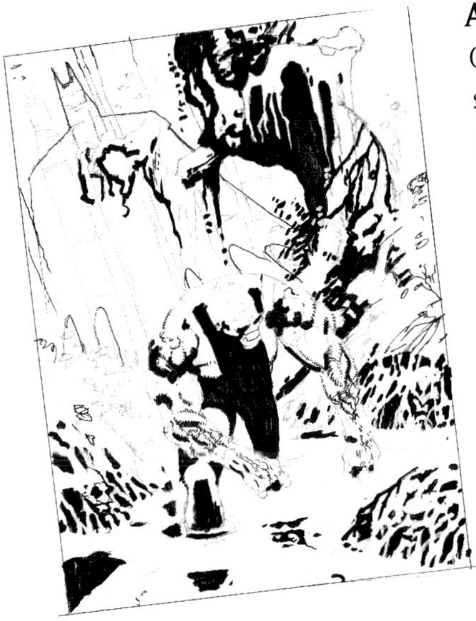

ART CONCEPT

On bottom third of card we see the partially submerged head of Killer Croc, his nose barely above the swamp waterline seen at very bottom of card; his red reptilian eyes, with their vertical-slit pupils, are dull but deadly; above his head, the top two-thirds of card is filled with his vision of Batman as Perfection Personified—a strong, vital "Dark Adonis" Batman.

DERMOT POWER'S SOLUTION

"I like this portrayal of Killer Croc better than my first one. I think I did a better job with the greens. I managed to keep all the tones across the whole thing the same. I think you can feel the weight of the sludgy swamp better because the color is much darker and murkier.

"Someone had come up with the idea of having little Batman heads throughout the card. You can see Batman's face in the reflections of the water, and in the trees in the swamp. They wanted to show how Killer Croc believes that Batman is always tormenting him, and so he is obsessed with Batman. I tried to make the Batman heads as obscure as possible, because I didn't want them to interfere with the composition."

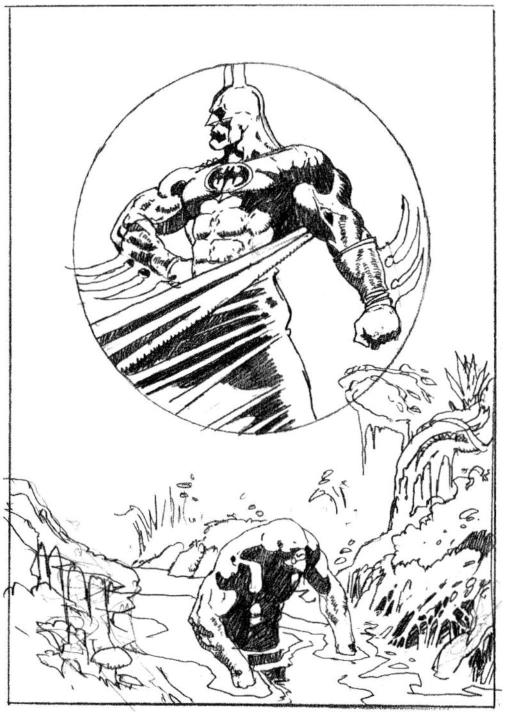

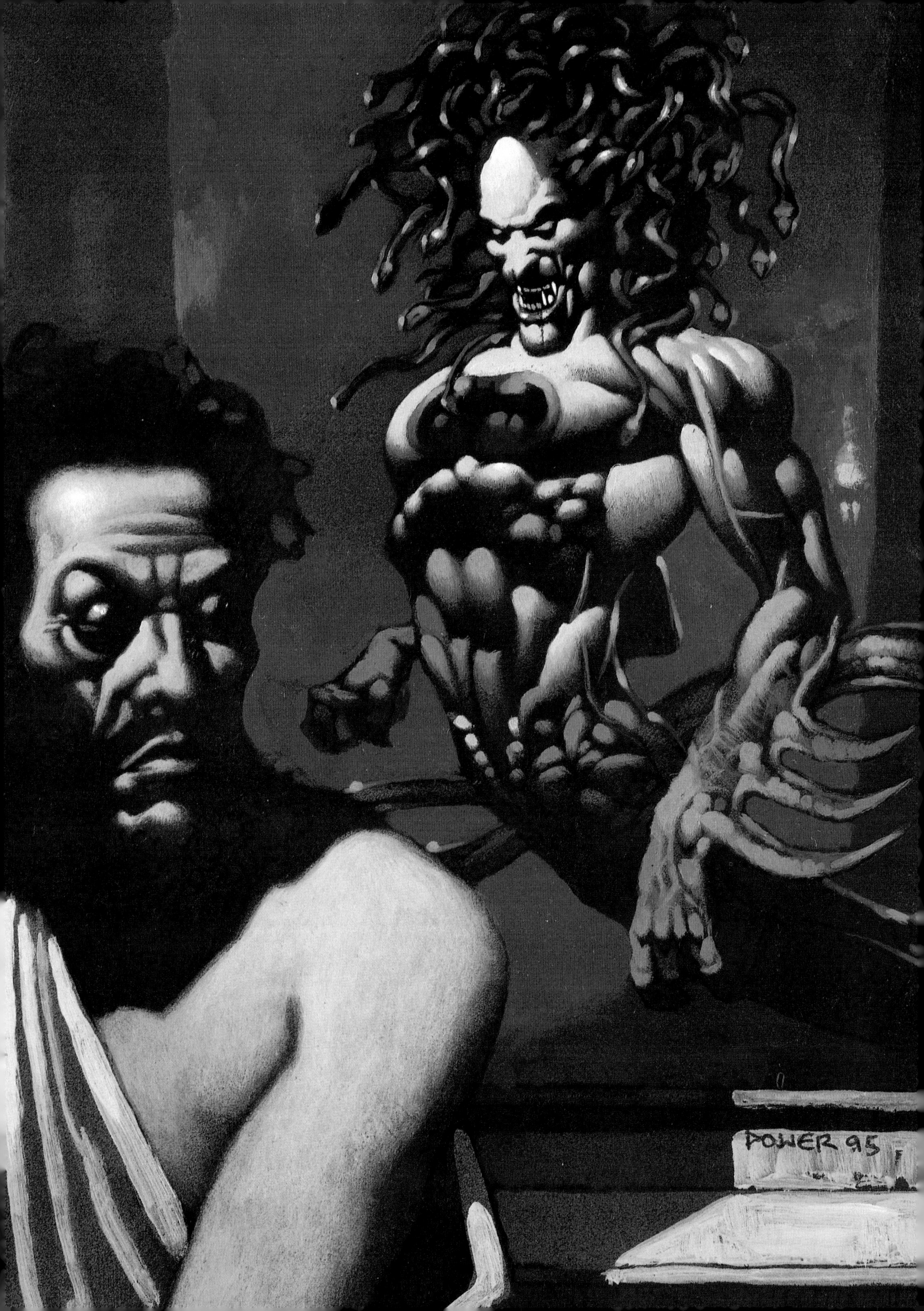
POWER 95

BY ZEUS!

Deep in the shadows of Arkham, Maxie Zeus chortles in madness:

"Hades has lost its *fiercest scourge,* and the flames of the underworld are *dampened!* The *Bat-Demon is slain*—and all the gods may now rejoice with the nectar of *ambrosia* and the joy of song! So declares immortal *Zeus, Lord of Olympus!*"

ART CONCEPT
Close-up mad Maxie Zeus in lower foreground left; beyond, we see the cavernous mouth of Hades filled with flames; flying out of the fire toward us (i.e., at Maxie Zeus's back) is a horrific Bat-Demon creature worthy of Greek mythology.

DERMOT POWER'S SOLUTION
"I really like Greek mythology, especially the movie *The Clash of the Titans,* where the hero goes off and battles Medusa. I was trying to make Batman a creature that you would see in that movie.

"I really like parts of this card, especially the color and the lighting about Medusa. I used a very high contrast on this painting's colors. The cool bit was taking Batman and warping his muscles and body into this weird snake-like creature.

"But when I think of the orange background. . . . I have a real thing about orange. I just don't like orange; I don't think that I've learned to use it properly. At least, I don't think that I used it well in this piece."

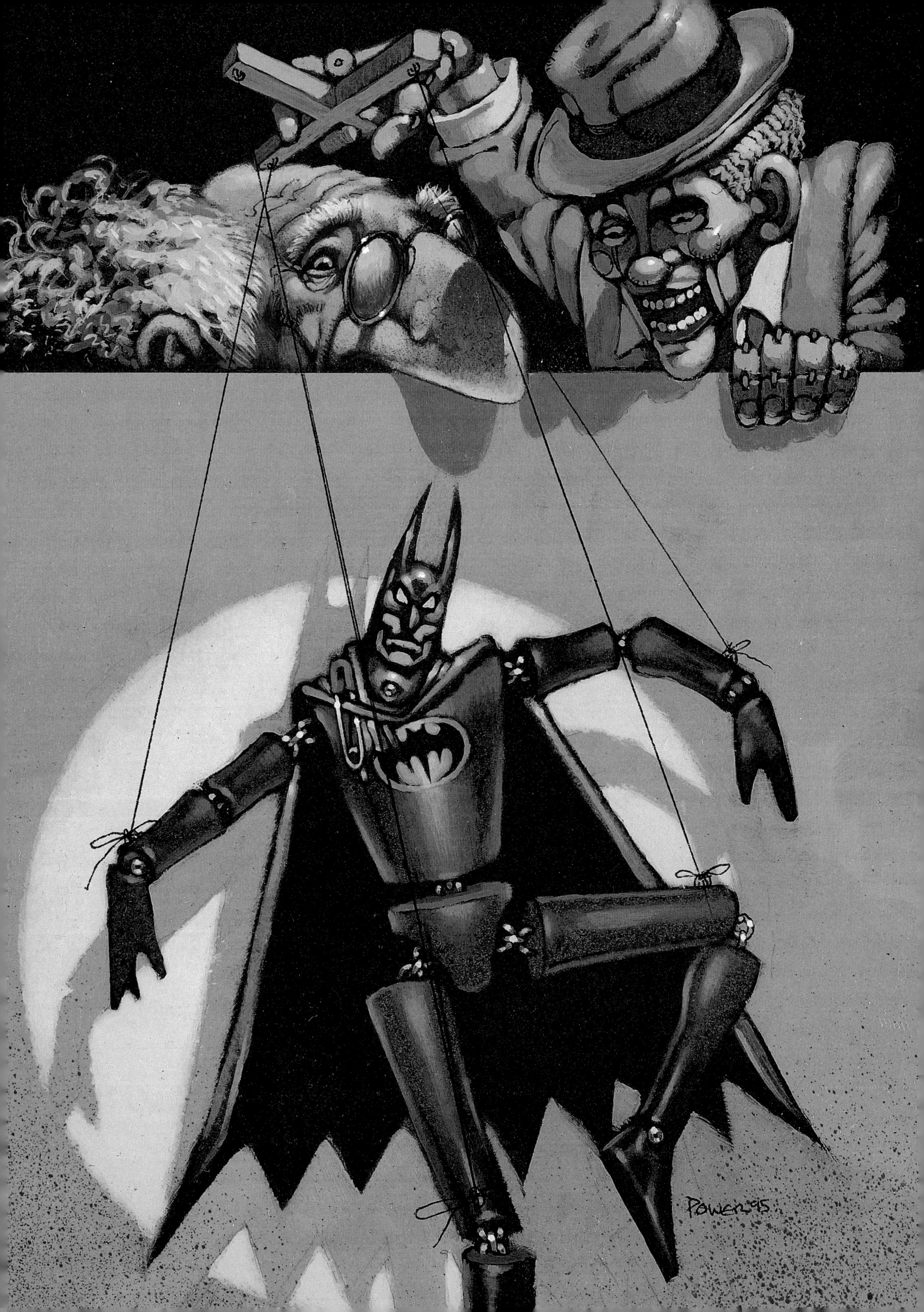
POWER '95

PULLING STRINGS

"Batman's *dead,* you know."

"So *you* say, gut Gatman can *never* die."

"Why *not?"*

"Gatman never *lived.* He's just a *puppet,* not flesh and glud."

"A puppet? Controlled by *whom?"*

"Guy who do you *think?* Guy the same one controlling *you,* you gig *dummy.* Guy *me."*

"But . . . why would a puppet-Batman be controlled by *you?"*

"*Revenge,* you glithering *idiot!"*

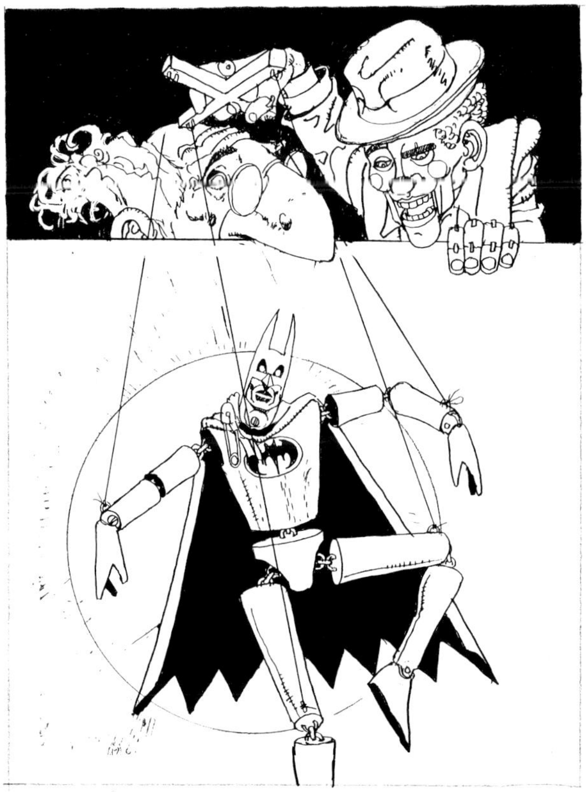

ART CONCEPT

Ventriloquist and his gangster-dummy Scarface (on Ventril's lap) are seen at top of card, partially behind & above a puppet-show backdrop; Scarface (the dummy) is apparently "alive," leaning over top edge of backdrop & holding cross-slats in each hand; strings from these cross-slats extend down to a loose-limbed herky-jerky Batman marionette, which is "dancing" on the puppet-show stage at bottom of card.

DERMOT POWER'S SOLUTION

"I was going for a magical, theatrical feel to this piece. I tried to do it so that the two characters, Scarface and the Ventriloquist, were up-lit. I don't think that comes across so well. But I like the fact that you can just completely exaggerate the elements of this piece.

"This is a simple, almost 'cartoony' piece. The interesting bit was taking Batman and making him look totally formalized and stiff looking. I also liked painting Scarface and the Ventriloquist in a completely unrealistic style."

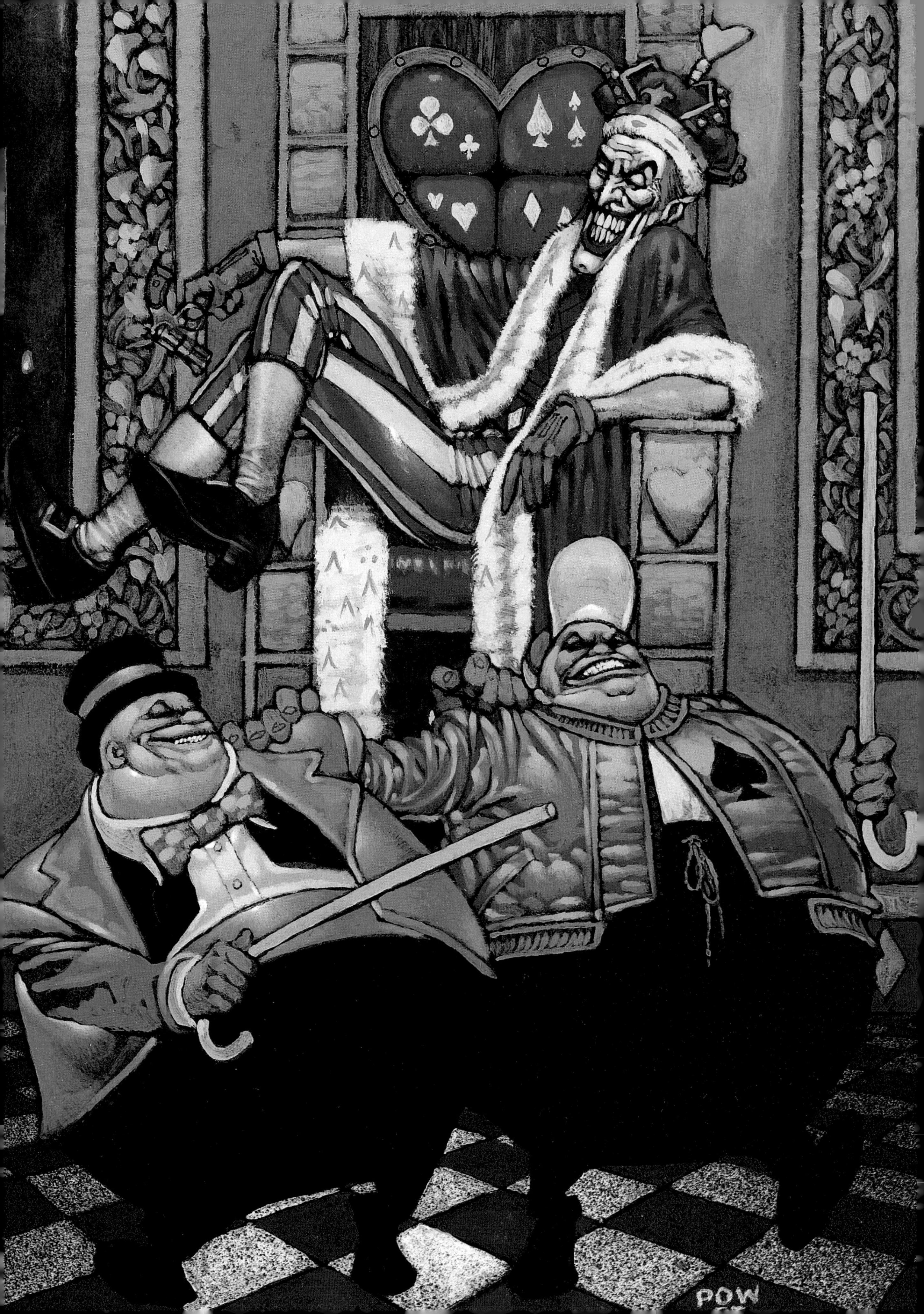
POW

TWEEDLEDEE
AND DUMBER

And as in chubbish thought they stood

The Batterwock with eyes of flame

Came ruffling through the Gotham hood

All righteous with some blame

One, two! One, two! And through and through

The Joker's gun went *BLAMMO-BAMM!*

He left it dead, his mania fed

And went on the laughing lam.

ART CONCEPT

Gotham street scene; Tweedledee & Tweedledum standing
off to side and/or in background, watching Joker blast his
.45 automatic at Batman-as-Jabberwocky-beast—based on
the Sir John Tenniel (public domain) illustration.

DERMOT POWER'S SOLUTION

"A lot of times, with these cards, they'll give me very specific
instructions," explains Power. "But then, if I can come up
with something better, they'll let me do it. The art
instruction isn't set in stone; in fact, sometimes it's quite
flexible. As long as I can make the card relate to the story.

"I originally did a drawing of Batman as the Jabberwocky
from *Alice Through the Looking Glass,* but that was too
obscure. I decided that since Tweedledum and Tweedledee
are such fun characters, I would make them really large
and just leave Batman out of it.

"I think that the two characters make a nice abstract
composition. I was very extreme when I exaggerated
them."

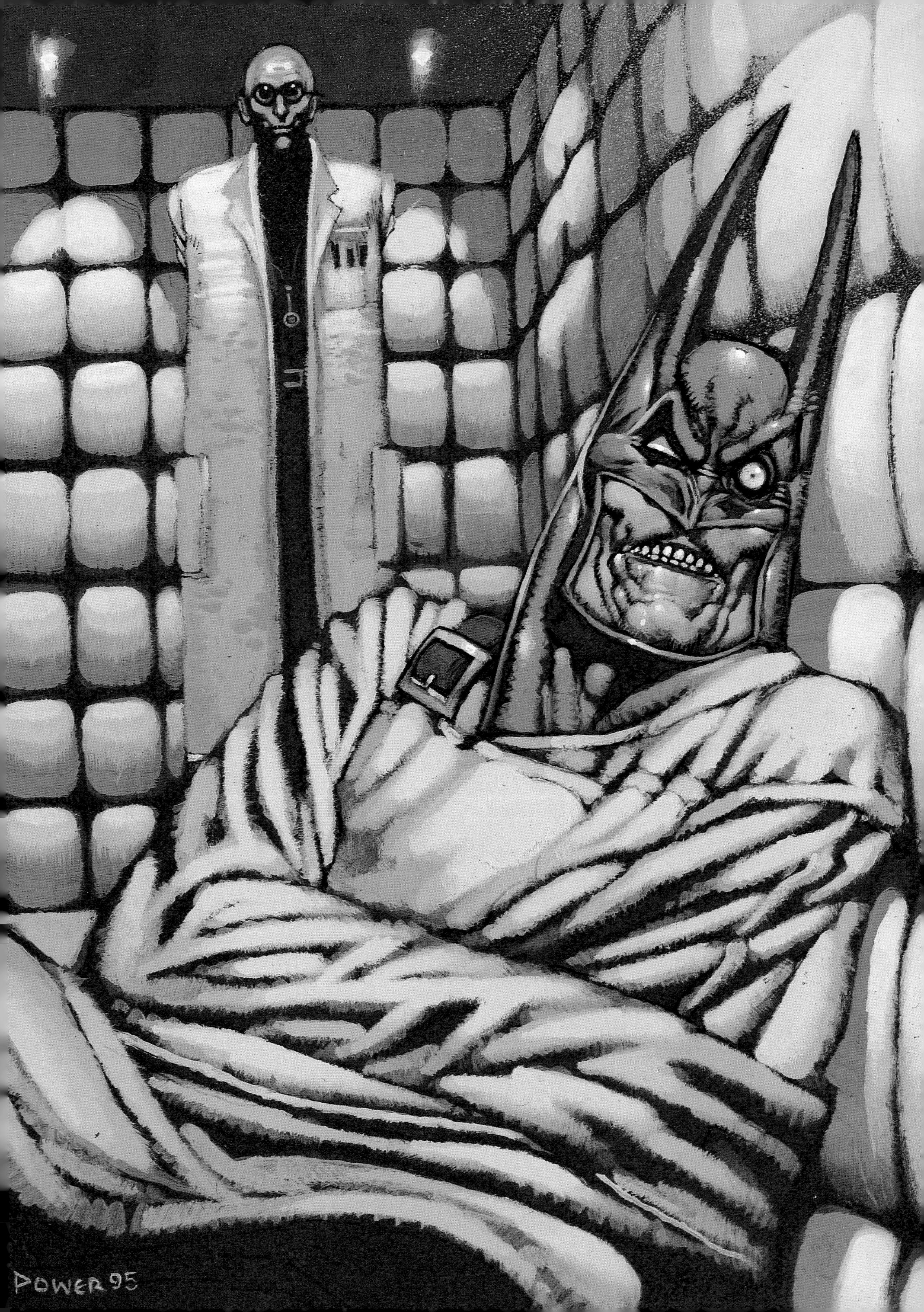
POWER 95

STRANGE ANALYSIS

Final Psychiatric Evaluation by Dr. Hugo Strange:

"Given the patient's lifelong delusions of grandeur (the result of overcompensated inadequacy), classic egomania, and the narcissistic streak of a sociopath, it is hardly surprising that his overconfidence (instilled by feelings of godlike power) should result in death at the hands of the Joker. The only true aberration is that I did not effortlessly kill him *first.*"

ART CONCEPT

Interior padded cell; shrink Hugo Strange smugly superior as he studies utterly insane Batman bound in a straitjacket.

DERMOT POWER'S SOLUTION

"The hardest part of this was finding reference for a straitjacket. You think that you know what one looks like, and then you go to draw it, and you don't!

"What's funny about this piece is that most of the cards in this set are about insane characters, or seen through the eyes of a madman, but this is the only scene that actually takes place in an asylum.

"Because the cards were originally intentioned to be so small, I wanted them to work as strong, simple images. So I tried to keep the color palettes simple—just one or two colors, and then just play with the tones of the color."

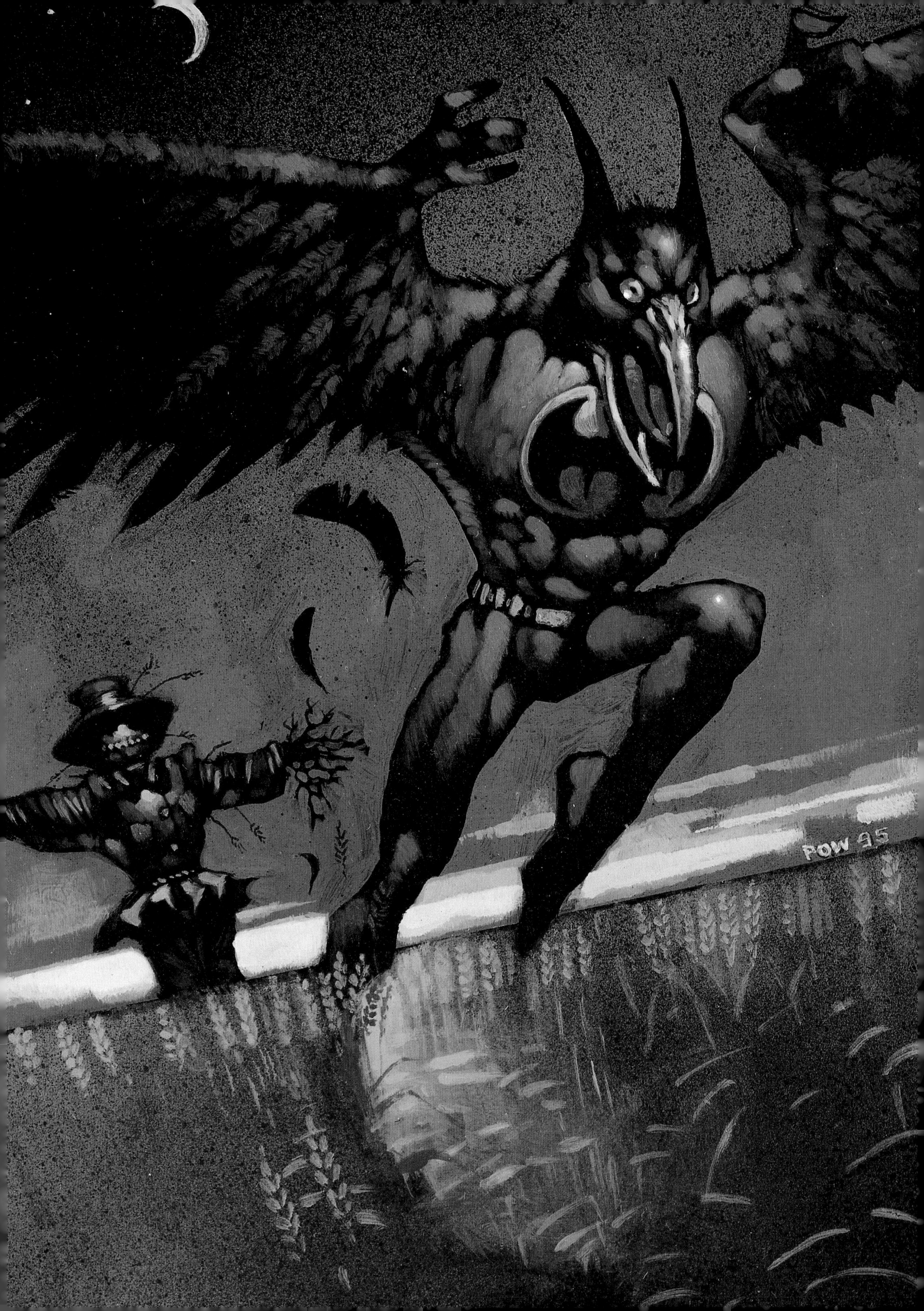
POW 95

MASTER OF FEAR

Scarecrow:

"Maybe I wasn't actually present, but Joker never could have done it *without* me. Who *else* could have softened the Batman for those final, fatal bullets? Without the baggage of silently screaming fear incrementally induced by our past encounters, the Batman would hardly have fallen prey to a garish green-haired clown with a gun. *I'm* the one who *truly* brought him down. It was *me—* and his crippling *fear* of me! *HROOOO HRAAAIIIII!*"

ART CONCEPT

In a field of dead, bent, & broken cornstalks, birdlike Batman as a "giant crow" is flying toward us in terror, fleeing the staked & sagging straw-stuffed scarecrow in background; the scarecrow's arms are outstretched on a cross-pole in limp booga-booga fashion. Scarecrow should resemble the Scarecrow from Batman's Rogues Gallery.

DERMOT POWER'S SOLUTION

"I remember liking that big, huge sky in the background. That big dark brooding sky over vast fields, with this flash of light from the sun going down and beautiful open skies with huge harvest moons, like something from *My Own Private Idaho,* something you'd see in an American road movie. . . .

"I don't know what part of America has this kind of landscape, but it contrasts so much to what we have in Europe that I find it fascinating. I'd love to go there, wherever that is."

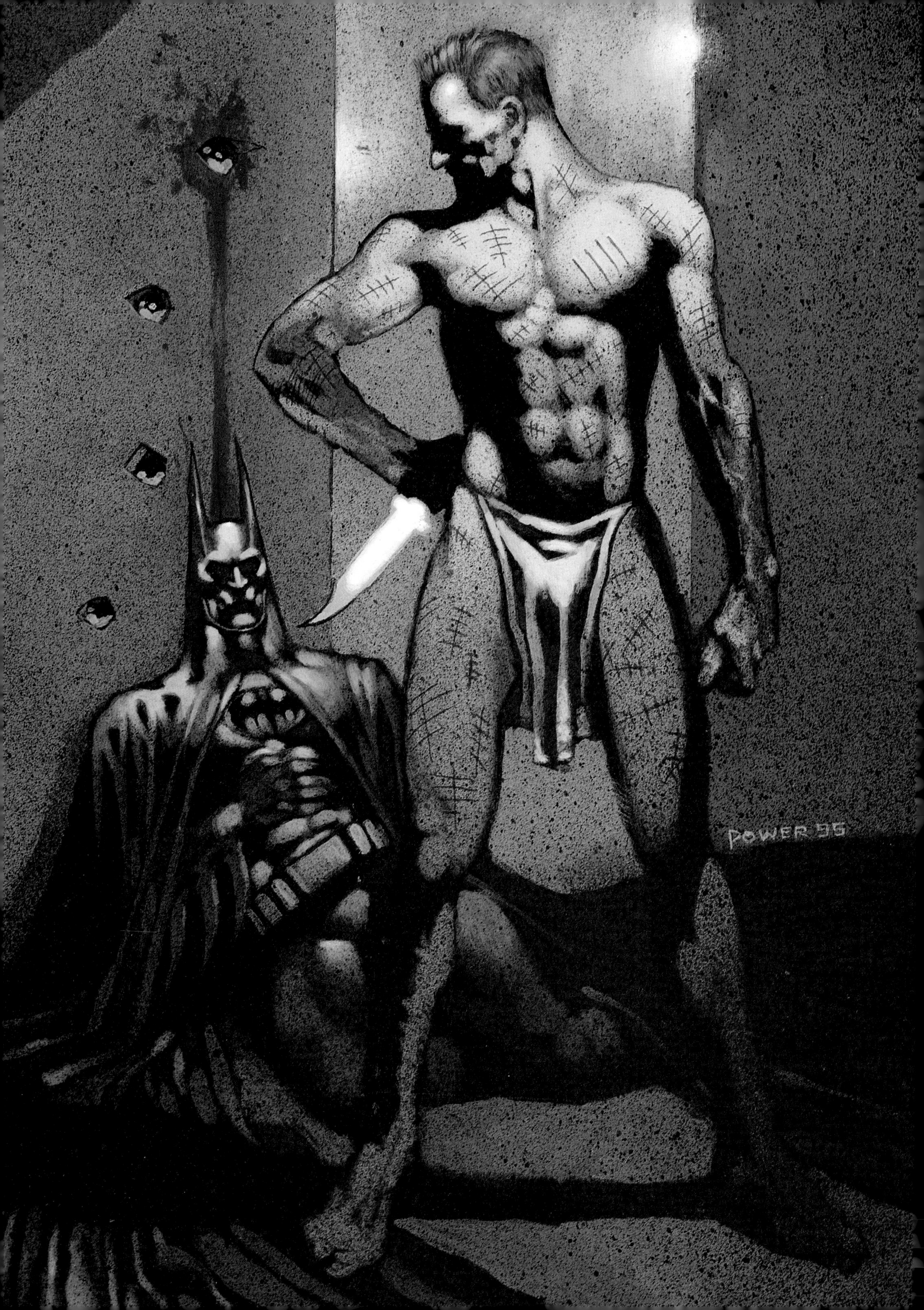
POWER 95

KEEPING SCAR

Mr. Zsasz:

"I live to kill, scoring each victim in my own flesh, a scar for every kill. Running out of skin, I was careful to keep one spot open, holding one future scar in reserve for the most special victim of all. Now he's dead, but my blade is clean . . . my final score never to be scarred.

"Or . . . I wonder . . . who *else* might be worthy of the *last notch?*"

ART CONCEPT

The serial killer Mr. Zsasz (holding knife) standing over dead Batman sprawled at his feet; Zsasz is wearing nothing but his loincloth, and every square inch of his exposed skin bears his "tally scars"—sets of four vertical lines with a fifth diagonal line through each set of four; one set of four, in a prominent position (say, over his chest/heart) is conspicuously minus the fifth diagonal scar/line.

DERMOT POWER'S SOLUTION

"It started to become a theme in my work—men in loincloths," jokes Power. "Really, though, you have to show Mr. Zsasz in a loincloth, because you have to show all the scars that he has, the tally that he's kept of his victims.

"The effort on a realistic, dark piece like this is deciding what to leave out, not what to leave in. I spent a long time on the lighting of this one so that people can figure out for themselves that Mr. Zsasz didn't kill Batman. Mr. Zsasz only uses a knife, and as you can see, Batman's been shot."

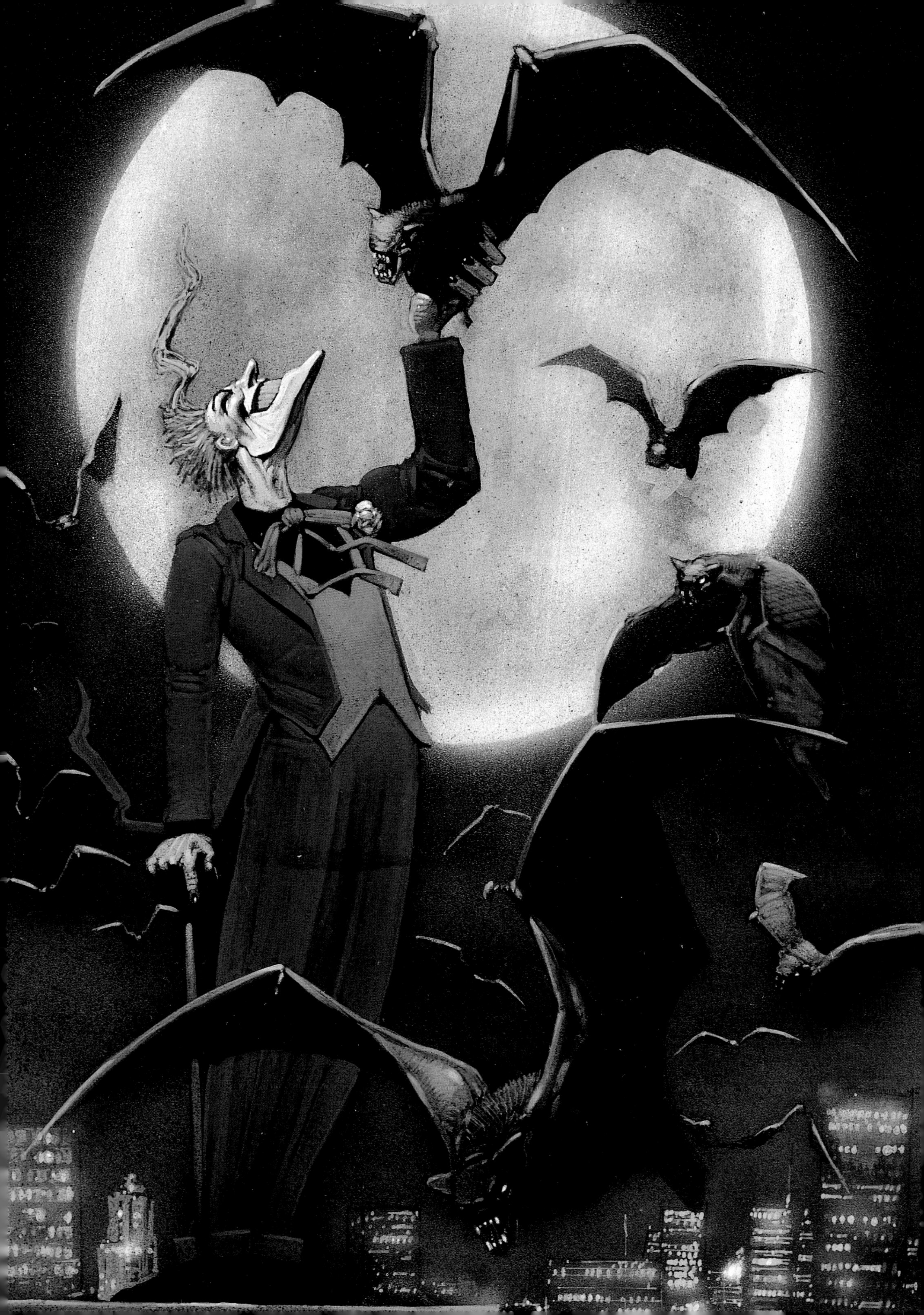

"Bats is dead and they say I done it but I know I didn't, not in *this* reality, not in the here and now, so do you think maybe I killed him *elsewhere* or *elsewhen,* in some *other* reality, some previous life when I was just as batty but Bats was *something else?*

"It's worth a *shot,* isn't it, since life is but a dream and maybe *one* of my dreams is where I *really* shot him. . . ."

ART CONCEPT

Joker has completely flipped out, speaking to a real bat he has caught—holding it spread-winged (one wing in each hand) right up in his face & madly imploring the thing.

CARL CRITCHLOW'S SOLUTION

"The bats were quite important in this shot. Joker was supposed to be sort of grabbing ahold of a bat. If I had put a big head in this picture, I couldn't have had a good bat-shape in, so the head things went out the window on this one. The little things going on are a bit more interesting, so I sacrificed the big head.

"On a subconscious level, I may have been putting in the big white moon in lieu of a big white Joker face, but I'm probably not quite that clever. The moon was just a sort of framing device, really."

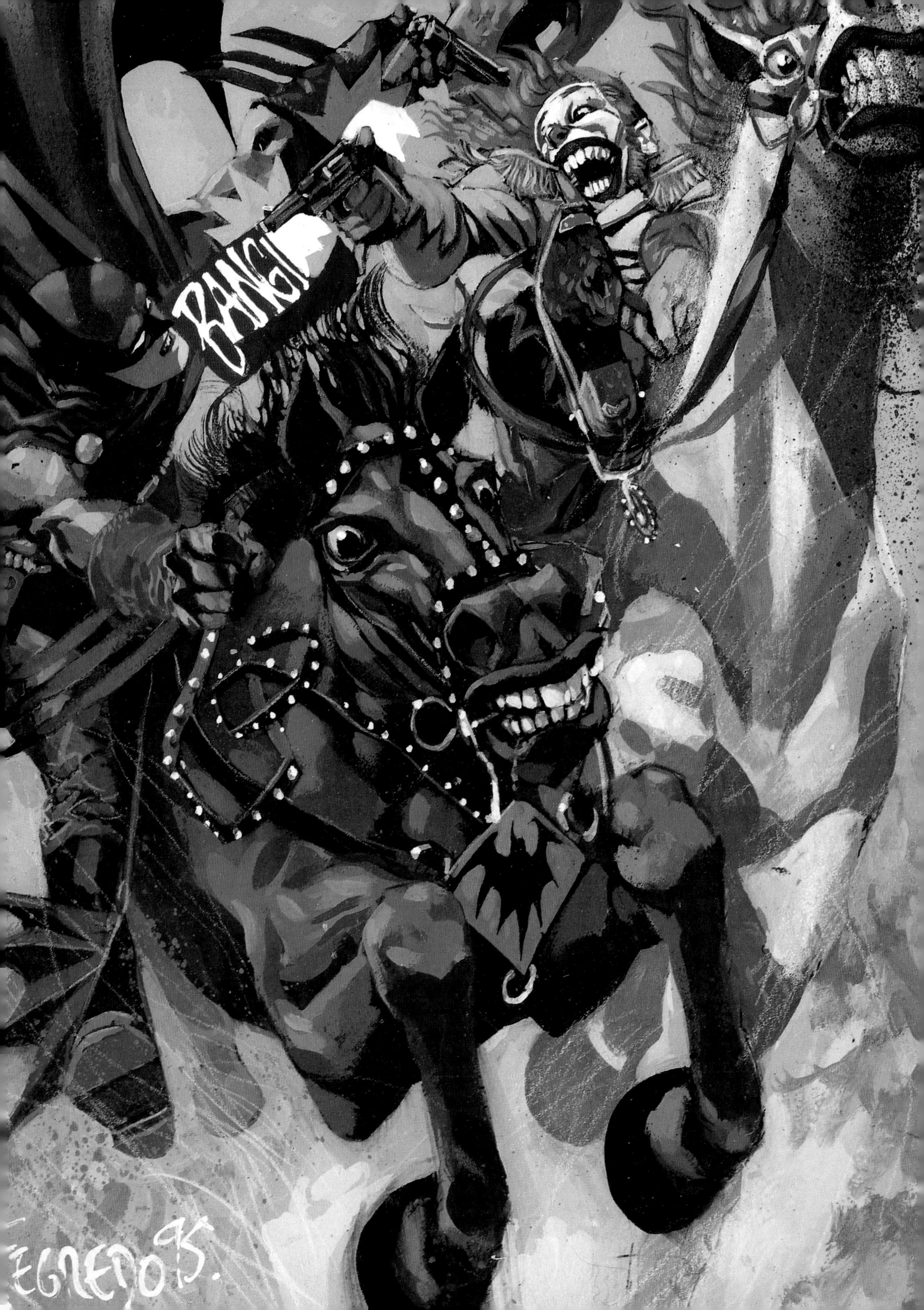
BANG!

Joker:

"Maybe during the War Between the Mental States of Sanity seceded from Insanity, at the Battle of Gigglesburg four score and seventy years ago when our sore fathers brought fifth on this continent a new laugh? Maybe I popped ole blue and gray Bats *then* and *there?*

"Nah . . . I think I was *Jack the Ripper* over in *England* at the time."

ART CONCEPT

Civil War setting; Batman as he appeared in Blue & Gray—with Joker as a Confederate soldier shooting at him.

DUNCAN FEGREDO'S SOLUTION

"All I know about the American Civil War," says the British Fegredo, "is what I've seen in movies—and read in comic books!

"But in this case, it really didn't matter. The cards I illustrated were all the product of the Joker's fevered imagination, so artistic license was allowed. If the painting had demanded a more accurate approach I'd have researched the uniforms, etc. But here I only wanted an impression of speed and action—overcomplicating the image would only have deadened the overall effect.

"I've always advised artists to learn to draw real life because you're going to have to draw it, whether you like it or not. Anything you can bring to a fantasy situation to make it more 'real' or convincing is a good thing. People, whatever they are wearing (be it a suit, T-shirt and jeans, or Lycra/spandex) should still look human, with convincing (even if exaggerated) human anatomy. I think the same applies to everything—clothes, vehicles, weapons, buildings.

"For instance, with this painting I had to do a bit of research to have a good idea of what a horse looks like. I'm sure anybody who really knows anything about horses would tell me 68 things I've done wrong, but there's enough there that gives an impression of height, power, and speed."

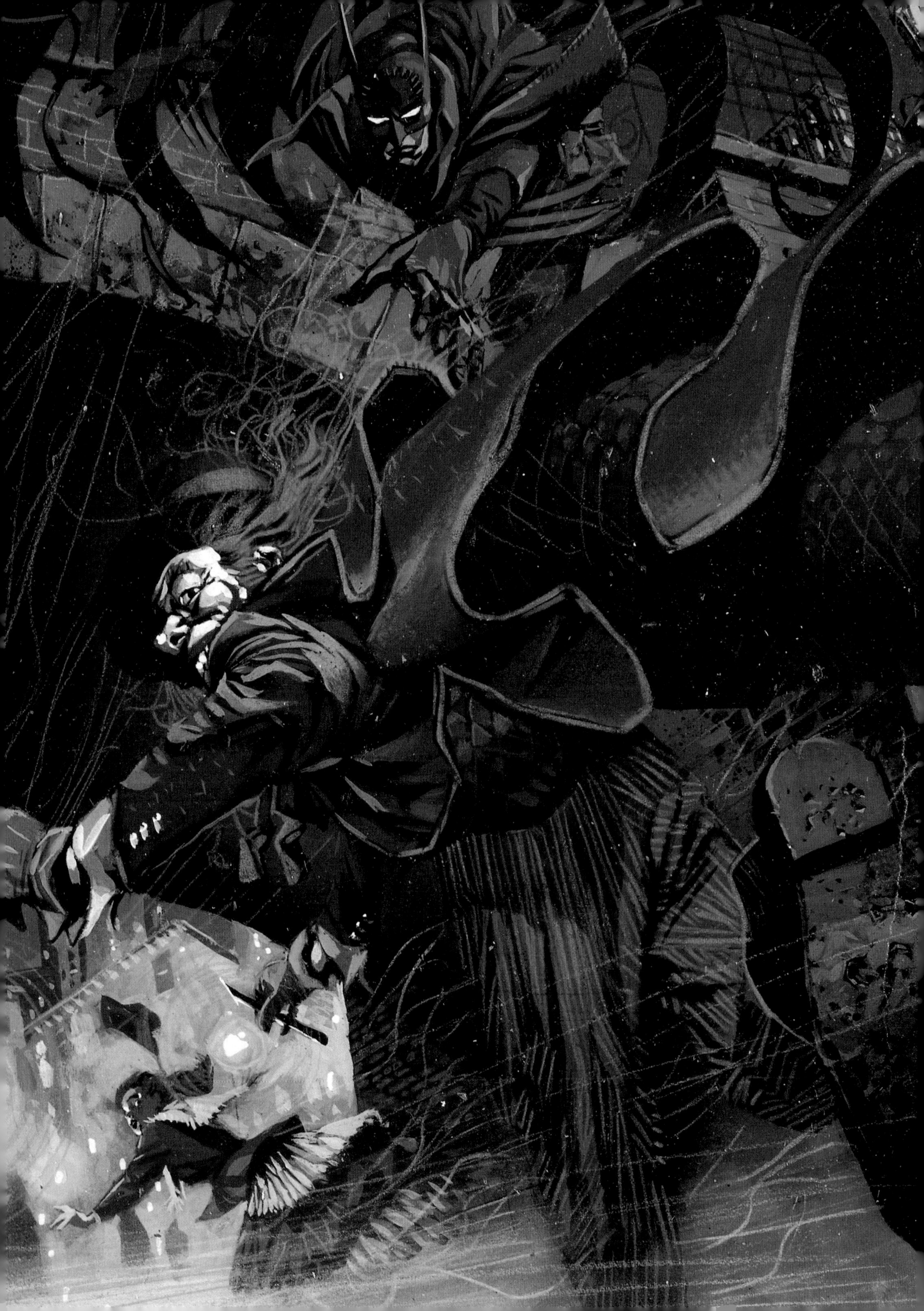

JACK'S WHACK

Joker:

"Speaking of Saucy Jack, maybe I made a trip to Gotham and ripped Bats *then*. After all, I *do* seem to recall a lot of fog by gaslight, the click of frightened heels on cobblestone, a black bag, gleaming scalpel, and. . . .

"No way. The Ripper ripped, but he didn't *guffaw*."

ART CONCEPT

Street scene from Gotham By Gaslight; Batman stalking Joker as Jack the Ripper—even as Joker/Jack stalks a Victorian streetwalker victim.

DUNCAN FEGREDO'S SOLUTION

"Somebody once said that my artwork made them seasick. I like to change perspective all the time. If you look at the cards, I usually try to choose an extreme viewpoint to heighten the excitement.

"Initially, I start with a script and I do a series of thumbnail roughs, just playing around and getting an idea of compositions. I draw a series of shapes at the same size and format as the cards, and try and work out the composition which would fit that card and make an exciting image. I decide where Batman would need to be, where the main characters need to lay.

"Like with this card, where you're in the position of falling closely behind the Joker figure. The perspective pulls you along in the Joker's wake to the inevitable collision with the Batman. The Joker may not know this is about to happen, but you, the viewer, do. And every time you look at this image, you're drawn inexorably to the same collision that never quite happens. It's an instant in time, with the conclusion left to your imagination."

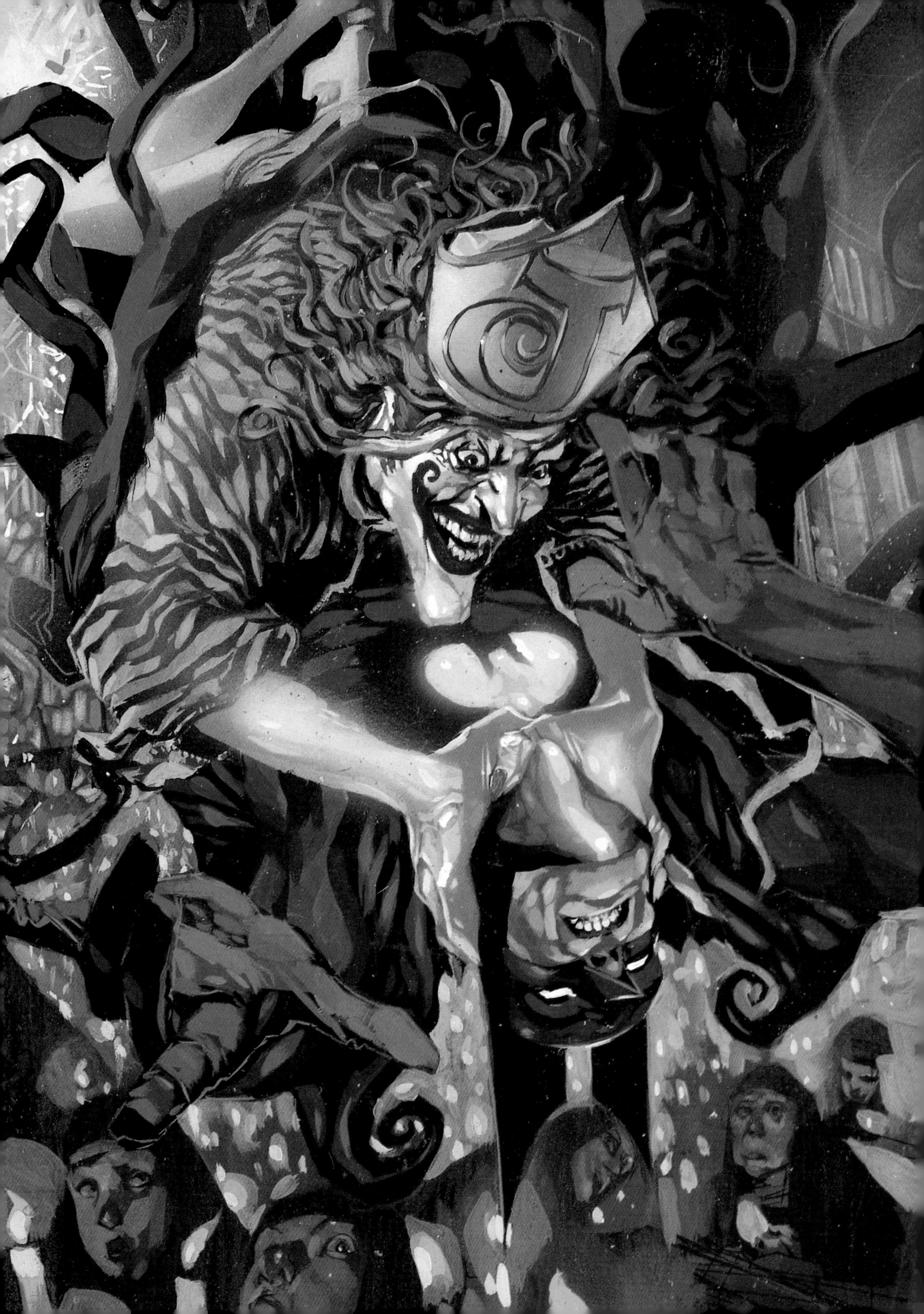

SACRED SCARE

Joker:

"I *must* have killed Bats! No one else has the Punch and Judy *panache* for such a hit! But if I can't remember doing it, then it *must* have been in a *past life.* Did I off him in some strangely skewed alternative future where church and state were hopelessly scrambled? Yes, I *do* seem to recall being a *holy terror* of prodigious—

"Wait a minute! How could either one of us live *past lives* in the *future?!*"

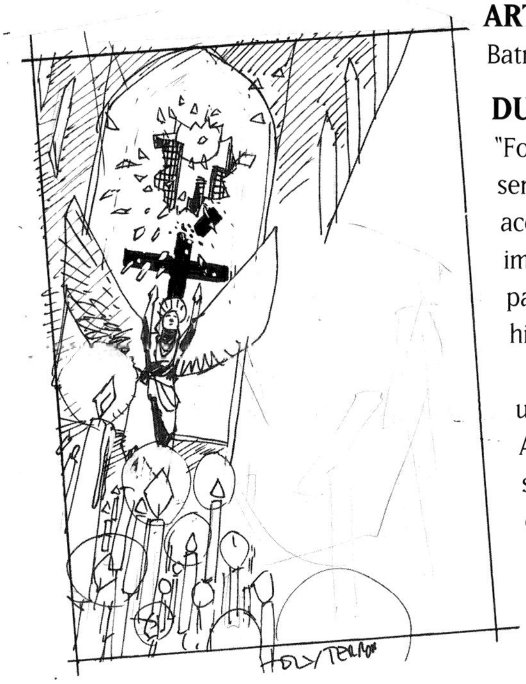
HOLY/TERROR

ART CONCEPT

Batman as seen in Holy Terror—with or without Joker.

DUNCAN FEGREDO'S SOLUTION

"For me, a painting usually ends up as the result of a series of accidents, happy or otherwise. The happy accidents are those that add to the spontaneity of the image. As for the bad . . . well, you can hope a particularly lousy bit of painting will be somehow hidden.

"After I figure out a layout, it's a case of drawing up the card to the scale I was going to paint them. At the same time, I try to work out the color scheme, to give it the right feeling. Is the picture cold, or do you want it to feel hot and dusty? And then you use the appropriate palette. . . .

"With this card, the original idea was to show the Batman and the Joker plummeting towards us through a stained-glass window in a church. I wanted Batman to appear as a demonic 'Fallen Angel.' Looking back, I don't think I chose a very involving viewpoint, and the window isn't prominent enough. Having said that, I *do* like the way the backdrop is split in two; the top half is a 'heavenly' glow, the bottom half, composed of a pattern of candle-carrying nuns, is, rather ironically, the fiery glow of hell. See? Accidents!"

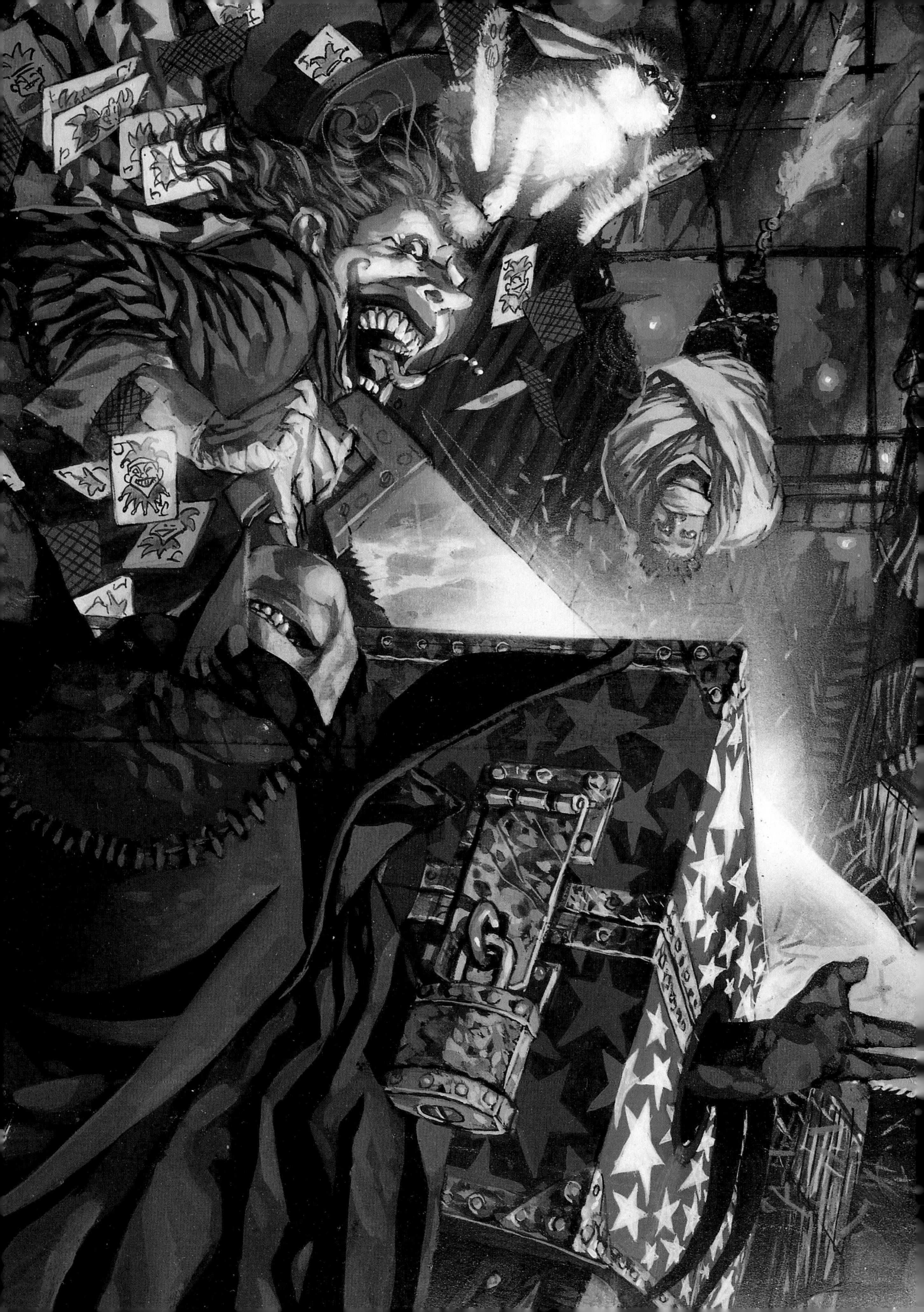

WHODUNIT HOUDINI?

Joker:

"Watch carefully! No smoke or mirrors, nothing up my sleeve—yet I shall confound all possibility by *sawing a bat-man in half,* after which you shall be dazzled by my extraordinary *escape artistry!* And for my *next* trick . . . pick a card, *any* card, just as long as it's the *Joker!* But whatever you do, don't punch me in the gut and ruin my *belly laugh!*"

ART CONCEPT

Joker as a stage magician, sawing Batman-in-a-box in half—as Houdini looks on.

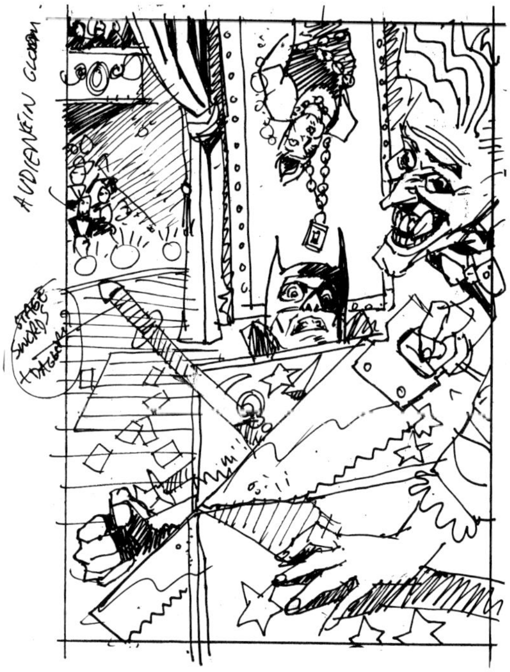
AUDIENCE IN GLOOM
STAGE SWORDS + DAGGERS

DUNCAN FEGREDO'S SOLUTION

Like many artists, Fegredo avails himself of technology: the photocopier.

"After I've settled on a sketch, I enlarge it on a photocopier and transfer the image to the artboard, trying not to lose the spontaneity and life of the original sketch. In a quick sketch, there may be accidental marks or exaggerations in anatomy and perspective that give life to the subject—more so than an anatomically correct and photorealistic image would have.

"This is one of my favorite ones actually. I like the aspect of this card that puts you right in there with Batman.

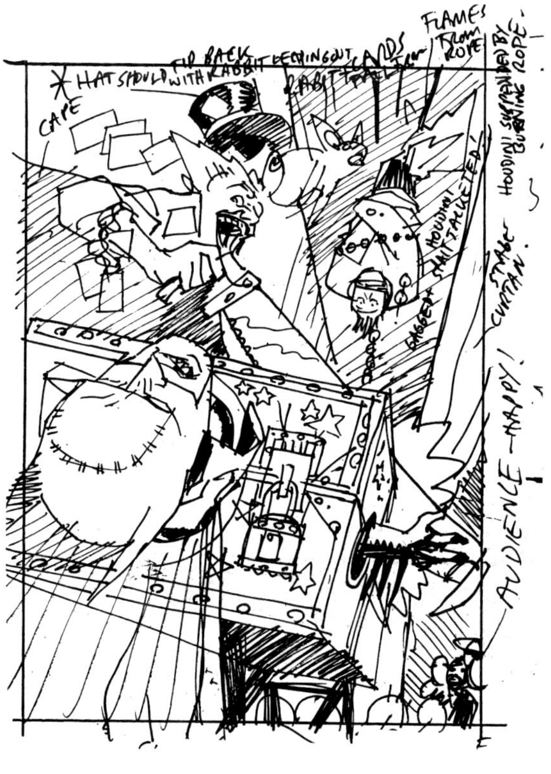
CAPE
FLAMES FROM ROPE
STAGE CURTAIN
AUDIENCE — HAPPY!

"I like the fact you're almost in the box, being sawed in half by the Joker, you've almost got Batman's point of view. At the same time, you see the original escape artist burning above, who's incapable of doing anything. He can see the Batman about to be cut in half by the Joker but there's nothing he can do, he's got his own problems. He's about to plummet to the ground when the rope burns through."

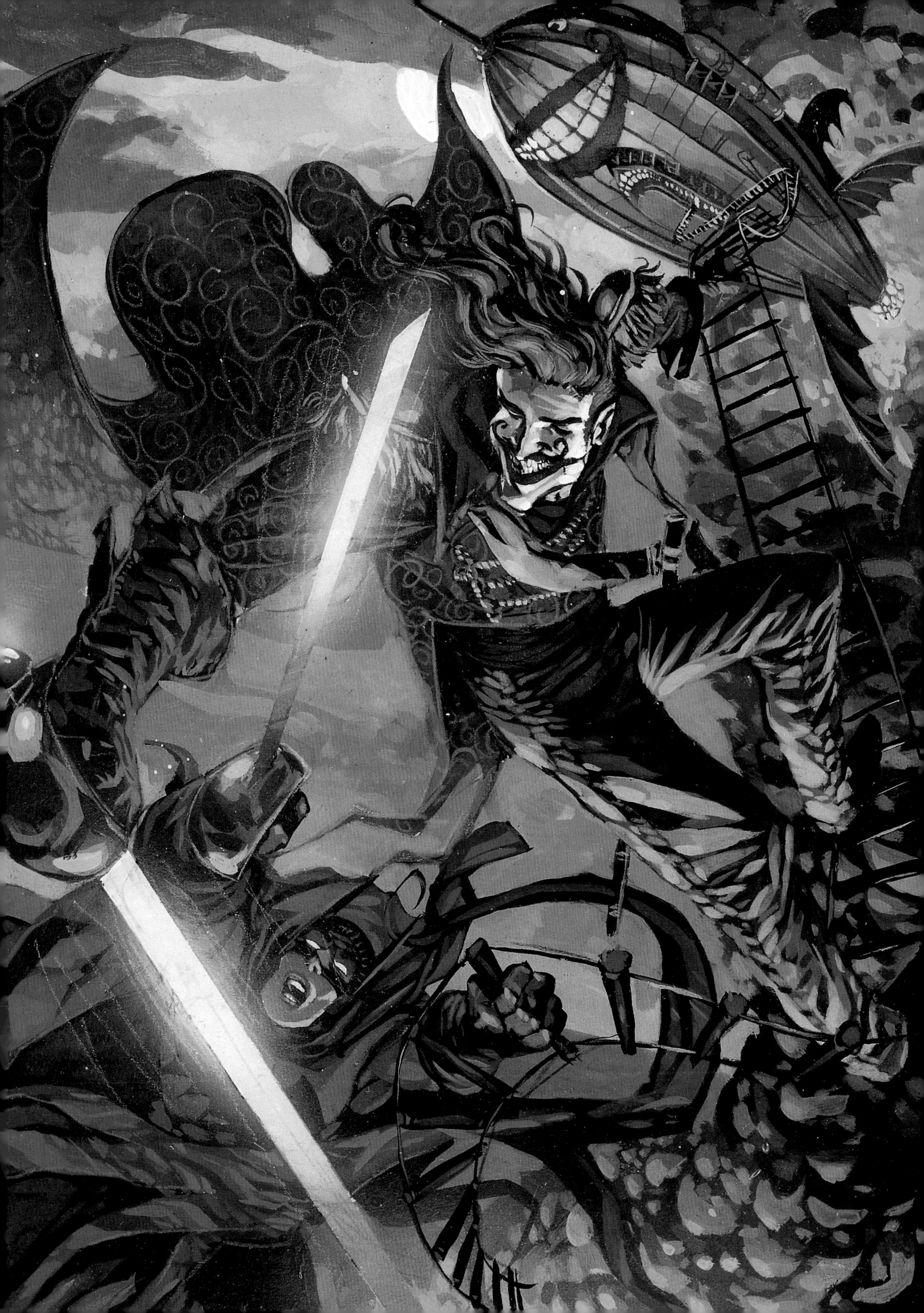

PAST MASTER OF THE FUTURE

Joker:

"Okay, living past lives in the future is out, but what if I were a Master of the Future back in the *past,* making the *future* nothing more than a quaint version of the *present,* which *itself* becomes the *past* as soon as it *happens!* Robur-Joker the Conqueror, wheee-*hah!*

"Except . . . if the future's the present and the present's the past, then I couldn't be then *and* now in two places at the same time. *Could I . . . ?"*

ART CONCEPT

Batman (and Joker?) in a Jules Verne scene from *Master of the Future.*

DUNCAN FEGREDO'S SOLUTION

"I tried to twist the perspective around so that whilst you, the viewer, are apparently at about the same level as the Joker, you can simultaneously see the airship far above, the Batman struggling to hang onto the rope ladder below, and beyond him, fire and smoke.

"I work in acrylics, generally. I like acrylics because you can work over them. They don't bleed or anything. I like the fact that you can thin them down and use them as watercolor, or you can use them thick. And if you make a mistake, you can just paint it out and work over them. I like that versatility.

"Initially, I paint the whole image in monochrome, usually black, blue, or brown. Using just one color at this stage enables you to balance the image right before getting bogged down with more colors. Then, I'll gradually work in other colors, trying to paint across the whole image, so as not to work one area up more than any other and paint too much detail.

"Sometimes I work with color crayons as well, for little details or little effects here and there. For instance, I wanted to give a feeling of richness to the Joker's cloak. If you look closely, you can just about make out the little swirls in crayon over his cloak. The crayon gives the impression of embroidery or something."

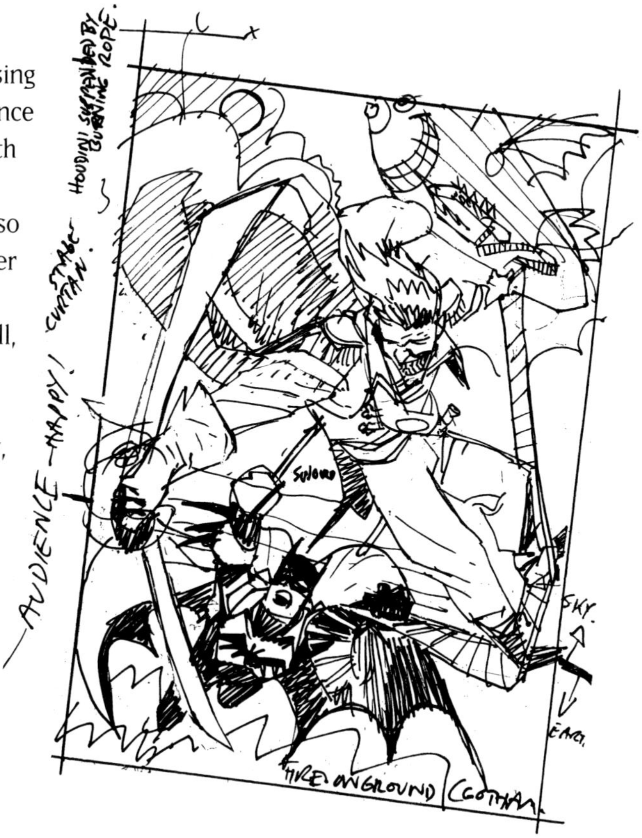

HOUDINI SUSPENDED BY BURNING ROPE.
STAGE CURTAIN.
AUDIENCE — HAPPY!
SWORD
SKY.
FIRE ON GROUND
GOTHAM

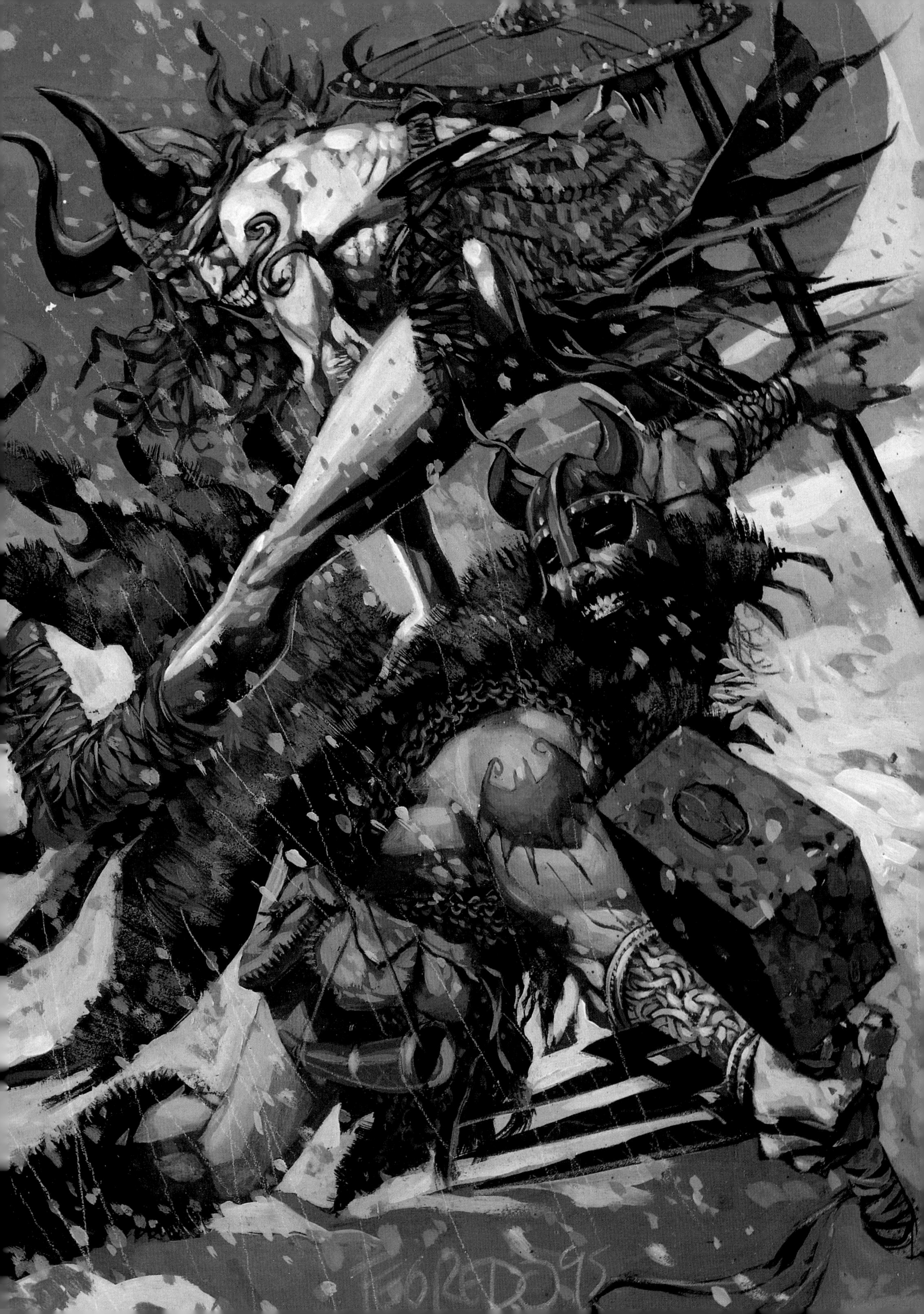

Joker:

"Maybe I hacked Bats back when I was a roving Viking reaver-raider—probably as that grinning trickster *Loki,* which means Bats was probably Thor. The gods of thunder and blunder, and what a pair we *made,* eh? Ragnarockin' the night away and—

"But what the Valhalla kind of sense does *that* make? If we were gods, we were immortal and if we were immortal, we couldn't die, so how could I *kill* him? And if we both lived forever, our past lives never would have *ended!*"

ART CONCEPT

Batman and Joker as Vikings battling in the snow—or on a Viking ship.

DUNCAN FEGREDO'S SOLUTION

"In this one, I kept the palette cold, because the scene is set in the snow."

Setting a palette hasn't always been easy for Fegredo.

"I sometimes do some pretty whacked-out colors when I paint, due to the fact that I'm color-blind.

"What I have learned over a period of time is that no matter how correct you can make your color, how precisely you paint, there is no way the printing process is ever going to fully reproduce the colors you've used. You get big shifts in the spectrum. You might find everything goes more green, more red, more whatever. Everything is going to change by the time it's printed. You just do the best you can. I try to get enough total contrast in the work, which also gets reduced in the printing process, so then at least I can end up with a strong image, whatever happens to the color."

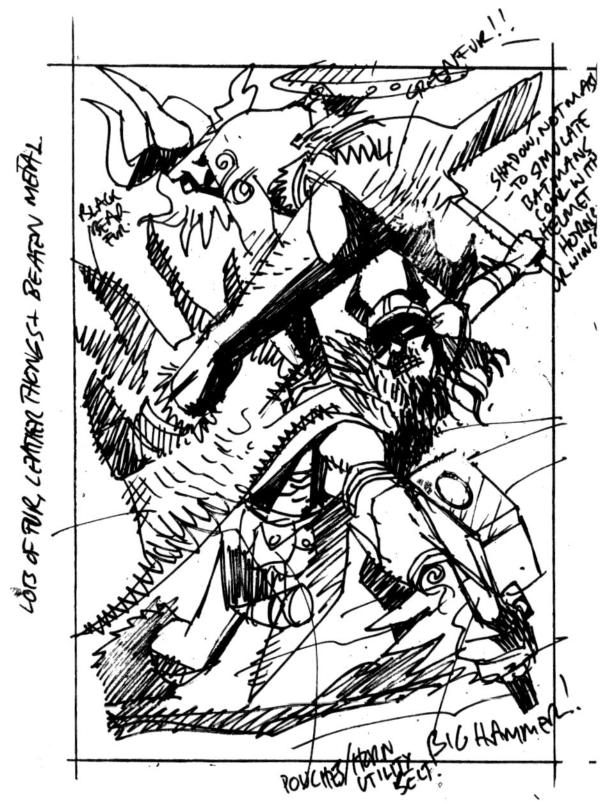
GREEN FUR!!
SHADOW, NOT MASK — TO SIMULATE BATMAN'S COWL WITH HELMET HORNS OR WINGS
BLACK BEAR FUR
LOTS OF FUR, LEATHER THONGS + BEATEN METAL
BIG HAMMER!
POUCHES/HORN UTILITY BELT

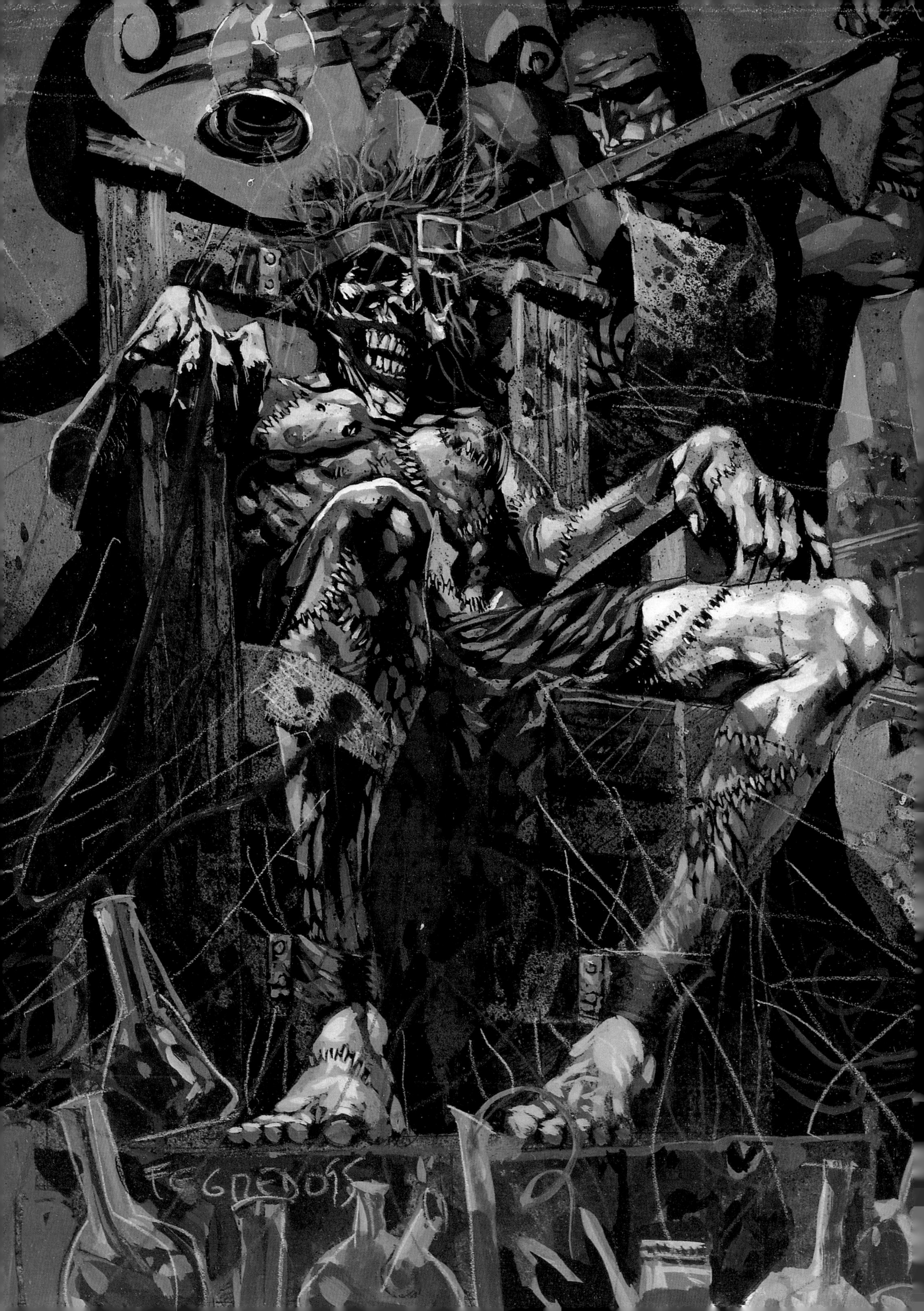

IT'S DEAD!

Joker:

"I'll bet I was a Bavarian baron who created a bat-monster just so I could destroy him. It's *aliiive!* No, it's *dead!* Or maybe I was the monster created by Bats and I killed my creator because he couldn't take a joke. But if I *was* a monster made from a dozen different dead pieces, was my past life actually a *dozen* past lives? And which one was *me?* The brain? Spleen? *Pancreas . . . ?*"

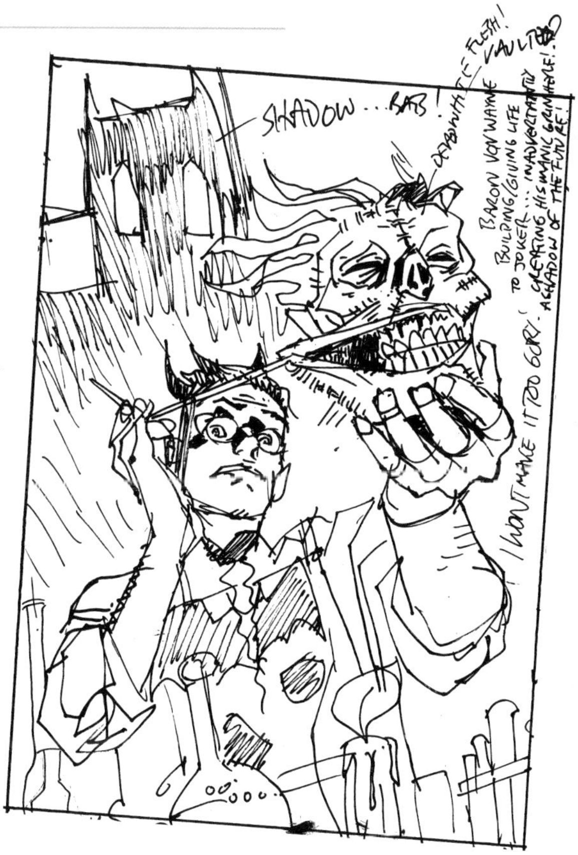
SHADOW...BATS!
I WONT MAKE IT TOO GORY!

ART CONCEPT

Joker & Batman as Frankenstein & his monster—or vice-versa.

DUNCAN FEGREDO'S SOLUTION

"There was an earlier version, an earlier sketch of Bruce Wayne covered in blood and whatever, holding in his hand, kind of Hamlet-like, a skull. Around the skull he was sewing dead flesh, and as Bruce pulled back the needle, the thread tugged the corner of the Joker's mouth into a gruesome death's-head grin—quite literally the Batman was creating the Joker's insane smile! This was unfortunately considered to be of questionable taste, so the concept was changed. Hopefully here we can print the sketch that shows the true abhorrent nature of my mind!

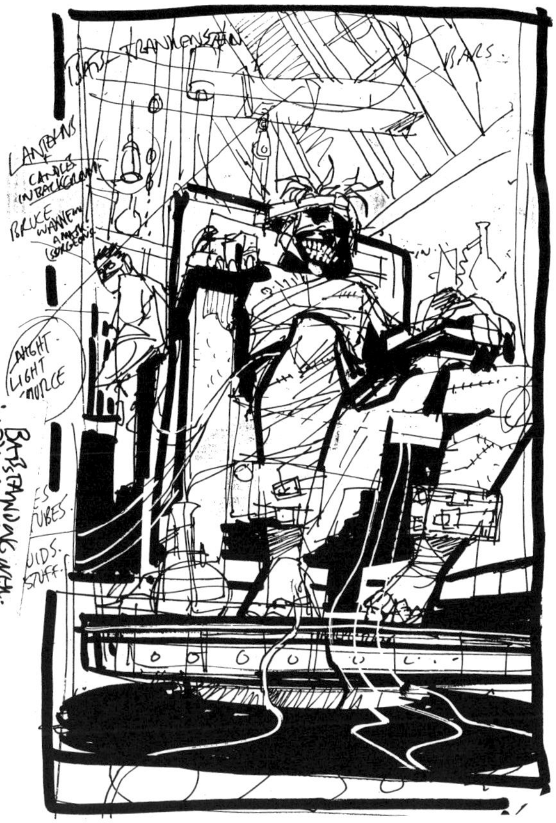
FRANKENSTEIN
BATS

"Even though the title is 'It's Dead,' I didn't want my card to be. I used colored crayon to strengthen the impression of lots of tubes and things. There's lots of little bits of crayon on there, just little fine details. It also livens things up a bit in areas that have become a little static.

"Each image I produced for this card set depicted the fevered imaginings of the Joker, hence the slightly off-beat frenetic approach to each card."

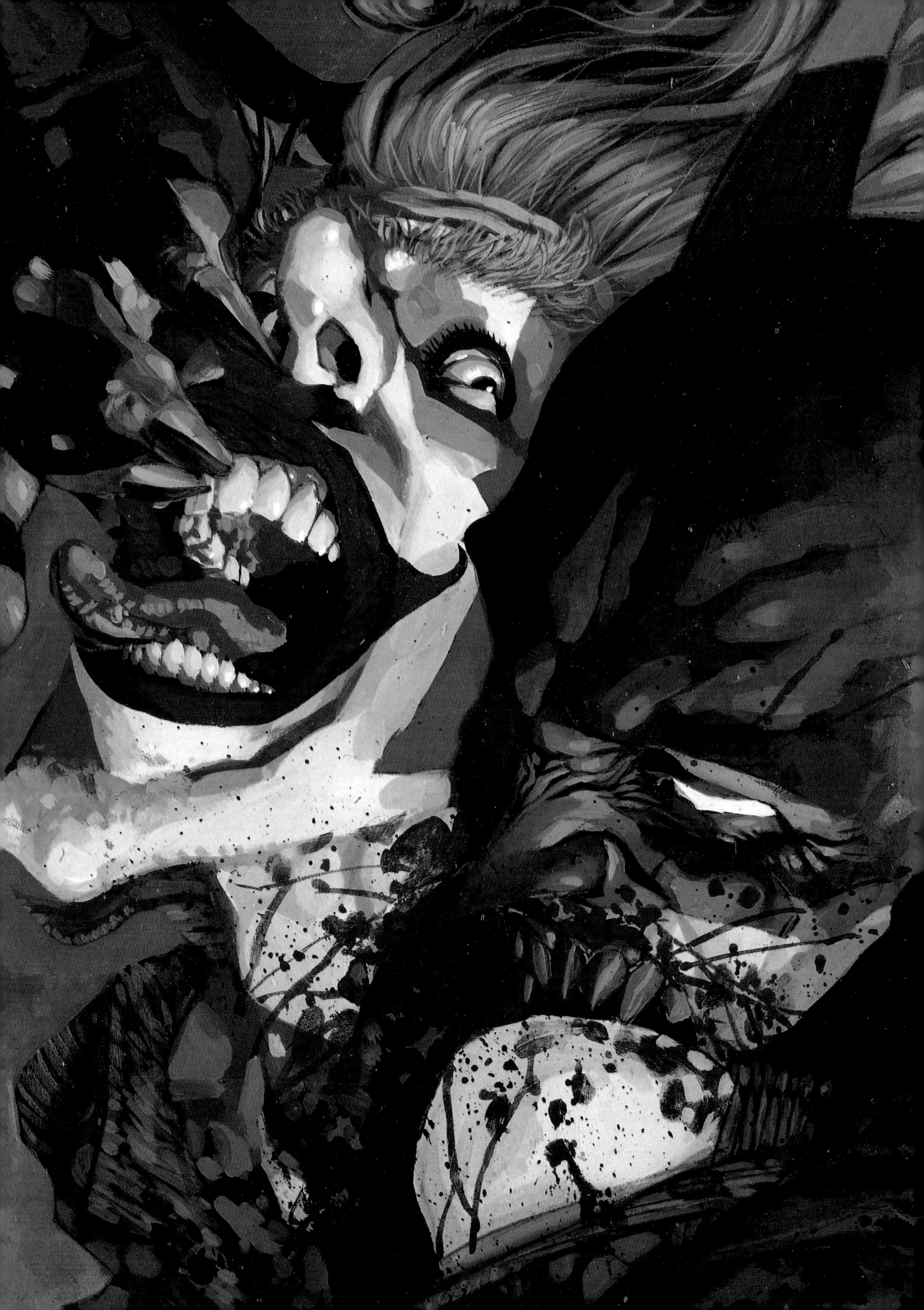

TEETHING

Joker:

"I *know* I braved the red rain in some other life, even led an army of vampires through a storm of blood which drenched Bats to the bone. This I *clearly* remember. Only problem is, Bats was *also* a vampire and it was my blood that got sucked. At least I *think* I remember this . . . but if vampire-Bats *did* slurp my plasma, how come *I'm* not a vampire? Yegads—*another* invalidated investigation!"

ART CONCEPT
Batman as a vampire sucking Joker's blood—from *Bloodstorm* [graphic novel].

DUNCAN FEGREDO'S SOLUTION
"Carl Critchlow drew the Joker as a completely distorted figure with absolutely massive teeth, which is actually fine. I drew the Joker with a big nose and a pointed chin, but rather than give him a cavernous mouth, I tried to give the impression that the lips are painted on, a big smiley face. If you look at the understructure, you can see his face distorted in a grimace at the same time. I kind of like the grimace and the smile there. I guess you always get that with the Joker, but it was fun trying to distort it slightly differently from the norm anyway.

"Originally I was going to paint Batman so you couldn't tell where the mask finished and his face began. There is still a slight aspect of that. You can see all the muscles, all the facial structures through the mask, which of course you wouldn't really be able to do. There is more of a beastlike nature in the piece."

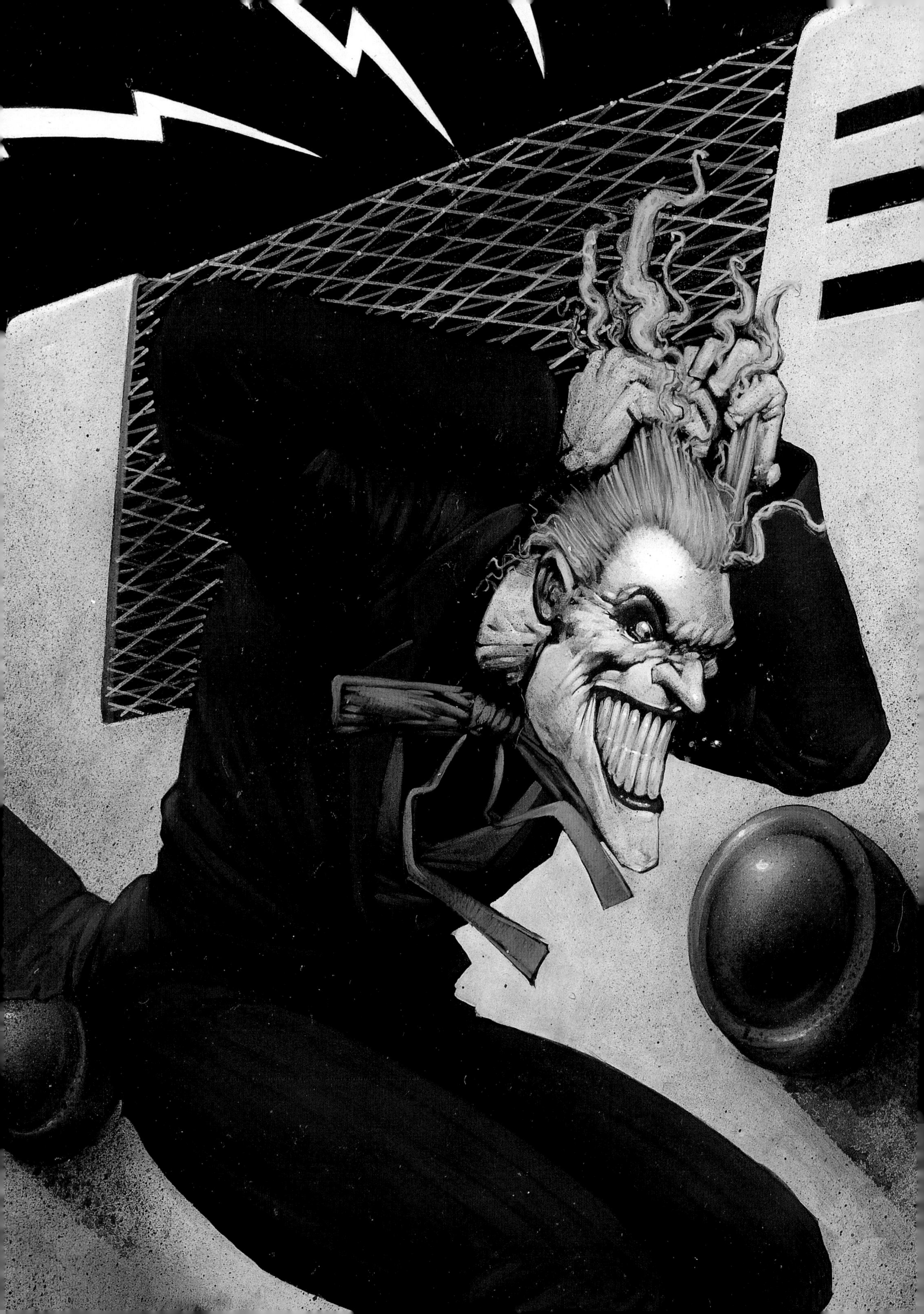

"If I *didn't* kill Bats here and now and I didn't off him there and then *either,* he can't possibly be—"

"We interrupt with this special news bulletin. Police Commissioner James Gordon has announced that the body of the Batman was recovered from the river last night and interred without publicity earlier today in a special memorial crypt located in Gotham Cemetery. . . ."

"*Whaaat?!*"

ART CONCEPT

Joker going truly nuts, tearing out fistfuls of his own green hair as he raves maniacally; on a table or shelf behind him, we see a large old-timey '30s-style radio.

CARL CRITCHLOW'S CONCEPT:

The many lines on the Joker's face were not the result of Critchlow suffering from too much "LPI" (lines per inch).

"He's supposed to have been terribly scarred after falling into a vat of chemicals. I wanted to try to get a bit of a suggestion of that in. The Joker was supposed to be this terrifying character.

"As to making his eyes so small, well, as big as I wanted to make the Joker's mouth and ferocious teeth, I just didn't have space. It wasn't a conscious decision."

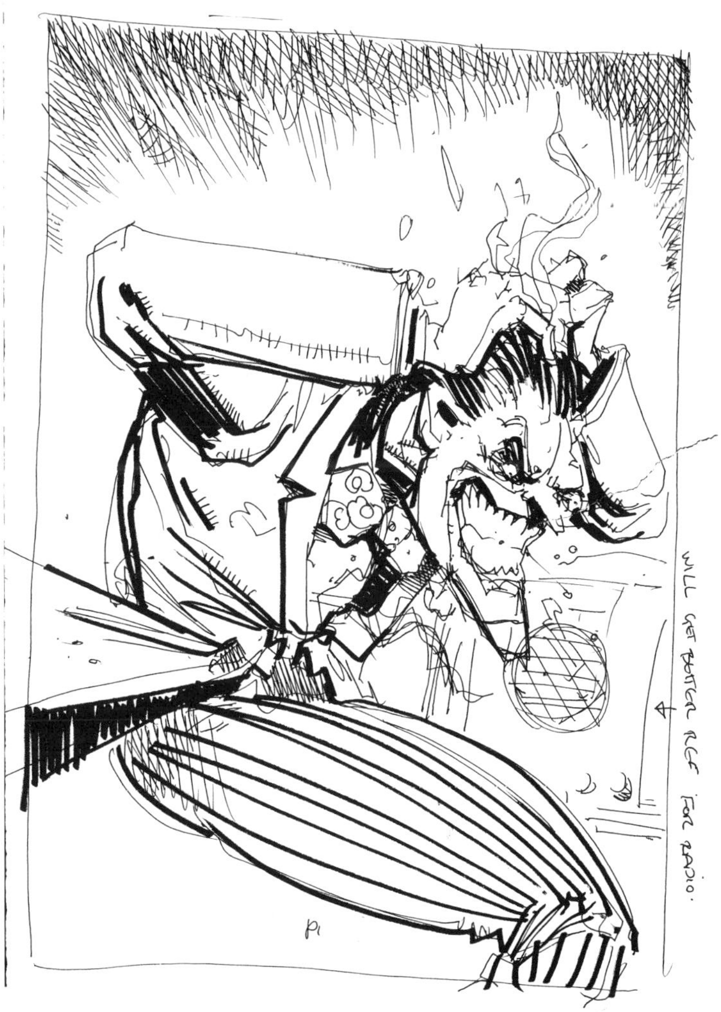
WILL GET BETTER REF FOR RADIO.

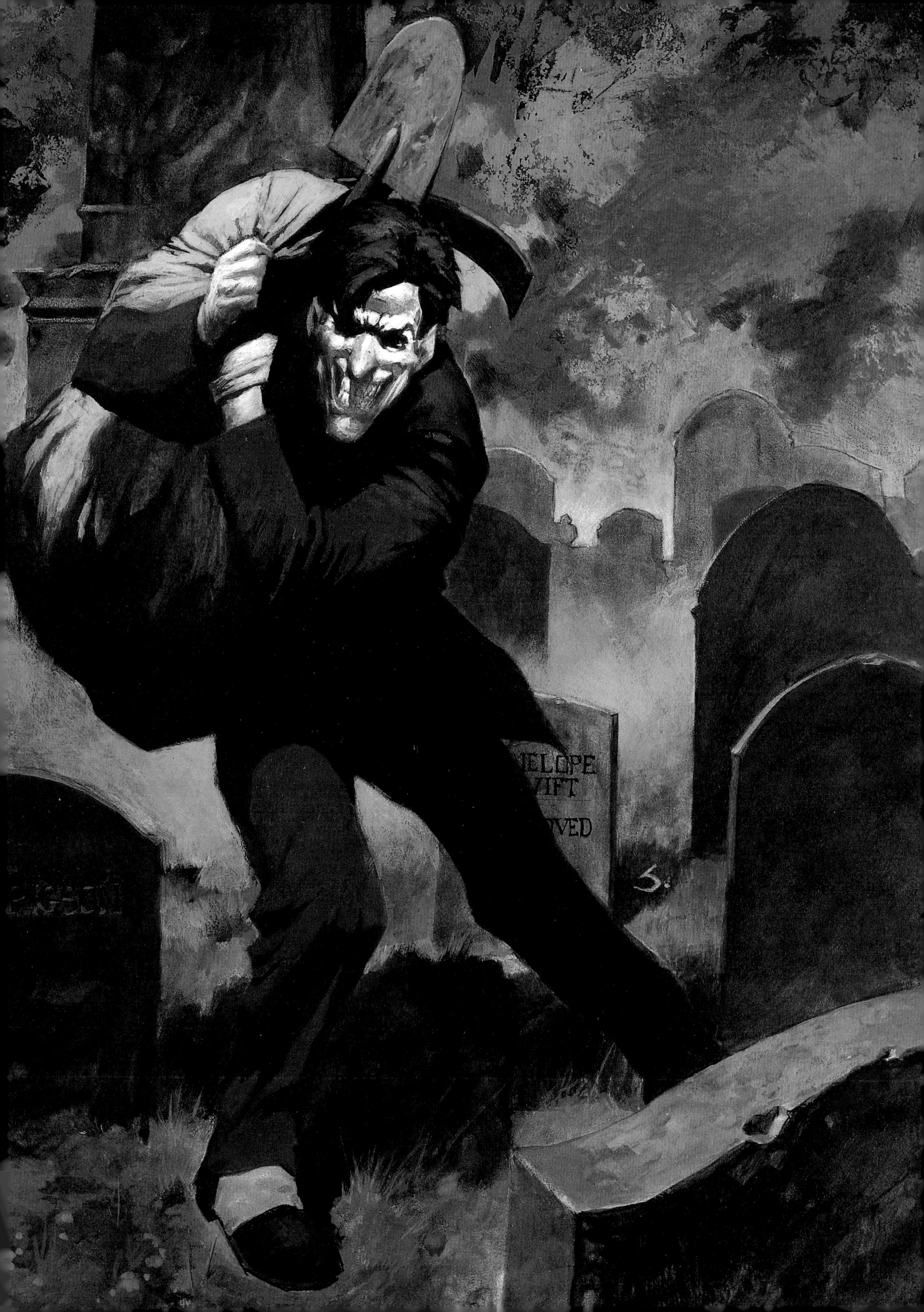

DIGGING BATTY

"Either he's dead or he isn't, and the only way to get to the bottom of it is by getting to the bottom of his grave or memorial crypt or ashtray or *whatever* they planted his batty body in. Ergo: Gotta *dig him up*—and *kill* him if he's *not already dead!*

"Heh heh *hweee.*"

ART CONCEPT

Crazy Joker with a shovel/spade over his shoulder, entering creepy Gotham Cemetery thru its wrought-iron gates—and with its graves & tombstones & crosses & angel statues & crypts & gnarled trees.

SCOTT HAMPTON'S SOLUTION

Hampton never tried to play off the other artists' images.

"I was totally in the dark as to what the rest of the set looked like. I think I had seen a few of Dermot's pieces up in the DC offices, but only one or two. Other than that, I did not know what Duncan or Carl or the others were doing."

But other artists influenced him.

"This was my homage to Bernie Wrightson. This is a classic Wrightson kind of pose, the knees bowing in together, and then splaying out, and being off-balance. And just the whole idea of a guy skulking around with a big sack, and shovels and picks and such. It's my tip of the hat to one of the premier talents in comics of all time.

"I had lit one tombstone—'Penelope Swift, Beloved.' I hate to say it, but the choice has no significance. That grave could not be as dark nor as silhouetted as the others, because I needed that bow of the knee. I wanted to clearly give the sense of the turning of the knee."

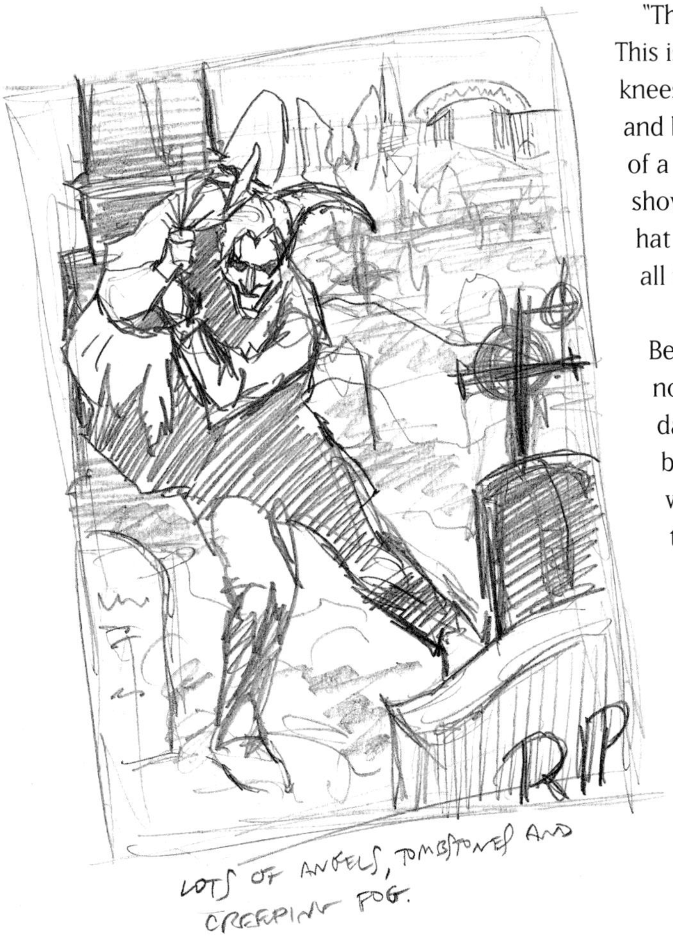
RIP
LOTS OF ANGELS, TOMBSTONES AND CREEPING FOG.

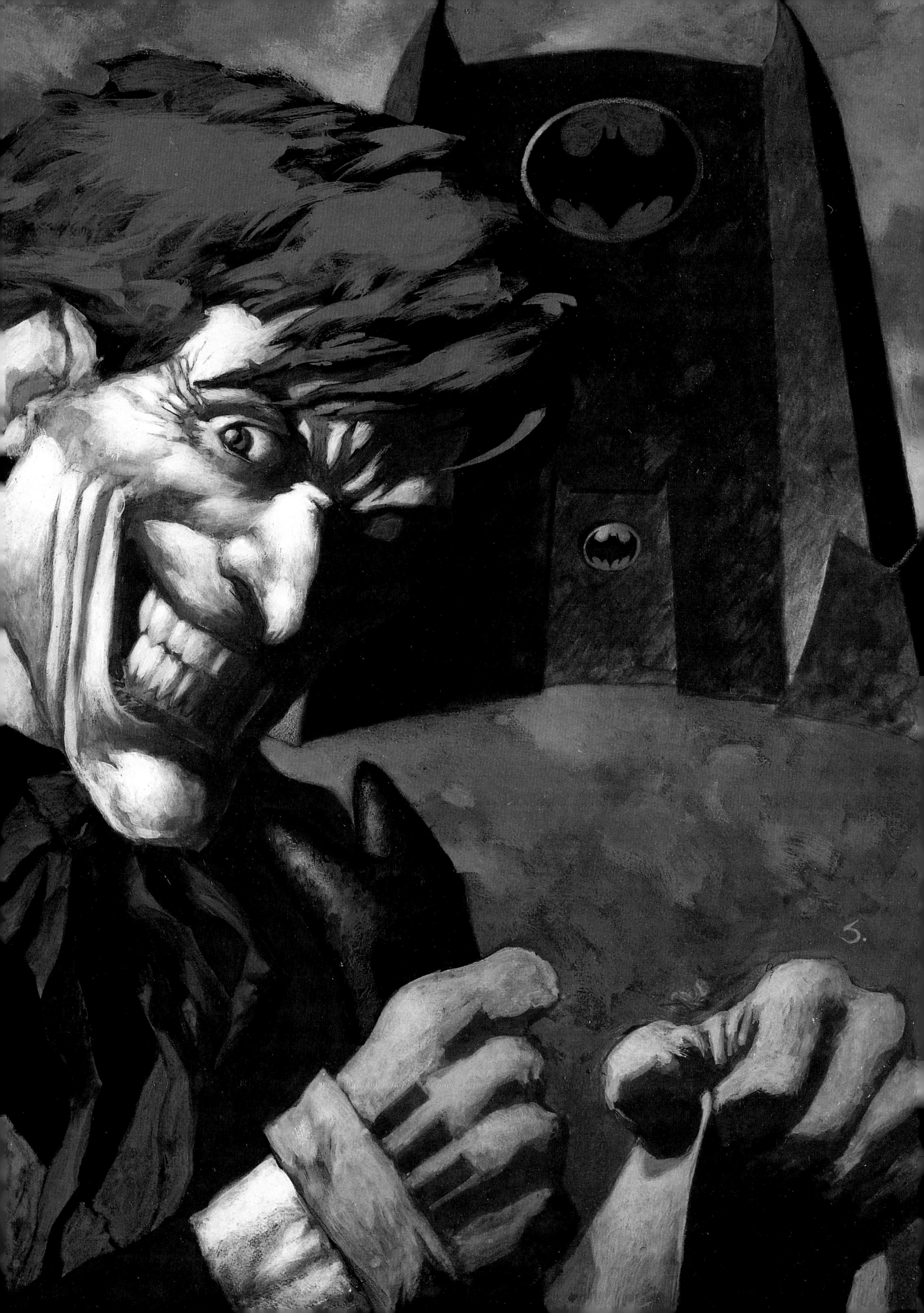

UNREST IN PEACE

"One way or another, this is where it all ends or ended, eh? Not bad for a box of polished rock. When *I* croak the big death-rattle, wonder if they'll do one with a mouthful of *teeth* chiseled over the entrance. Abandon hope, all ye who giggle here—but nevertheless, Bats, dead or alive and ready or not . . . here I *come!*"

ART CONCEPT

In creepy Gotham Cemetery, Joker (with his shovel/spade) is standing before & beholding impressive Bat-Crypt—stone crypt with the bat symbol and "R.I.P."

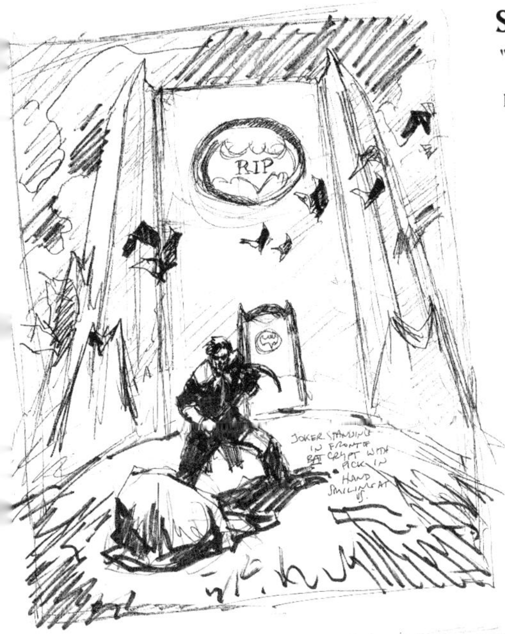
RIP

SCOTT HAMPTON'S SOLUTION

"This one was a lot of fun, and I think that it was one of my most successful paintings in the set. Initially, I had done the sketch as the Joker standing full-figure with a big sack, with the emphasis really on the Bat-Crypt. The editor thought that the Joker wasn't big enough, wasn't important enough in the piece, and wanted me to get him further into the painting, closer to the mausoleum.

"I resisted changing it, at first, because I had spent some time trying to come up with the design of the Bat-Crypt. I thought that I was going to lose all that if I just popped the Joker in. But he was right, he was dead right. The Bat-Crypt is not a stark and interesting enough image on its own.

"Getting the Joker, with his creepy grin, in there, and showing him pulling out one of his tools from the sack, a crowbar, I guess, getting ready to go and bust into the Bat-Crypt. . . . It's a much more interesting image."

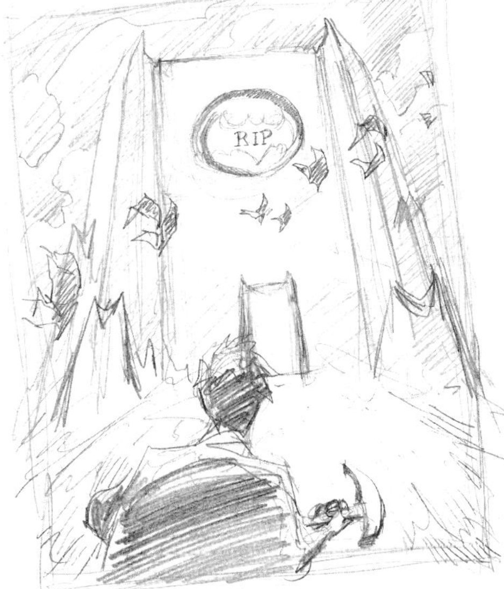
RIP

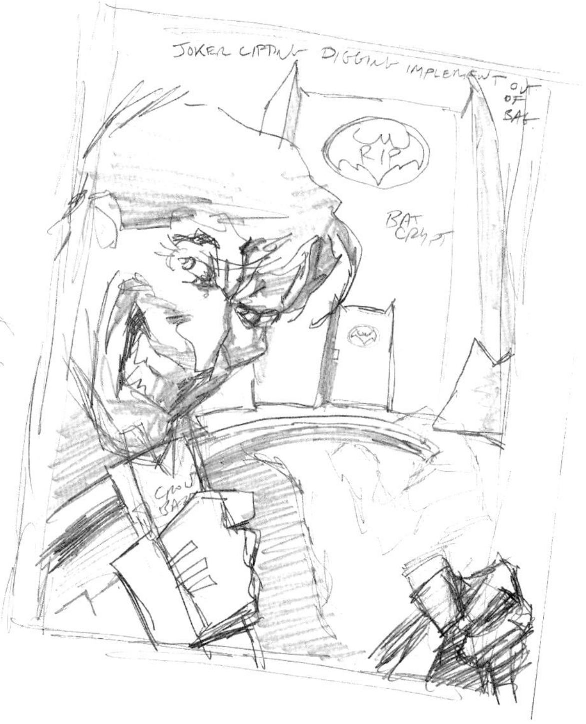
RIP
BAT CRYPT

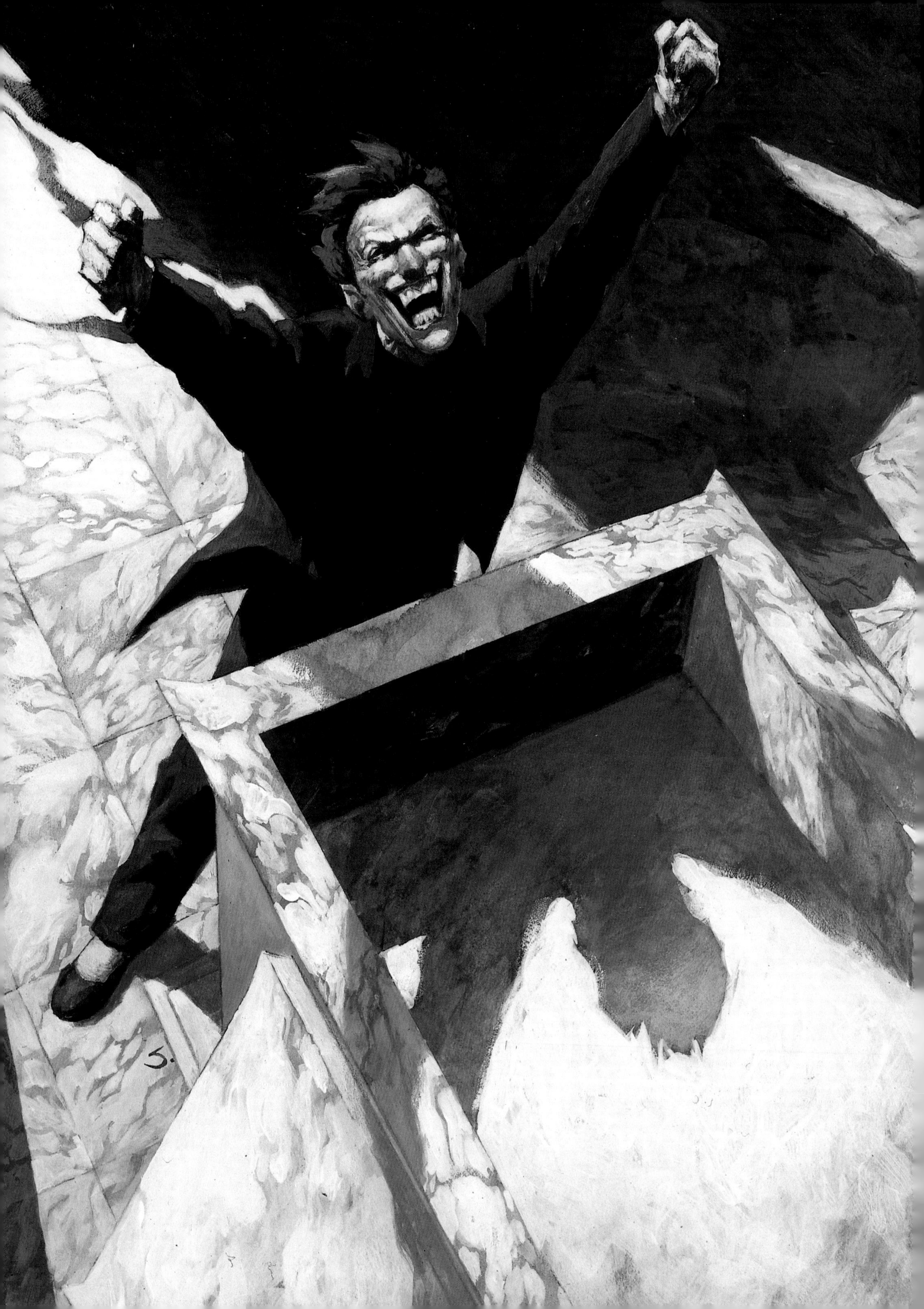

SHADOW OF THE BAT

"*Ahah!* Just as I *suspected!* I'm *not* going mad—mainly because I'm *already* mad, but I was *right* about not killing Bats! No body, no bones, no dust! His coffin is *empty!* It's nothing but—"

"Bait for a *trap,* Joker, and you've just *taken* it."

ART CONCEPT

Interior of Bat-Crypt with a dark coffin/catafalque on a dais in center of crypt; Joker has just lifted (or removed) the lid, revealing that the coffin is empty—and the shadow of the bat is falling on crypt wall or floor near/above/beyond Joker—prominent to us but unnoticed by Joker.

SCOTT HAMPTON'S SOLUTION

"I painted this card twice. It's a very similar shot, but the Joker is seen not so close up, and his head is down. The emphasis is on his green head of hair, and the hands going up. In both shots, he's basically saying 'YES! I knew I was right!' and is oblivious to the shadow creeping in.

"I had done the first painting, but it didn't show the face. Then I redid it, to show the face.

"The emphasis here is the look of satisfaction on the Joker's face, not on the empty sarcophagus—which is the key to the mystery. The Joker is happy that he didn't unknowingly kill Batman because he wants to *knowingly* kill him, and savor it for years to come."

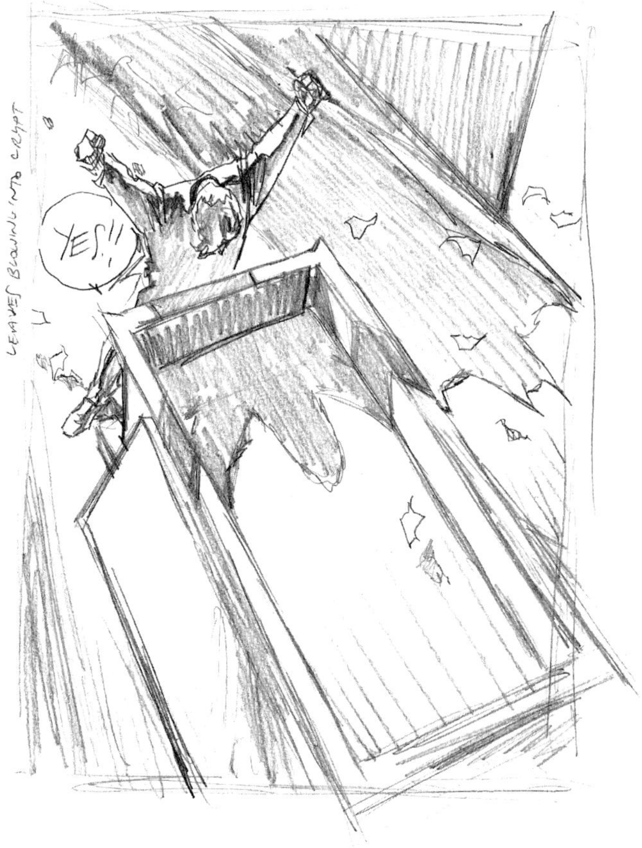
YES!!
LEAVES BLOWING INTO CRYPT

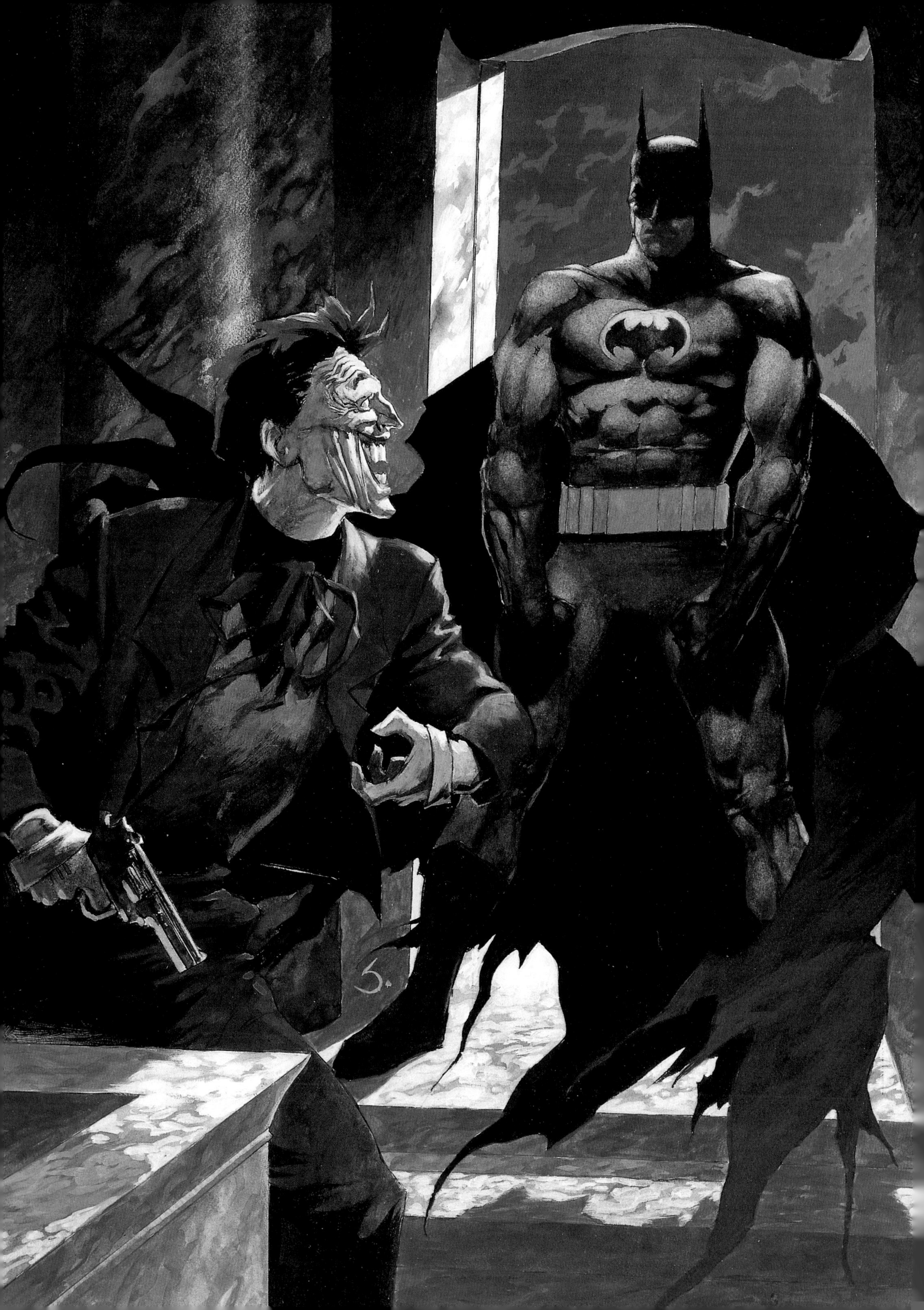

THE BAT IS DEAD, LONG LIVE THE BAT

"*Bats,* old buddy! You're *alive!* My life has *meaning* and *purpose* again! Thank the stars you're *not dead*—because now I can *really* kill you!"

"You get *one warning,* Joker. Don't *try* it. . . ."

ART CONCEPT

Interior Bat-Crypt; Joker spinning away from the empty coffin with his .45 automatic now in hand—to face (and point gun at) grim Batman, who stands blocking the path.

SCOTT HAMPTON'S SOLUTION

"This takes place seconds after the card before it. The Joker turns and sees Batman standing in the doorway. Still cackling with glee, the Joker is pulling out his gun. Stupidly cackling, because the Joker never wins for long. . . .

"This whole last sequence of eight images is the most like actual comic book storytelling in the whole card set. It's from moment to moment, some of them are within seconds of one another. To me, these are some of the most engaging images I did."

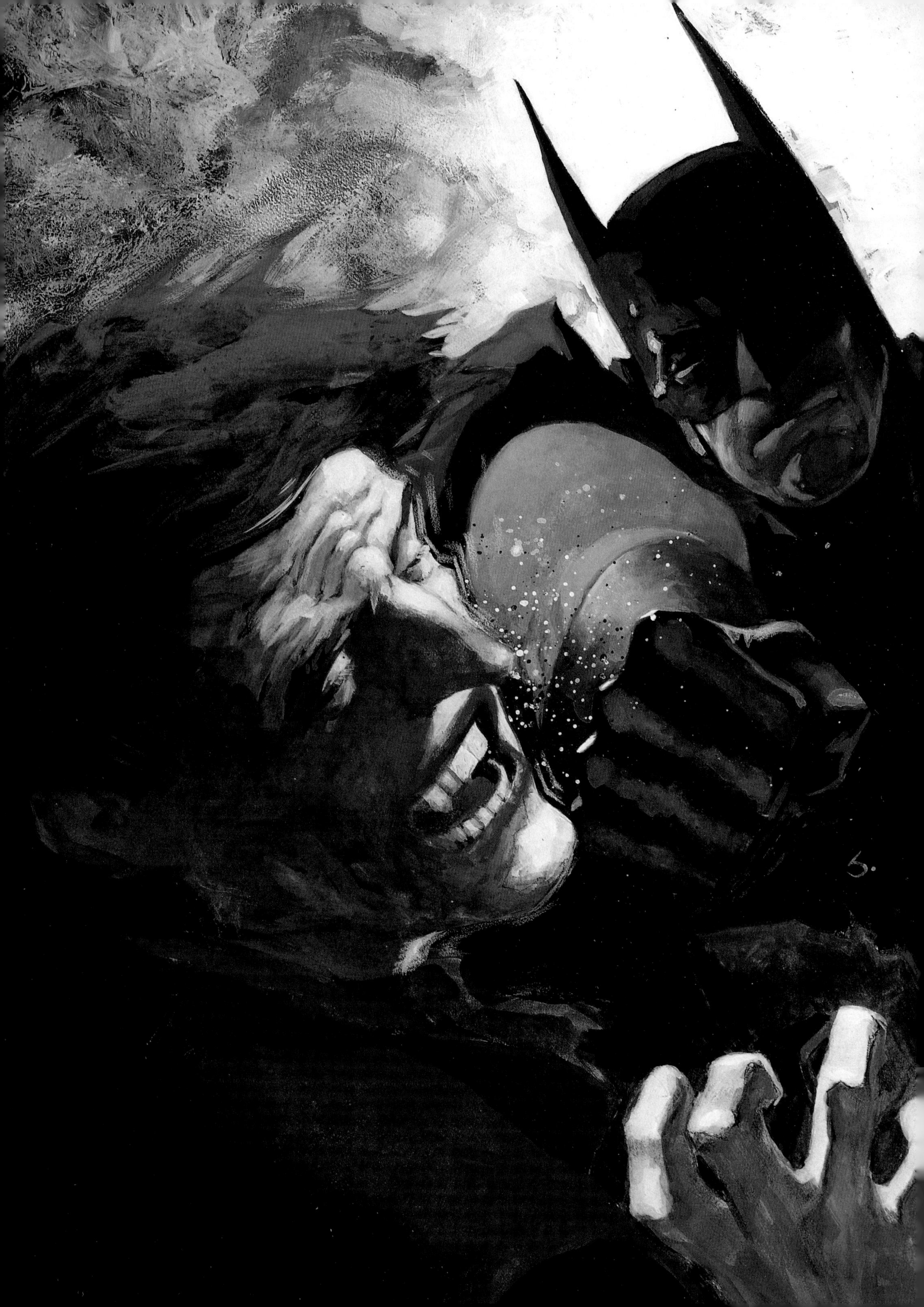

SNAPPED TRAP

Even as the Joker sweeps his .45 automatic up into firing position, a dark jagged blur rushes forward. The movements, too swift to see, are felt in rapid succession—a sharp pain in the wrist which sends the gun flying, followed by a shocking jolt to the face, catapulting the Joker's mind through a warped void of purple spinning lights. . . .

ART CONCEPT

Interior Bat-Crypt; Batman lunging forward & smashing a hard straight right into Joker's face; the .45 automatic is flying. . . .

SCOTT HAMPTON'S SOLUTION

"In the previous card, Batman was done in watercolor. In this one, Batman is done in acrylics and lots of opaques. It helped to convey the sense of Batman knocking the Joker, hitting him. You can barely see the gun falling out of the Joker's hand.

"Just doing a shot that was nothing but 'rock 'em—sock 'em' was kind of fun for me. It's the sort of thing that I often think is very obvious, and so I avoid it, but in this instance I felt like it was the only appropriate shot to follow up on the two previous images."

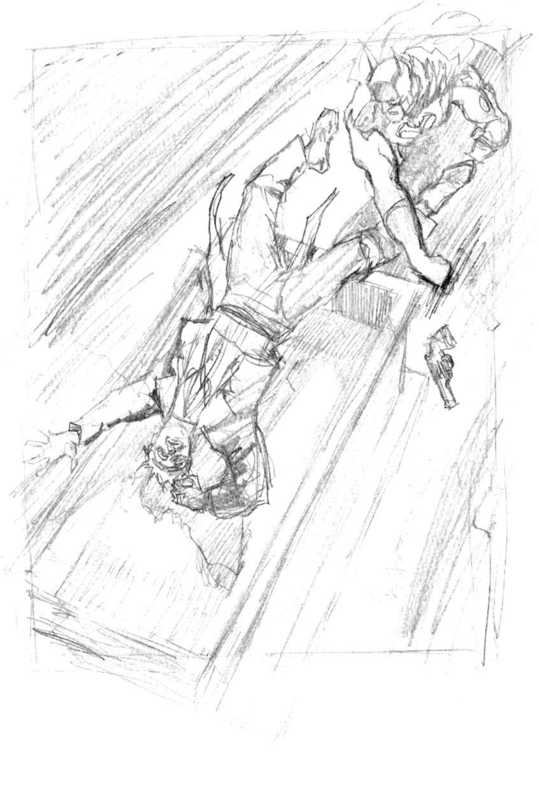

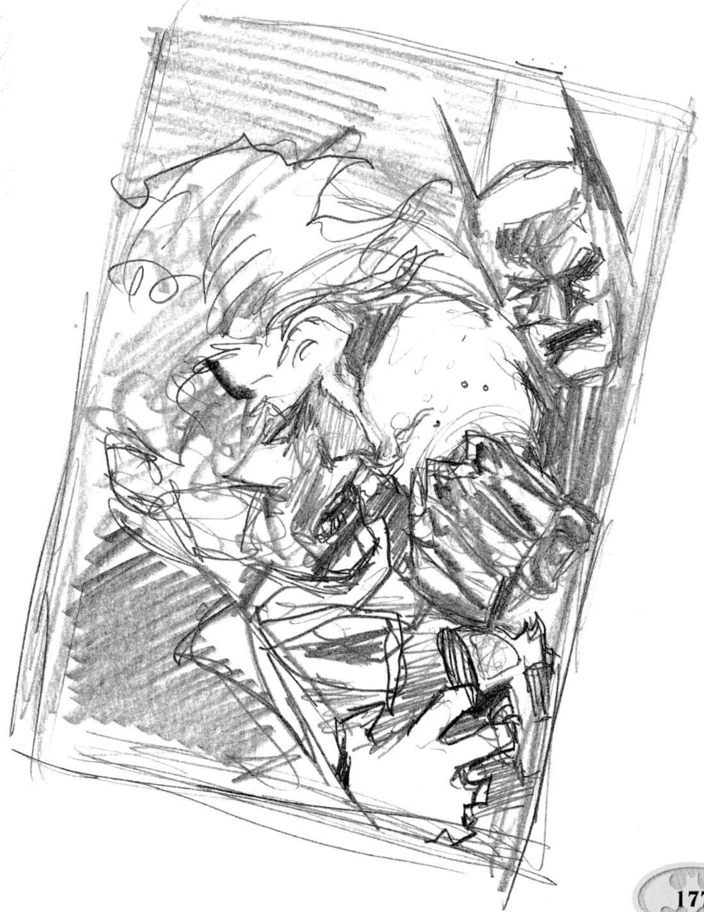

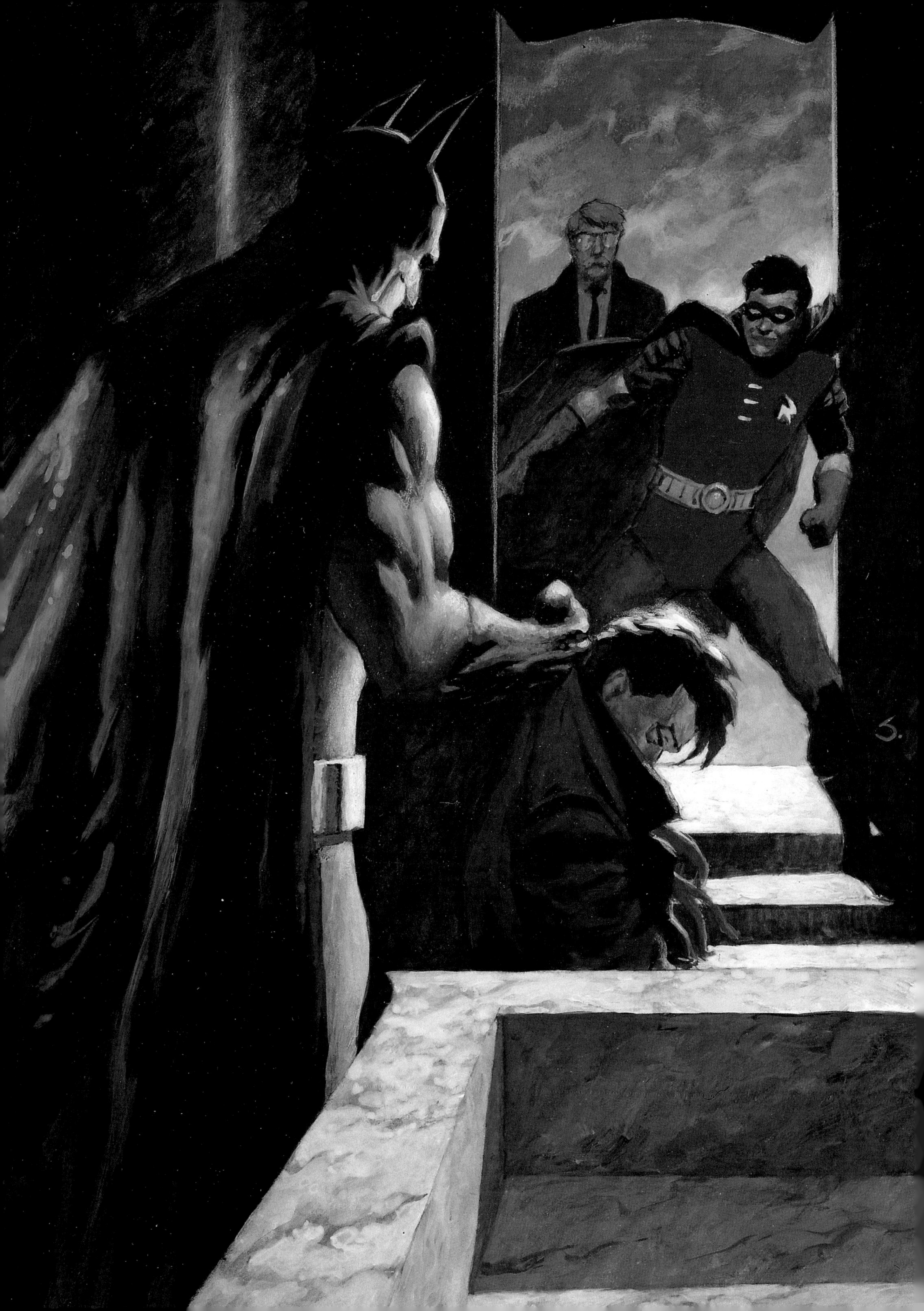

ACCOMPLICES

"Your trap *worked!* And it's a good thing you let Gordon in on your *plan*—because you really had us *worried,* man!"

"I couldn't take any chances, Robin, not with someone as dangerous as the Joker. My 'death' *had* to be convincing. Nothing else could occupy his warped mind and flush him from hiding before he harmed anyone."

"Except *himself.*"

ART CONCEPT

Interior Bat-Crypt; stunned & groggy Joker is on his hands & knees (or seat of his pants), with the shadow of the bat falling over/near him from offstage—as Robin (grinning) and Gordon (more reserved, but relieved & satisfied) rush in.

SCOTT HAMPTON'S SOLUTION

"Getting lots of characters to do things in paintings that are going to be used as trading cards is problematic. If you don't have decent reproduction, you can basically just say adios to any detailing or subtleties that you put into the paint.

"This card tells the story, which is the first thing that it needs to do. You can see what's going on, and tell what is happening. But compositionally, it's not very interesting or very dynamic. The Batdoor to the Bat-Crypt is dissecting the composition, which is never good. I would like to think that there was a different way to compose this piece, but with the spatial restraints. . . .

"When you bisect an image, there's no visual tension. It's too 'samey,' it's too pleasing to our sense of symmetry. And it's almost impossible to not have an image like that look . . . boring."

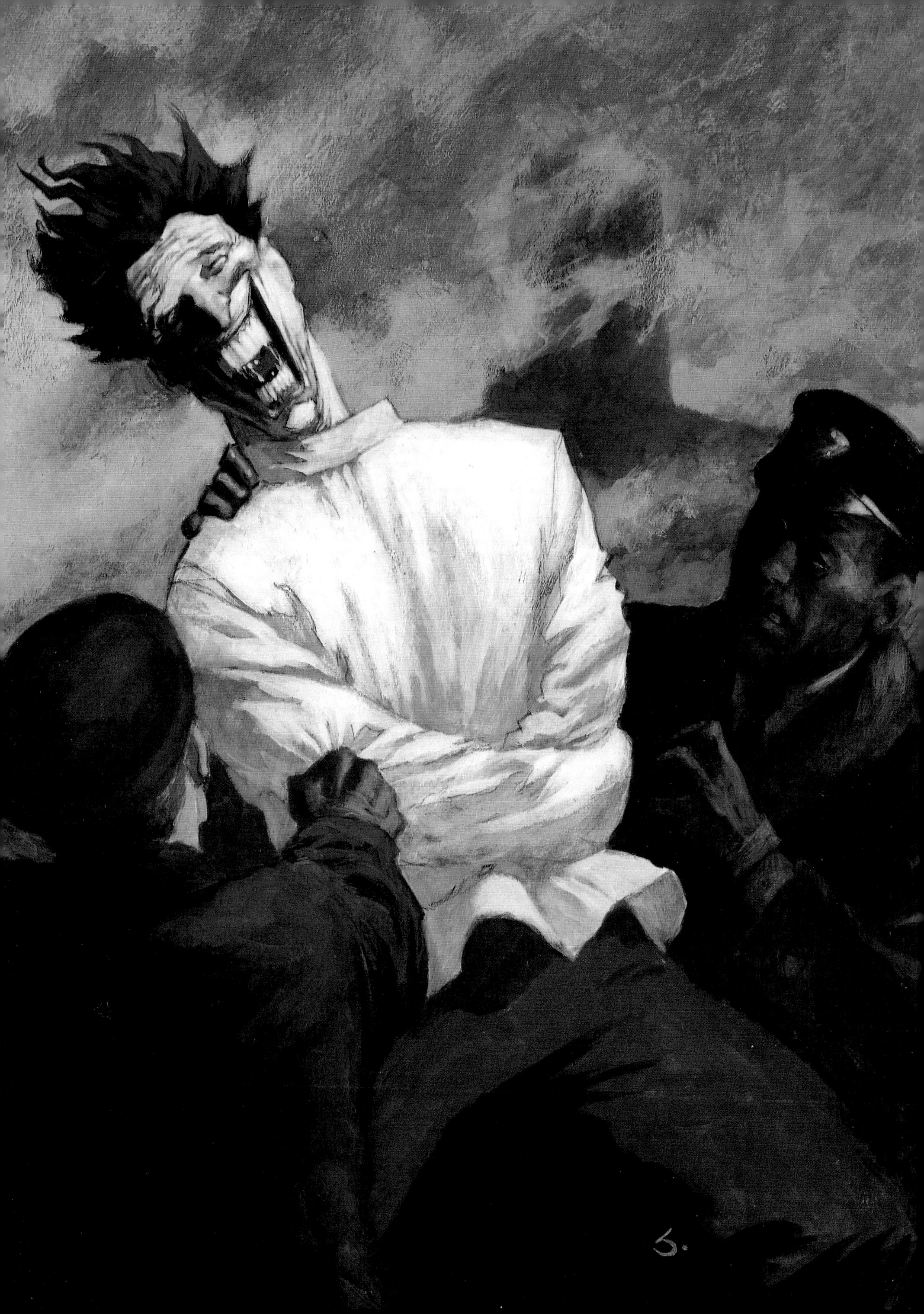
5.

BACK TO ARKHAM

"He's alive . . . he's *aliiive! HYEEHAHAHAHAHAAA!*"

Atop the monument to his own false passing, a dark figure watches as the maniacal laughter fades. Even then he remains perched on the crypt, surveying the silence of surrounding graves, wondering how many hold victims of madness and violence. No one new, anyway, not delivered by the hand of the Joker. . . .

ART CONCEPT

Exterior shot Gotham Cemetery; his cape whipping in the wind Batman is perched atop his crypt—as seen on the Shadow of the Bat card [page 173]—as two uniformed cops lead handcuffed & insanely laughing Joker toward a waiting squad car or paddy wagon.

SCOTT HAMPTON'S SOLUTION

"The Joker is in a straitjacket, howling with glee as they cart him away. He's howling with glee because he was right, and even though he was defeated, he knows that he—and Batman—will live to fight another day. And you can't really tell it, but the Bat-Crypt is looming in the background.

"I had not wanted the Bat-Crypt to command too much attention, but I think I went a little wild with my palette knife and obliterated the Bat-Crypt to the point that you can't quite tell what it is.

"I use almost no reference. Often I'm terribly lazy about reference. I paint out of my head, almost all the time. Luckily I've been doing this for a while, so it usually turns out okay.

"Dermot actually did some research, and came up with a real straitjacket. I didn't; decent reference shots for straitjackets were hard to come by. I knew, basically, that it was white and it wrapped around, and that was enough."

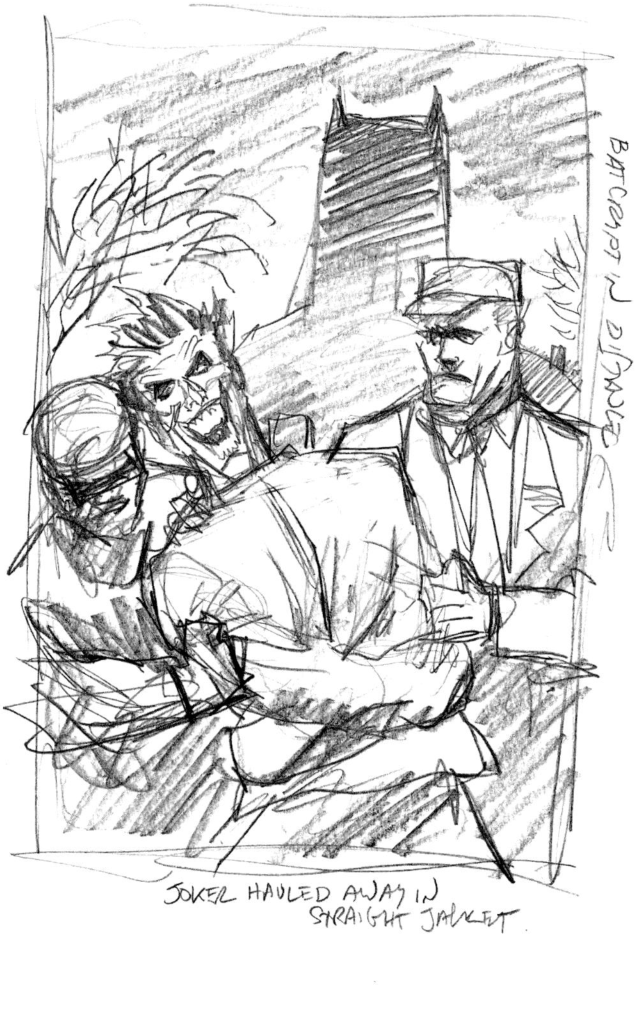
BATCRYPT IN DISTANCE
JOKER HAULED AWAY IN STRAIGHT JACKET

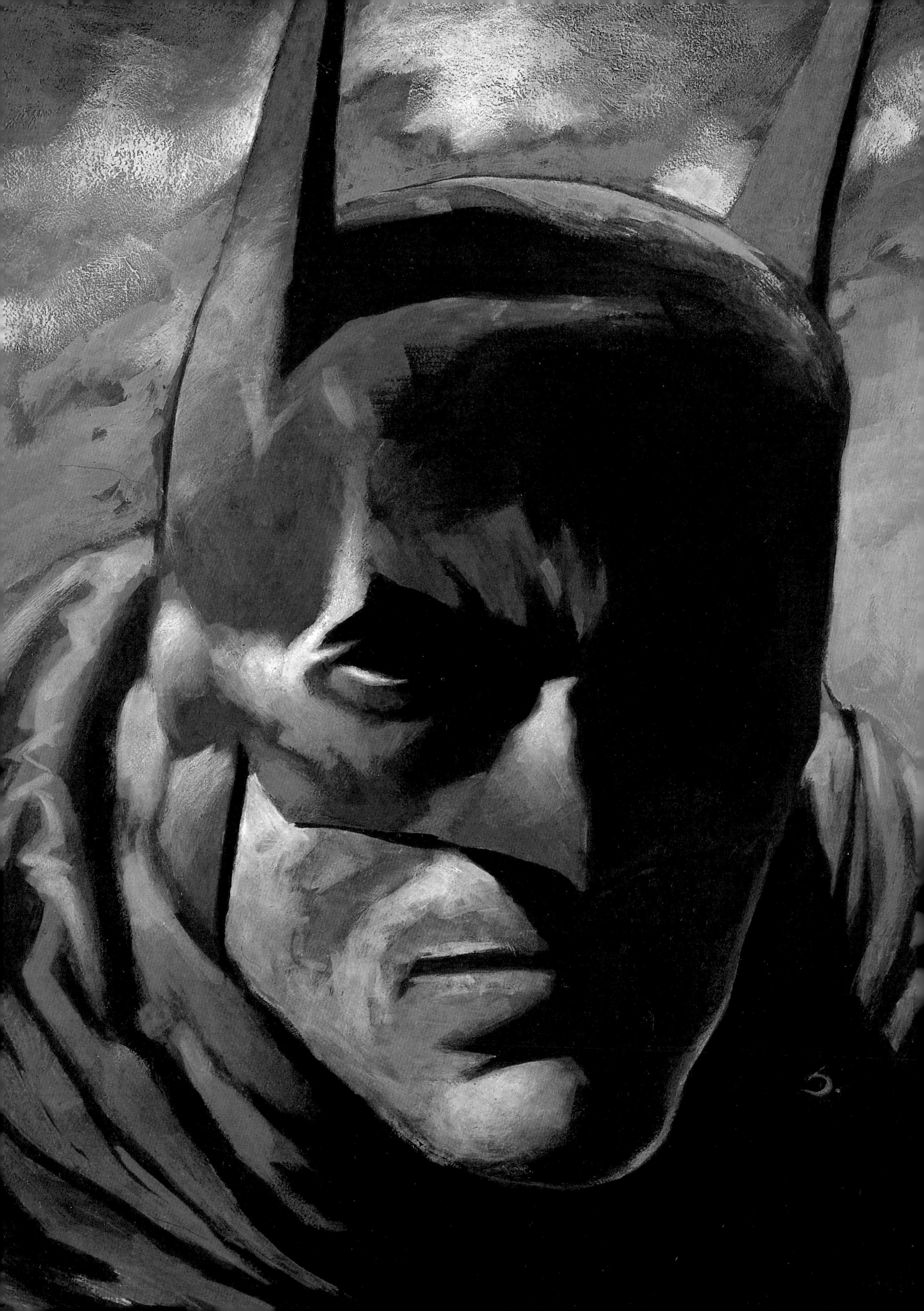

CREATURE OF THE NIGHT

He turns to the rising wind, his jaw set against its bracing rush, his face a mask of nocturnal menace, protector disguised as predator. Something gleams deep within his eyes: a spark of vitality, an awareness that he still lives, even here in this place of the dead. Then a distant shriek cuts the gloom, and his eyes narrow to kill all light. He rises to the terrible sound, knowing that his death, in the end, was *worth* it.

SCOTT HAMPTON'S SOLUTION

"We were playing with a lot of different ideas for this card. A big shot of his face was not among what anyone had suggested to me. But ultimately I argued, and the editors agreed, to go forward and let this be the last card—this shot of Batman, just his face.

"In the end, it's a final bit of punctuation, rather than just another scene. We had begun the set with the one card of Batman swinging into action, but the card where the story really begins was the card with the portrait of Joker. I wanted to book-end the set, and I got to do a real close-up shot of Batman, which you haven't seen all set.

"You can get some of the subtleties with what's going on with the flesh tones in the card. The way I paint, especially when I get a chance to do something like this, where I can really go nuts with some areas of paint, is that I like to work a lot of color in, and then manipulate it. That's what I'm doing with the flesh that you can see of his face.

"What everyone had expected was a final shot, with everything being dismantled, flying over the mausoleum or something. But for my money, this is better."

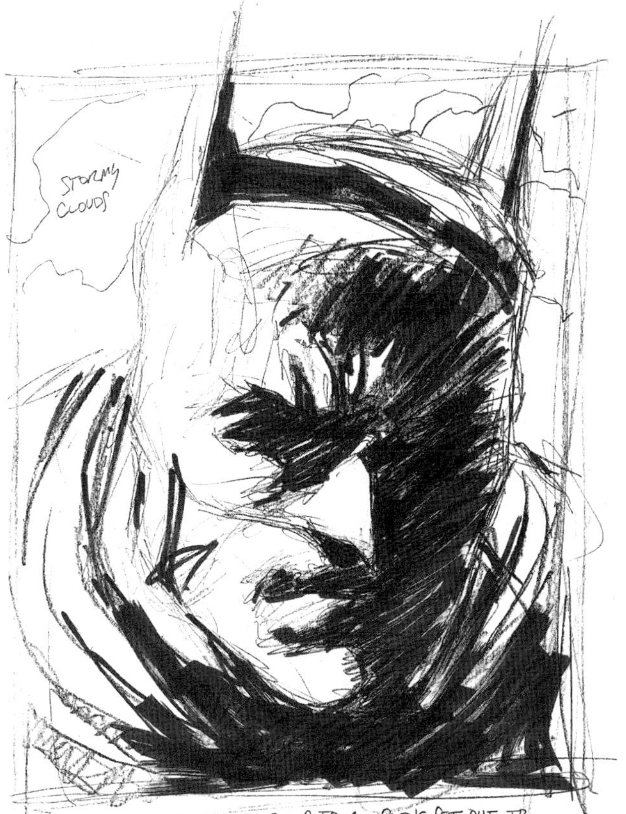
STORMY CLOUDS

PORTRAIT OF BATS TO CLOSE THE SET OUT TO BALANCE PORTRAIT OF JOKER THAT OPENS IT.

THE ULTIMATE CHASE CARDS

After the story was completed, Fleer, the card set manufacturer, made a request: They wanted more.

"We had to come up with 'chase' cards," Larry Daley explains. "The idea is to randomly insert them into packs, so that people will go after them to complete their collections." Indeed, chase cards are the brass rings of trading cards: To find one is akin to winning the lottery. Since they are rarer, they usually come with bells and whistles such as chrome finishes, thicker stock, or even holographic reproductions.

Daley is quick to point out that the chase cards had to fit with the overall concept: "Editorially, we tried to make them fit into the set. We had wanted the tone of the story to be about characters reflecting on what Batman meant to them, what impact he'd had on their lives. With the Master Villains chase cards, we asked Doug Moench, 'How would these villains kill the Batman?' This gave Doug the opportunity to play with the characters—I think he really captured the voice of each villain."

A second subset of chase cards was dedicated to an entirely different vision of Batman. "With the fantasy set," recalls Daley, "we approached illustrators who don't normally work on Batman and asked them to come up with their personal interpretation of the character."

HOW WOULD THE MASTER VILLAINS KILL BATMAN?

Black Mask

Two-Face

Catwoman

The Riddler

The Penguin

Poison Ivy

Rā's al Ghūl

Scarecrow

Bane

The Joker

BATMAN AS A FANTASY CHARACTER

Ken Kelly

Vincent Di Fate

Joe DeVito

Romas

Nick Jainschigg

James Warhola

BLACK MASK
Horley/Parente Studio

BLACK MASK, HOW WOULD YOU HAVE KILLED THE BATMAN?

"By exposing the man *behind the mask*. Depending on the nature and identity of that man, I might kill him in any number of ways. I might flay his face. I might wrap his head in transparent, smothering plastic. A shotgun blast to the face is always effective. I might even *return his mask*—after first filling it with a special *poison* absorbed through the *pores. . . .*"

DOUG MOENCH ON BLACK MASK

"Black Mask is a character that I created in 1984. He is, in a way, the dark side of Batman. He had a similar upbringing, and his parents died when he was young. However, he himself set the fire that burned their house down and killed them.

"Black Mask is obsessed with the power of the mask. Members of his gang wear different ritual masks to protect their identities; he also controls his henchmen through them.

"He's based on a 1940's pulp character, and that's where he got that sort of fortyish double-breasted gangster suit. I thought that we needed a film-noir type of villain in Batman."

ARTISTS' COMMENTS:

"Black Mask was the only character I was supposed to paint that I didn't know," recalls Paolo Parente, of the Milan-based Horley/Parente Studio. "I was totally unfamiliar with him. The editor sent us references, including Dermot Power's Black Mask card. I saw a guy looking like a gangster, so I decided to sketch a pose where he fired a machine gun. This was the one character that I didn't know anything about, so the only thing I could think of doing with him was to put him in action.

"I didn't want the mask to be black, so I made it bluish; the rest of the card was done in bright warm colors to go with the gunfire."

TWO-FACE
HORLEY/PARENTE STUDIO

TWO-FACE, HOW WOULD YOU HAVE KILLED THE BATMAN?

"Such severe punishment must be meted judiciously, and only after the due process of a *trial.* . . . Which reminds us . . . we have this coin, a very *special* coin, both sides heads, no tails, one side pristine, the other scarred beyond recognition. Before executing the Batman, we would have to *flip* this coin . . . one side *life,* the other *death* . . . and let *fate* guide the verdict."

DOUG MOENCH ON TWO-FACE

"Two-Face is former Gotham City District Attorney Harvey Dent, who was borderline psychotic to begin with. After a crime boss threw acid in his face, Harvey went to the other side.

"As Two-Face, he flips a coin with a scarred face and a pristine one to apply his twisted form of judgment. If the scarred side comes up, then he commits a crime. In effect, the coin becomes judge, jury, and executioner."

ARTISTS' COMMENTS

"I think that every Batman villain represents Batman's dark side," chuckles Alex Horley, "and they complement him. That's why I like Two-Face: he leaves his dark side free.

"I also like the fact that he uses a coin, so in some way he leaves it to God to decide what to do to his enemies."

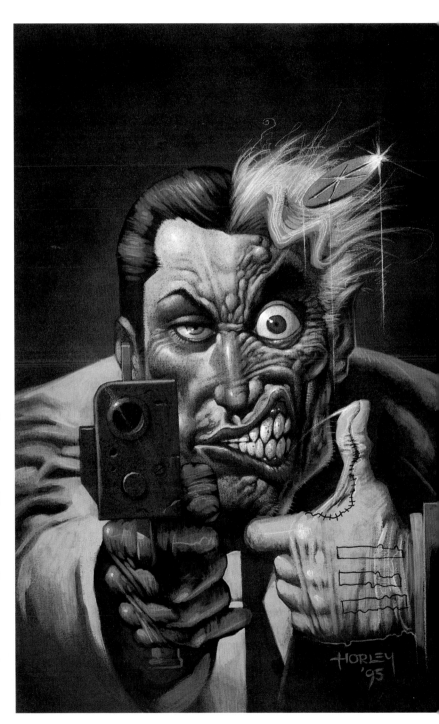

CATWOMAN
HORLEY/PARENTE STUDIO

CATWOMAN, HOW WOULD YOU HAVE KILLED THE BATMAN?

"*I wouldn't.* I'd pick him clean of everything he had, including his heart and mind, but I would never eliminate him. I'm a *cat-burglar,* not a killer, and I've never murdered anyone, nor would I, least of all him. Without the Batman, the night just isn't the same. It may pose less menace for me personally, but it also loses all *magic* and *mystery.*"

DOUG MOENCH ON CATWOMAN

"Catwoman is Selina Kyle. After her mother committed suicide and her father pretty much drank himself to death, she walked out into the night and found a way to survive.

"Eventually, she was captured while shoplifting. She was sent away to a Dickensian orphanage where she was mistreated. Upon escaping, Selina vowed to never again be subjected to anyone else, to always be independent and survive on her own.

"Catwoman is obsessed with the other creature of Gotham's night—Batman. I think that Batman is also obsessed with her, but he can't allow himself to admit she is the perfect woman for him."

ARTISTS' COMMENTS

"This one was painted and drawn by me," says Paolo Parente.

"I just inked the sketch," recalls Alex Horley, "I like this card. I think it has good coloring."

"Catwoman was very difficult," Parente continues. "We had to submit something like ten sketches before getting one approved. I really loved the costume from the movie *Batman Returns,* but it's extremely different from the one in the comic books. I tried to mix the two, but it didn't work out. Then the poses were too aggressive, she was too muscular, not feminine enough.

"In the end, I came up with a composition that was dramatic and powerful, full of energy, and it worked."

THE RIDDLER
HORLEY/PARENTE STUDIO

RIDDLER, HOW WOULD YOU HAVE KILLED THE BATMAN?

"With immense pleasure, believe you me. I'd have to work it so that all of Gotham would be mystified by the ingenious fatal foreplay—there would probably be some sort of *ransom* involved—and Batman's actual death, of course, would have to be choreographed with painstaking precision, so as to provide the perfect punch line to the most regal riddle ever rendered."

DOUG MOENCH ON THE RIDDLER

"The Riddler's raison d'être is to match wits with the Batman. To that end, he plans very complicated capers and then leaves clues for Batman to find; then he tries to pull off the caper before Batman gets there to stop him."

ARTISTS' COMMENTS

"The Riddler is a fun character, because he's so mean," explains Parente. "He was a little too muscular in my first sketch, so I made him thinner. He has this baseball pose, using his cane as a bat. It looks as though he's going to hit you in the face. I wanted to give him this funny face, sort of a grim grin. I really like this card."

THE PENGUIN
HORLEY/PARENTE STUDIO

PENGUIN, HOW WOULD YOU HAVE KILLED THE BATMAN?

"If I knew the answer to *that,* Batman would have fed the worms a *long time ago!* After trying everything from Trojan Penguins to Uzi Umbrellas, dive-bombing gulls to poison parasols, he just stood there time after time, smiling that grim little smile of his. Still, no matter how many times he may have bested me, I always knew that eventually, I'd have won in the end. . . ."

DOUG MOENCH ON THE PENGUIN

"Penguin is one of nature's mistakes. He was this little runty-looking guy who was mistreated as a child and jeered at by other kids. They also made fun of his name, Oswald Cobblepot, and of the way he walked like he was waddling, and so on. So that's how that started.

"He grew up with the overwhelming desire to prove himself and he became obsessed with birds in general, and penguins in particular."

ARTISTS' COMMENTS

"This was the card that was the most fun. I mean, I *love* the Penguin," says Horley. "I really tried to make this image a good mixture between the comic book and the movie version of the Penguin, and it worked. He's really mean and he makes these extremely bad jokes with a smile on his face. So I imagined him throwing a grenade to kids playing catch. He has a big smile on his face because he doesn't care.

"The funniest things on the card are the little toys hanging from the umbrella, like the caricature of Batman. Those were fun to work on."

POISON IVY

HORLEY/PARENTE STUDIO

POISON IVY, HOW WOULD YOU HAVE KILLED THE BATMAN?

"With a *kiss,* of course. Just as the Midas Touch turned everything to gold, *my* toxic touch brings *death.* A brush of our lips and his heart would race, fever would inflame his blood, sweat would burst from his brow, his mind would swoon, his muscles would contract, his swelling tongue would choke his throat . . . and when the kiss was *broken,* he would fall *conquered at my feet.*"

DOUG MOENCH ON POISON IVY

"Pamela Isley was a botanist who did experiments with plants; somehow she acquired a toxic touch from plants. She uses various spores and aromas to attract men (mainly Batman), put them under her spell, and use them for various things. Poison Ivy's kiss is lethal: if she kisses you, you are dead."

ARTISTS' COMMENTS

"I painted this one twice," remembers Parente. "The first time around, I was really insecure. I used too much airbrush on her skin and on her costume in order to have this smooth, very feminine effect. Since she's going to kiss you, I wanted to make sure that she was quite charming, inviting, demure. She's cute."

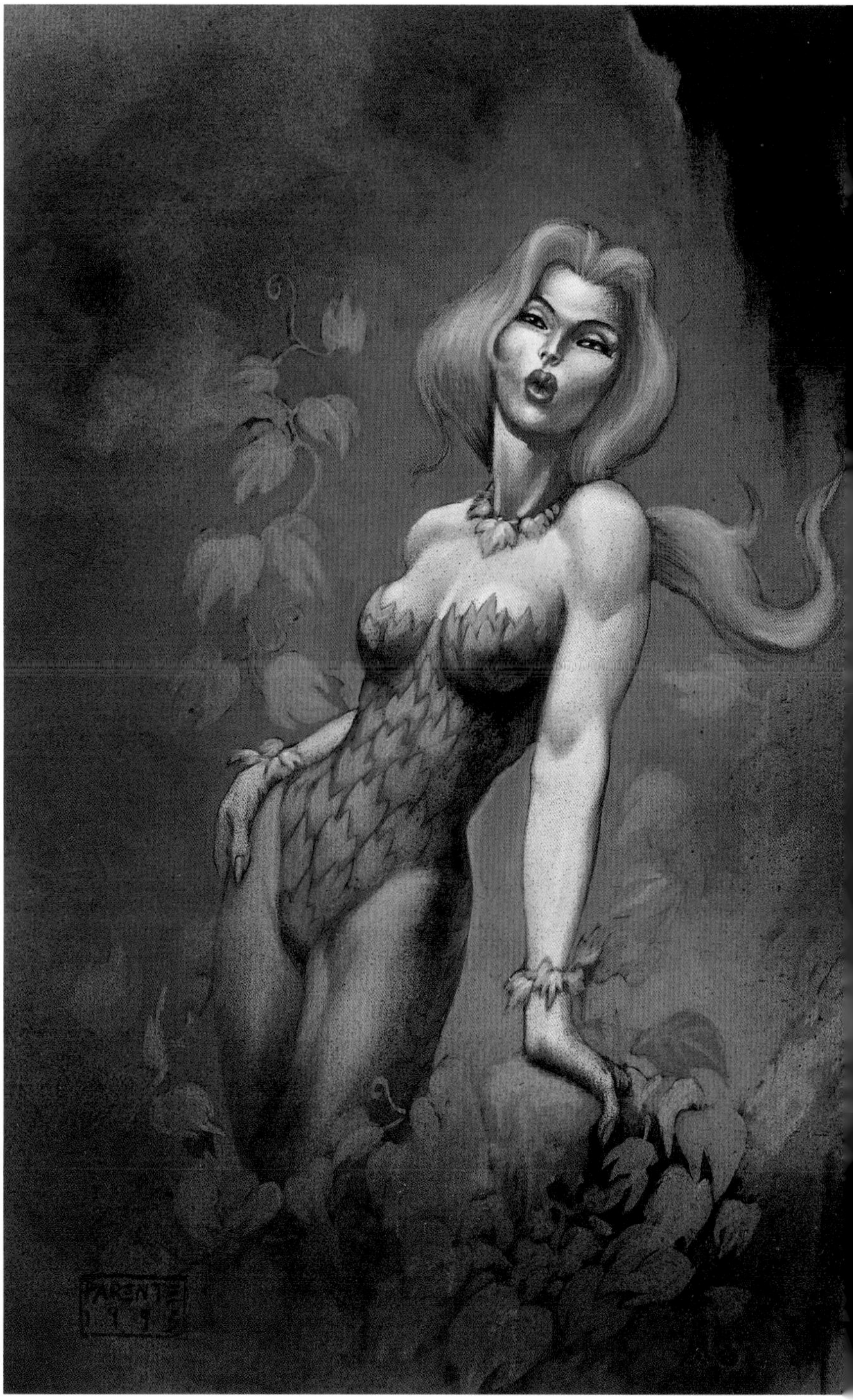
PARENTE

RĀ'S AL GHŪL
HORLEY/PARENTE STUDIO

RĀ'S AL GHŪL, HOW WOULD YOU HAVE KILLED THE BATMAN?

"The truce between us would perforce be broken, no doubt at *my* whim. Were that to happen, I would give the Detective one last chance—to wed my daughter, sire my heir, and join me in reshaping the world. Only when he refused, as he has in the past, would I end his existence, probably with my bare hands—as a demonstration for my League of Assassins."

DOUG MOENCH ON RĀ'S AL GHŪL

"Rā's al Ghūl is a guy who is convinced that the world is a mess and needs to be changed. Where he goes wrong is that he feels that he knows better than everyone else how to change it. To that end, he does all kinds of nefarious things. He is Batman's one, or at least main, globe-spanning opponent, the one who is concerned with the world as a whole, rather than just confined to Gotham.

"Rā's al Ghūl respects Batman and considers him the only man worthy of his daughter Talia. He has actually tried to get Batman to sire an heir with his daughter."

ARTIST'S COMMENTS

"This is a character that I really didn't know very well, but Rā's al Ghūl turned out to be a real pain!" exclaims Parente. "The way I sketched him, he kept looking too much like another character entirely. I had to change it— but I thought that he looked far more evil in the beginning!"

SCARECROW

HORLEY/PARENTE STUDIO

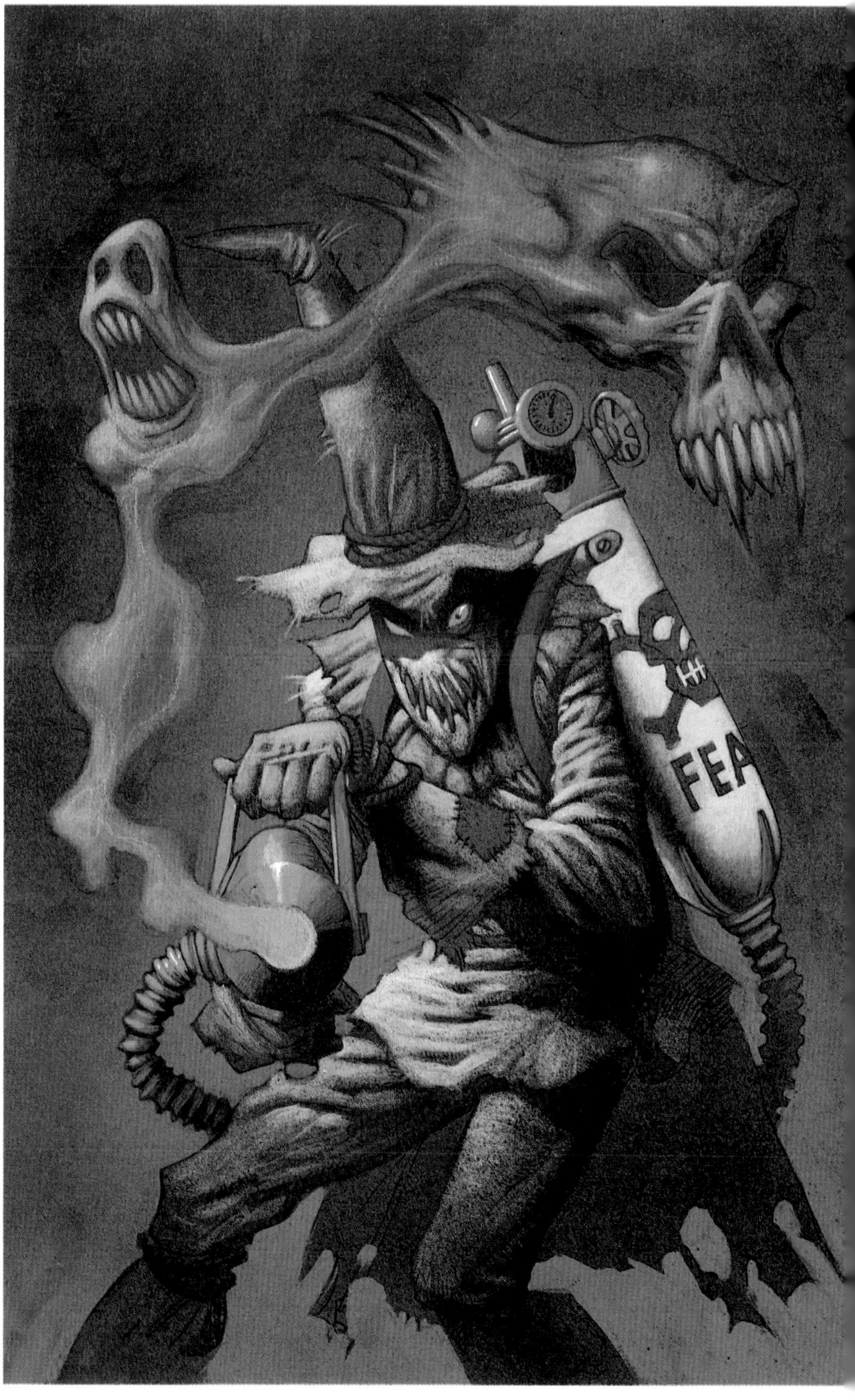
FEA

SCARECROW, HOW WOULD YOU HAVE KILLED THE BATMAN?

"Not with something so crude as *bullets in the back*. My philosophy of fear relies on hallucinations of more *primal* phobias—hookworms feeding on your brain, a clammy caress in a pitch-black room, midnight giggles and sobs from under your bucking bed, blindness caused by writhing maggots bursting from your eyeballs—real *screaming jeebies* to stop the Batman's *heart cold*."

DOUG MOENCH ON SCARECROW

"Scarecrow's real name is Jonathan Crane. As a child, he read the legend of Sleepy Hollow and noticed the similarities between himself and Ichabod Crane. He was ridiculed and terrorized by the other kids because he was weird, tall, and geeky looking.

"Sick of being frightened by others, he decided to become the master of fear. He took chemistry classes in college and developed a gas that terrifies people, giving them visions of what they fear the most."

ARTISTS' COMMENTS

"The Scarecrow was drawn by me," says Parente, "and painted by Alex. I was very happy that they agreed to this sketch, because I wanted to portray the Scarecrow in an unusual way. He usually uses those little things to spray his victims, and I thought, 'that's no fun!'"

"We equipped him with this huge gas tank," Horley recalls. "Scarecrow's very visual. He's skinny and he's trying to scare you with a chemical monster. It's funny."

"We decided that Alex should paint this card," Parente remarks, "and he did a great job. I loved the way he did it."

BANE

Horley/Parente Studio

BANE, HOW WOULD YOU HAVE KILLED THE BATMAN?

"I thought I did *worse* than kill him: I snapped his *back* and left him a *helpless cripple.* His spirit should have been *crushed* when I broke his body, but somehow he survived. Somehow he recovered. Somehow he *returned*—stronger and more indomitable than *before.* I *defeated* him, you hear me—but *still* he haunts my *nightmares!* With another chance at him, I would not stop until his *heart ceased to beat!*"

DOUG MOENCH ON BANE

"Bane was born in prison on the (imaginary) island of Santa Prisca. He got his hands on a drug called Venom, which is a combination of steroids and speed. He mainlines it straight into his cerebral vortex, through tubes feeding into holes in the back of his skull. When he pumps Venom into his brain, he becomes a fighting machine."

ARTISTS' COMMENTS

"I like Bane just because he's huge and I like to paint huge muscles," says Horley. "I like huge bad guys. I like Lobo for that reason."

"Alex used colored pencils on this painting," recalls Parente, "as well as on the Penguin and Two-Face. Colored pencils are good for creating textures and for details. Sometimes, you want to add some more color, or a different shade, and it's faster to do it with pencils. They work with acrylics beautifully."

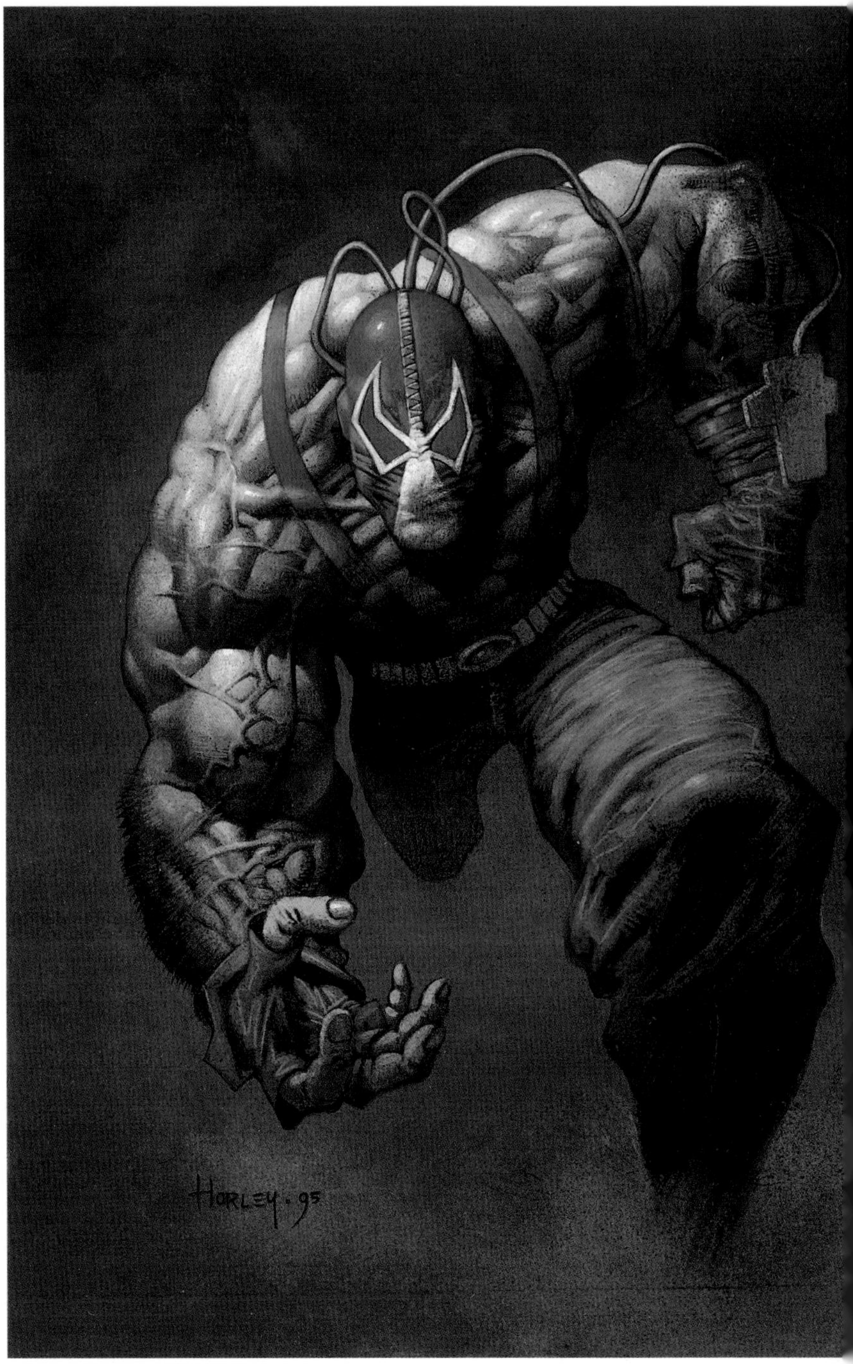
HORLEY · 95

THE JOKER
HORLEY/PARENTE STUDIO

JOKER, HOW WOULD YOU HAVE KILLED THE BATMAN?

"Surely you *jest!* They're all saying I *did* kill him! After all, who *else* could have snuffed Bats? Wait a minute—this isn't some sort of *trick,* is it? A way to convince me that I *didn't* kill him—or worse a way to make me *confess* that I did? Well, it won't *work,* you *hear* me? Somebody *blasted Bats* and you can't tell me I *didn't*—even if he *did* slap me back in *Arkham! HYAHAHAHAHAAA!!"*

DOUG MOENCH ON THE JOKER

"I think the Joker probably is the best of the Batman villains. He certainly has the best look of any of them.

"He is simultaneously funny and chilling, very scary and also very absurd. It's vital that you have both, you've got to balance the two things. And obviously, the Joker is completely insane.

"The Joker would be the one villain most capable of actually killing Batman, because his combination of insanity, comedy, and terror makes him completely unpredictable. He's the one guy Batman can never anticipate; you never know what he's going to do next, and that's what makes him dangerous."

ARTISTS' COMMENTS

"I think the Joker works pretty well in this painting, even if his skin is a little bit too dark," says Horley. "The skin is a little bit too blue. In the comics, it's white, but white is too flat a color. I like volume and shapes, so I tried to interpret what white is.

"I like the character because he is kind of the dark side of Batman; Batman hates him, I think, because he sees a lot of himself in the Joker. I think the Batman villains are the most complex of all comic book villains."

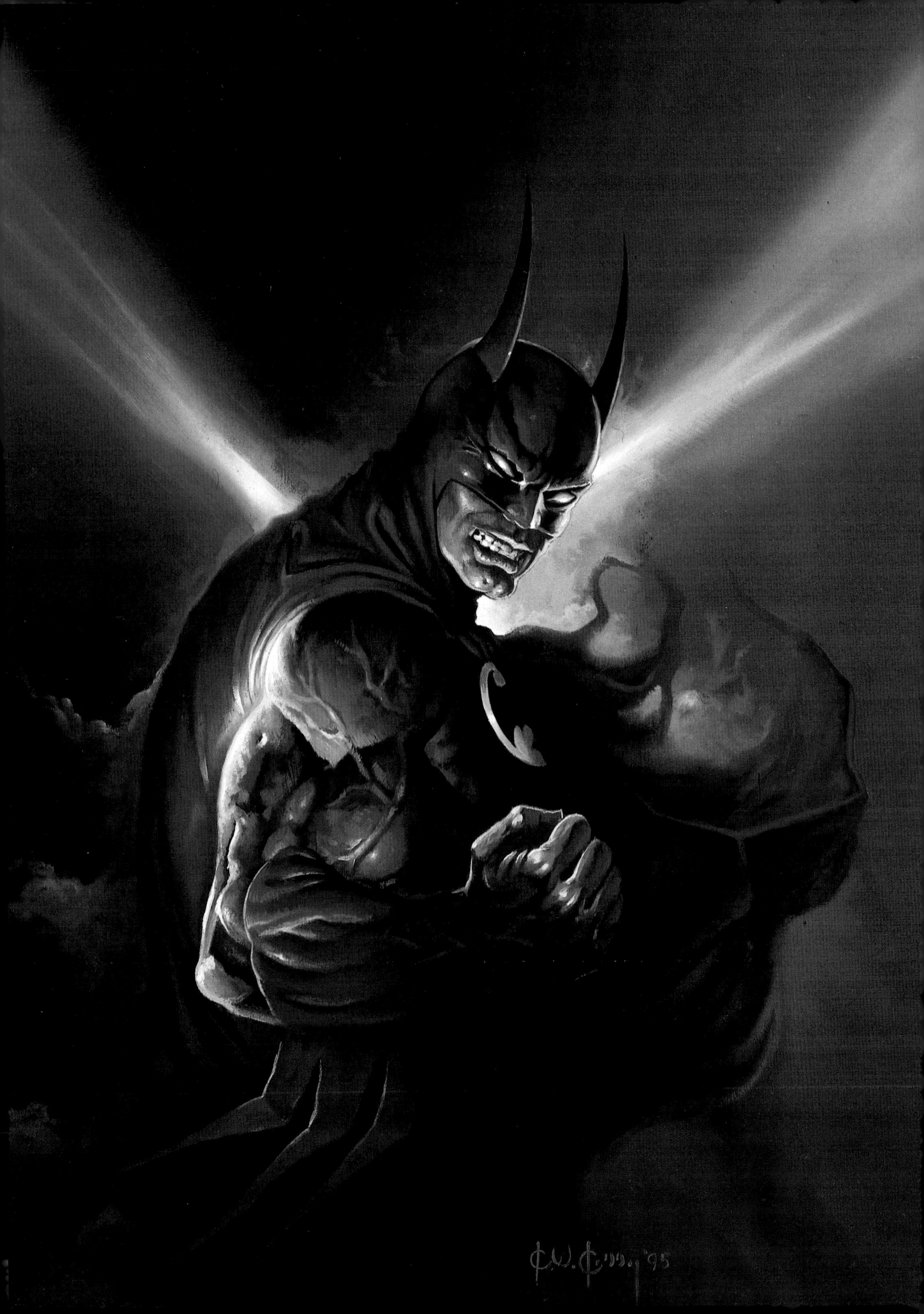

For Ken Kelly, the biggest problem that artists have with oil painting isn't technique. It's patience.

"A lot of people are frustrated by the first few days of oil painting, and they quit. The first two days you spend on an oil painting. . . . It looks like hell. It looks like a six-year-old is messing with paint. You have to just mentally keep going and get past that very rough stage, until you start seeing what's to be, when some of the colors are starting to blend, and you're getting what you want."

Kelly's first step is a thumbnail. "I used to do a color rough, and I would if it's requested, but if it's not requested, I don't.

"You see the illustration in your mind, and it's usually very correct, and very exciting. Then you have to transfer it to paper. What you're concentrating on in that first thumbnail sketch is getting what you have in your head down on paper as best you can. You're trying to catch that spontaneous explosion in your brain. This is where the painting comes from, everything else is building on those blocks.

"I go from the thumbnail sketch to as finished a sketch as I need. Then I put it on transparency paper, and transfer it with an opaque projector onto the Masonite board.

"Once it's on the board, I go over the lines with permanent marker, so that when you get to your turpentine and the first coat of oil, and you soak the board down, it doesn't wash away and you're left looking at a blank board, having to do it all over again.

"Once that dries, I start building with paints. Yellows, reds, blues, blacks. I have no rhyme nor reason to the order that I put my colors down. It doesn't matter if you start with the lighter or the darker colors first. What matters is that you stick to it, and that you finish."

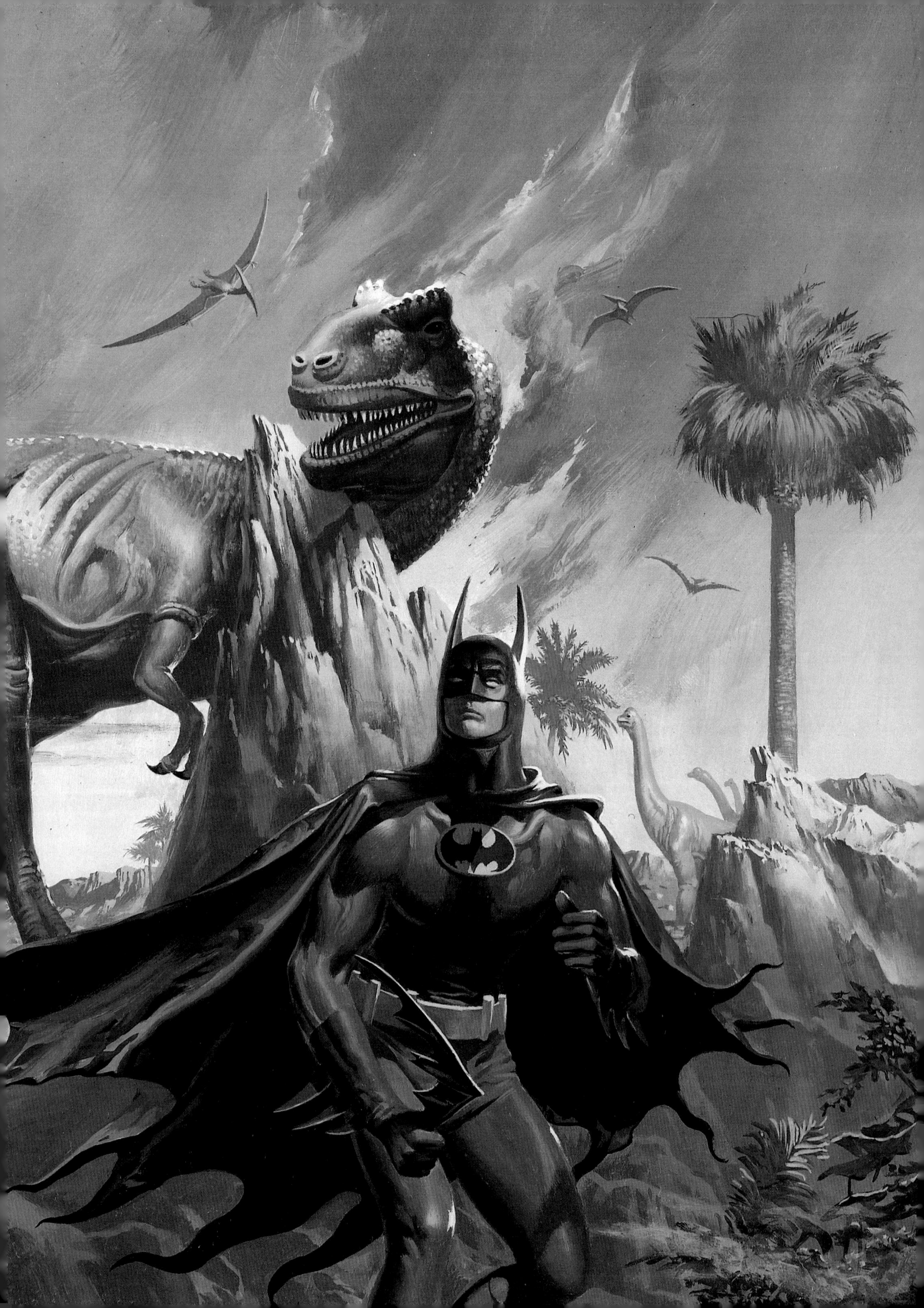

VINCENT DI FATE

Vincent Di Fate's career spans over three decades.

"I've done about three thousand professionally-published book and magazine covers, as well as movie posters and so forth. I've done things for *National Geographic* and I've done a number of things for NASA. I've done virtually every novel ever written by Robert A. Heinlein, most of Arthur C. Clarke's work, a good deal of Frank Herbert's work, especially the *Dune* novels."

This assignment brought Di Fate back. "When I was a kid, I'd go with my older brother to the store and he'd buy up all the Superman comics. That was okay, though—that left me with Batman."

Di Fate starts with a thumbnail sketch and color rough, but doesn't rely on a "trace-off" (a tracing of the thumbnail onto the final board). "In the length of time that I've been working in the field and with the high volume of work that I've produced over that time, I've learned to paint in a variety of different methods that all somehow manage to resemble each other."

He paints on Masonite board "because it's sturdy" with an undercoating of gesso "which seals the surface. I do at least some minimal amount of drawing on the Masonite whether it's a quick pencil sketch or a finely-tuned pencil drawing, depending on the amount of time that I have and the nature of the subject matter."

Di Fate paints in both oils and acrylics, although the Batman card was done exclusively in acrylics. "With acrylics, because of the fast drying, you create the illusion of halftone, mostly by dry brush or glazing. But they're not as flexible as oils."

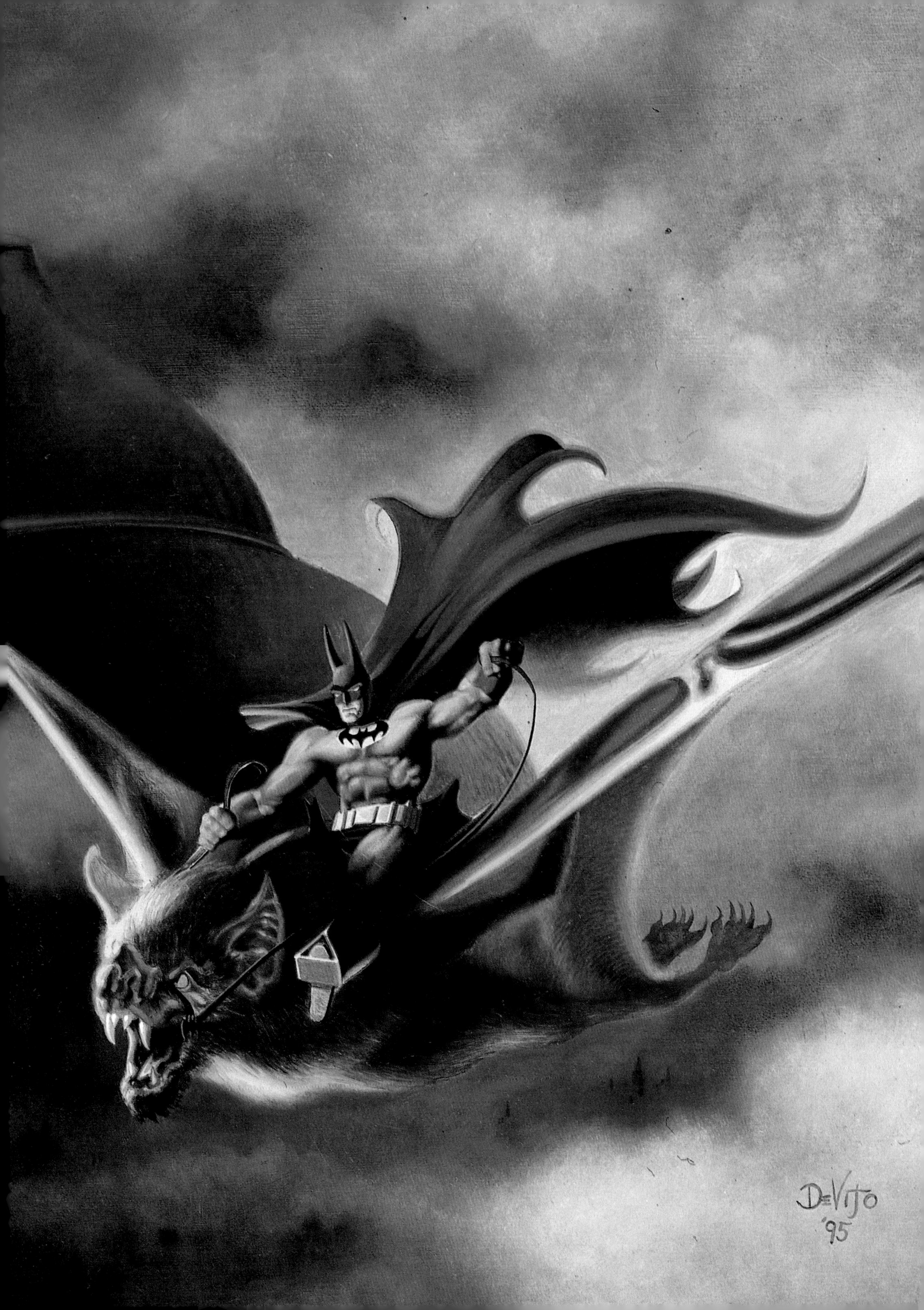
DEVITO
'95

JOE DEVITO

Being technically proficient isn't the only important thing to Joe DeVito.

"There's a big difference between being able to render something, and being able to create a picture. It's up to the artist to make the viewer look where he wants the viewer to look, because the artist is telling the story. It's not an arbitrary thing."

DeVito knows of what he speaks. "I've worked in many subject areas, though mainly science fiction/fantasy, horror, and comics. I was the last one to work on the Doc Savage *Man of Bronze* paperback series. Doc was the prototypical super hero.

"My oil painting technique is basically a traditional one, using hand and brush. I do thumbnail sketches to establish a concept and a composition. I then transfer that drawing to my board. Before painting, I always do a small color sketch to establish color, value, and edge relationships. Once those are done, I'll gather reference and I will do a finished drawing, just to get my outlines and proportions correct. And I transfer that to my board, do a color sketch. And then I'll paint."

All the while, DeVito is conscious of where he wants the viewer's eye to travel. "The way you do that is through the controlled and skillful use of opposites. With this painting, the whole background is monochromatic, somewhat on the cool side, and more or less blurry. The bat itself is warm, so it stands off against the cool background. In addition, the sharp rim lighting, a very hard and intense yellow, and a very warm color, stands out against the blurry cool blue behind it. This contrast draws your eye to Batman and the bat rather than letting it wander aimlessly around the painting. The picture itself is simple to look at because it was composed that way. Had the clouds been more detailed and the city beneath more highly focused, it would have been much more confusing to look at."

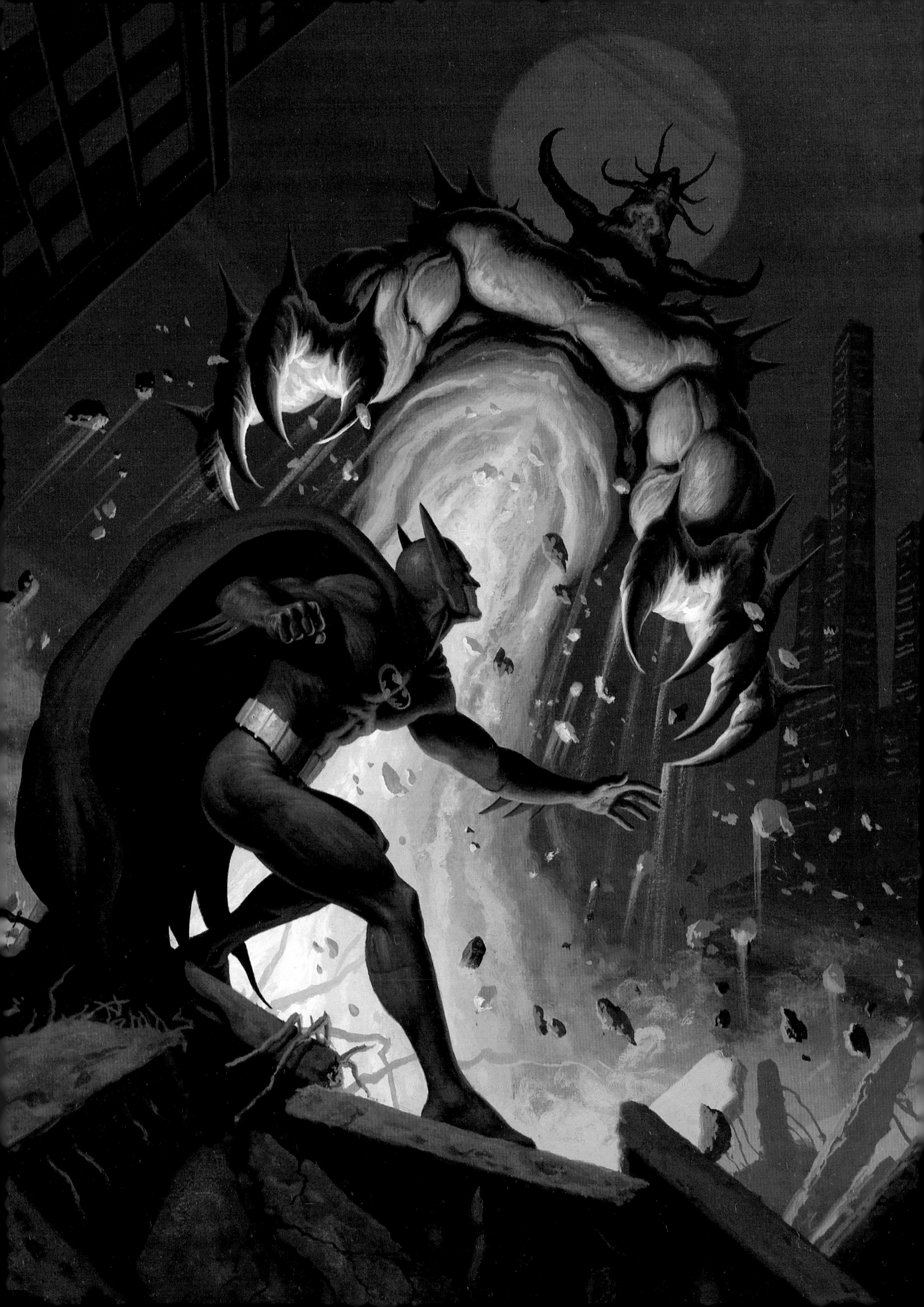

ROMAS

Although Romas never worked with super heroes before this card set, they were part of his background.

"I read all that stuff when I was a kid," he says, "Batman and the other super heroes, and they fascinated me."

How does he describe his fantasy illustration career? "Doing absolutely what I was born to do. Making the unbelievable believable, making something that doesn't exist real, is an absolute challenge."

In his creative process, Romas starts with "simple, very little pencils and then you bring those up. I just start roughing things out with a pencil, then I finish with a resolved 6 x 10 pencil sketch, and fax three or four variations to the editor."

It's rare that Romas does a color rough. "I just don't have the time. If there are figures involved, which in my work there normally are, I find models and I shoot reference; then you just elaborate on what you have to get to what you need."

After he's settled on an image, he does a full-size drawing for the painting "and then I transfer it to the board that I paint on. I make these little sheets with graphite fixed with lighter fluid, transfer sheets in other words. Then I put that under the drawing, between the drawing and the board, and I trace my drawing down on the board, and that's what transfers it.

"I paint in acrylics. Whatever is in the background goes down first, then I come forward to the foreground. The figures are the last thing you do because they're usually in the front, they're the objects closest to you."

Although it's rare for him to work in oils, "I ended up going back and painting a lot of Batman with oils on top of the acrylic because there was a lot of nice rendering I wanted to do on that figure. I wanted to model the anatomy through the costume, just to get some nice softness."

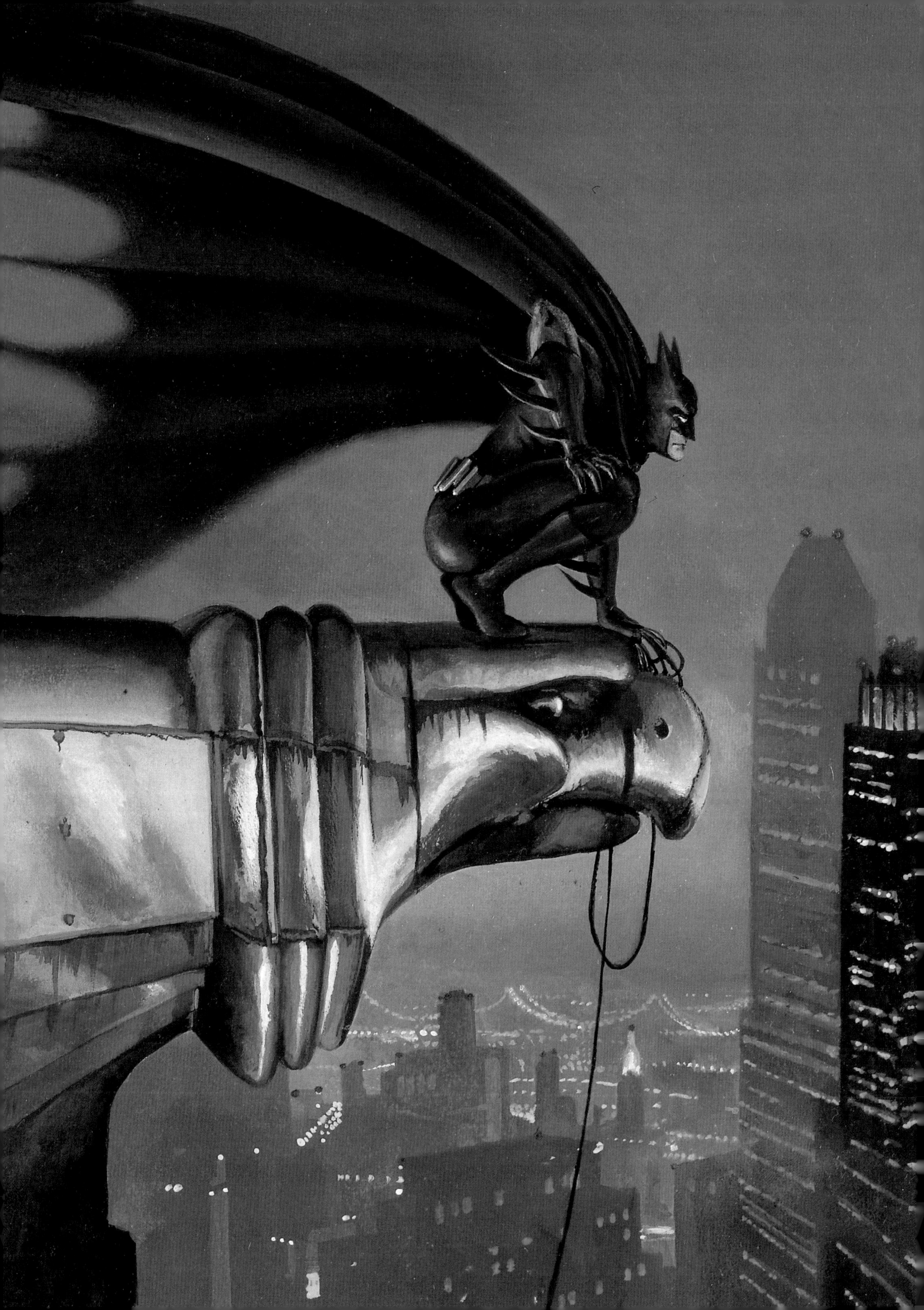

NICK JAINSCHIGG

For Jainschigg, the beginning of the process is purely cerebral.

"The first step, for me, is not to draw thumbnails. The first step is to roll my eyes back in my head and sit real dazed, grumpily marching around the house and making bowls of cereal and cups of coffee for myself. Then, when the idea actually hits, I do several hours' worth of thumbnails, almost uninterpretable to anybody else but me.

"I just try to decide the compositional direction that the picture's going to take. I always try to go for the more dramatic composition. That's sort of a big stage, trying to figure out what's the most dramatic way to show the character.

"I have a cheap paper sketchbook and I just work my way through it. It's easier that way, having one book where all the thumbnails are."

After that, he makes a color rough "on whatever's handy." Although Jainschigg paints in oils and acrylics, he uses colored pencil for the "little touches" and most of his color roughs. "I can define little colored notes a lot more easily than by mixing up separate little batches of acrylic."

He eschews any sort of projection of the rough image onto the final board. "The image can get static and dead and I really wanted the impression of Batman sort of leaning forward to the wind. I try to leave the painting with a fairly matte finish throughout. It's easier to see the hot spots, and I also find that when the painting is finally photographed, the printing almost always has a gloss which kicks up all the color relationships."

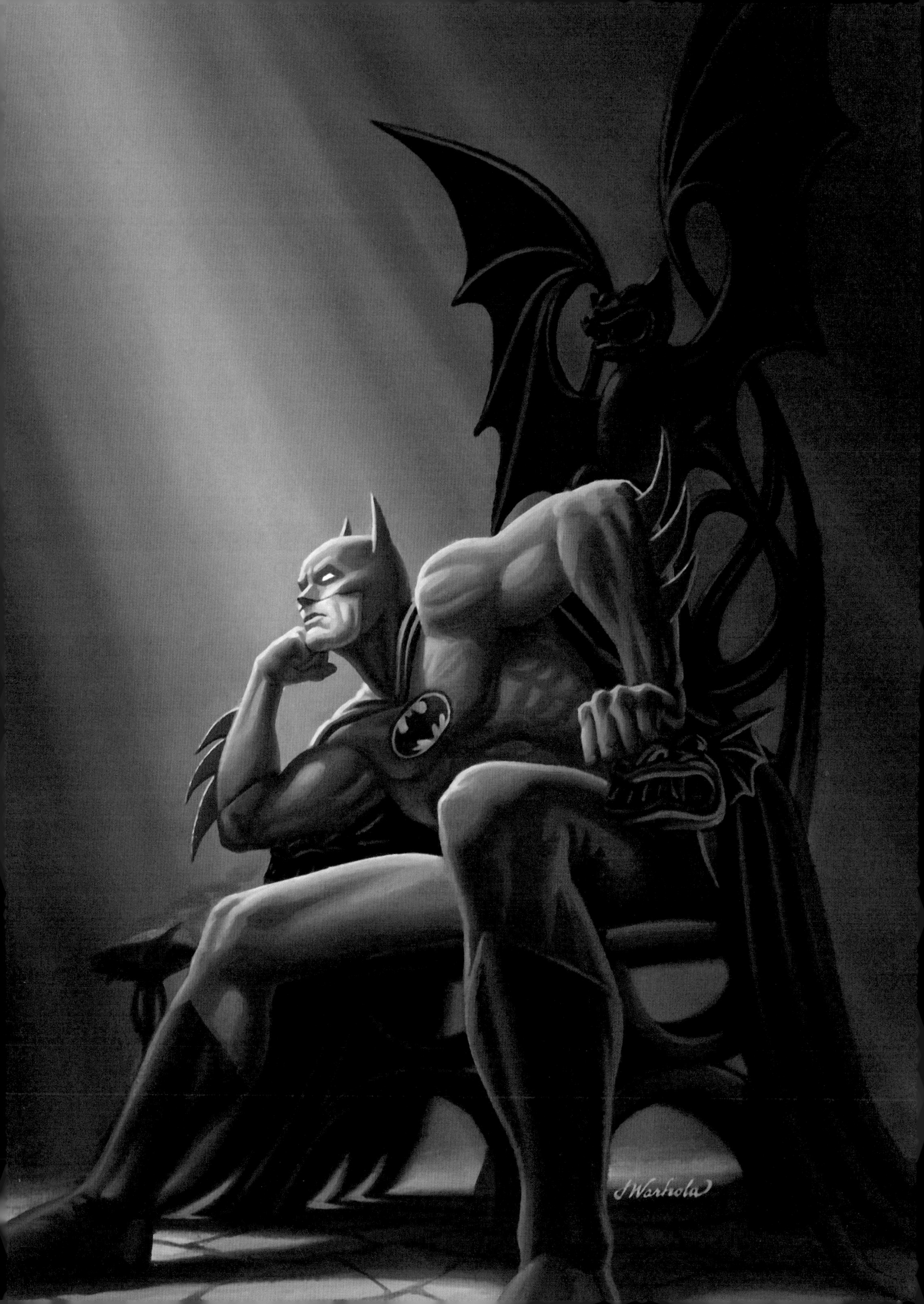
J Warhola

JAMES WARHOLA

As James Warhola discovered, talent can take you only so far.

"I was just average. I only got good through a lot of practice, and I'm talking about painting and drawing fifteen hours a day for several years. It just requires that."

Warhola's hard work paid off. "For the last fifteen years or so, I've done about 300 covers, mostly science fiction and fantasy book illustrations. For the last several years, I've also been doing mostly children's picture books."

Like most artists, Warhola starts with "small sketches, a little bigger than your thumbnail, but very small sketches nonetheless. Then I'll work up tighter sketches (approximately 4 x 6 inches) and when I get those approved, I might shoot some photo reference to help me paint as realistically as I can."

Warhola will sometimes sculpt what he's trying to paint "just to get some of the forms right and the designs right. I'll just sculpt it real quickly, and put an actual light on it, and so I can get that three-dimensional feeling."

Then, "I compose another master drawing very carefully and I work out all the problems and all the perspectives, and just get the drawing as perfect as possible.

"From there, I transfer the sketch onto a Masonite board and I coat it again with a thin layer of gesso. That kind of locks in the drawing. I can still see the drawing pretty clearly, but when I start painting on top of it with oils, it stays there—if I want to rub something on, I still have my drawing underneath.

"I usually do a monochromatic underpainting and let that dry. I work out all my values at that point, lights and darks. When it's dry, I start with the next final layer of paint, which is full color."

BIOGRAPHIES

Carl Critchlow was born in Liverpool, England, in 1963. He attended art college, where one of the teachers introduced him to serious comics. He has done work for role-playing game companies, the British comic magazine *2000 A.D.,* and *Judge Dredd/Batman.* Currently, he is the penciler on the monthly *Lobo* title and would like to do some painted Lobo work.

If he could be any Batman character, he'd like to be Batman so he could drive the Batmobile.

Duncan Fegredo was born in Leicester, England, in 1964. One of his older brother's friends used to get "lots and lots of comics" and was nice enough to share. After obtaining a graphic arts degree, Fegredo decided to pursue a professional comics career and learned to paint. Past work has included *Scarecrow: New Year's Evil* and the *Kid Eternity, Enigma,* and *Girl* miniseries, all from DC Comics. He's also a frequent trading card, pinup, and cover artist: "I've done loads of stuff."

When he was nine, Fegredo used to dress up as Batman. As he wasn't allowed out after dark, his crime-fighting career was largely uneventful.

Scott Hampton was born in Highpoint, North Carolina, in 1959. "I never received any formal art training. I just gleaned knowledge from my brother Bo, who studied under Will Eisner at the School of Visual Arts in New York City" (and who is also a successful comics illustrator). Some past works include *Batman: Night Cries, Batman: Dark Past,* and the second chapter of *Books of Magic.* He is also a frequent contributor to book covers, trading card sets, and posters.

Hampton's wife is Letitia. His cat is Roxanne.

Doug Moench was born in Chicago "as the blues song goes," and never let schooling get in the way of his education. One of the preeminent Batman writers for 15 years, he still has many Batman-related projects in the works. Additionally, Moench was involved in a DC-produced custom comic book celebrating the century and done for the U.S. Post Office.

Moench has never been afraid to do the uncommon. "When I was 15, you were ridiculed if you read Bugs Bunny at that age, but I saw some magic in what these guys were doing."

Ruth Morrison, born in Madison, Wisconsin, tripped over a *Wonder Woman* reprint book early in her life and has been hooked ever since. She has contributed articles for *Disney Adventures, InQuest,* and *Wizard* magazines. Her comics work includes stories in *Wonder Woman* #120 and in *Wonder Woman Secret Files.*

Anyone who doesn't believe in the validity of super hero secret identities has never seen Morrison without her makeup and contacts.

Dermot Power was born in Dungarvan, Ireland, and now lives in London. After graduating from art school, he thought that comic illustration would be easy—until he tried it. His work has been seen on *Wizards of the Coast* cards, in *2000 A.D.,* and in the *Batman/Judge Dredd* graphic novel. He's dabbled with conception illustration and costume design for movies and "loves things that are very magical." He can be reached at Power@dircon.co.uk.

If Power could be any Batman character, he'd like to be Batman, so he could jump off tall buildings and swing around.